CONTENTS.

INTRODUCTION.

PAGE

TECHNICAL BOOKS AND THE WRITERS OF THEM, WITH SOME PARTICULARS OF FIREARMS INVENTIONS, THE HISTORY OF GUNMAKING ON THE CONTINENT OF EUROPE, IN ENGLAND AND IN THE UNITED STATES OF AMERICA, AND THE DEVELOPMENT OF THE PRACTICE AND ART OF SHOOTING ON THE WING . . . 1

PART I.

ANCIENT BOOKS (1472—1850).

BOOKS WRITTEN PRIOR TO 1600			.	.	15
SIXTEENTH-CENTURY MANUSCRIPTS			.	.	23
SEVENTEENTH-CENTURY BOOKS			.	.	24
EIGHTEENTH-CENTURY ENGLISH BOOKS			.	.	42
FOREIGN EIGHTEENTH-CENTURY BOOKS			.	.	50
BOOKS PUBLISHED 1800—1850, IN ENGLISH			.	.	58
,,	,,	,,	FRENCH	.	71
,,	,,	,,	GERMAN	.	75
,,	,,	,,	ITALIAN	.	79
,,	,,	,,	SPANISH	.	80

PART II.

MODERN BOOKS (1851—1894).

ENGLISH BOOKS:—   PAGE

    GUNS AND SHOOTING—GUNMAKING—GUN TRADE—
        PROOF OF GUNS 85

    RIFLES—THE VOLUNTEER MOVEMENT—MONOGRAPHS
        OF SPECIAL ARMS 97

    GUNNERY—BALLISTICS—FIELD TRIALS—ART OF RIFLE
        SHOOTING 101

    CURRENT ENGLISH SPORTING BOOKS . . . 106

    SELECTED ENGLISH BOOKS ON FOREIGN SPORT . 115

        EUROPE 116
        ASIA 117
        AFRICA 120
        AMERICA 122
        AUSTRALASIA 128

FRENCH BOOKS:—

    CURRENT WORKS ON SHOOTING 129
    GUNS—GUN MANUFACTURE—GUNNERY . . . 138

GERMAN BOOKS:—

    GENERAL WORKS — MILITARY RIFLES—MUSKETRY—
        GUN-MAKING—SPORTING 148

ITALIAN BOOKS 155
SPANISH BOOKS 157
VARIOUS LANGUAGES 160

A Bibliography of Guns and Shooting.

*BEING A LIST OF ANCIENT AND MODERN ENGLISH AND
FOREIGN BOOKS RELATING TO FIREARMS AND THEIR USE,
AND TO THE COMPOSITION AND MANUFACTURE OF
EXPLOSIVES; WITH AN INTRODUCTORY CHAPTER
ON TECHNICAL BOOKS AND THE WRITERS
OF THEM, FIREARMS INVENTIONS AND
THE HISTORY OF GUNMAKING, AND
THE DEVELOPMENT OF THE
ART OF WING SHOOTING.*

Compiled and Revised to Date.

BY

WIRT GERRARE.

FORMERLY EDITOR OF "THE GUNMAKER," "THE SPORTING GOODS REVIEW," ETC., ETC.

The Naval & Military Press Ltd

Published by the
The Naval & Military Press
in association with the Royal Armouries

Unit 10 Ridgewood Industrial Park,
Uckfield, East Sussex, TN22 5QE
Tel: +44 (0) 1825 749494
Fax: +44 (0) 1825 765701

For a full listing of all N&MP titles, visit:
www.naval-military-press.com

MILITARY HISTORY AT YOUR FINGERTIPS

Online genealogy research:
www.military-genealogy.com

In reprinting in facsimile from the original, any imperfections are inevitably reproduced and the quality may fall short of modern type and cartographic standards.

PART III.

APPENDICES.

	PAGE
A SHORT BIBLIOGRAPHY OF EXPLOSIVES:—	
BOOKS RELATING TO GUNPOWDER	163
MODERN HIGH EXPLOSIVES, ETC.	165
AMMUNITION, GUN WOUNDS, ETC.	168
TECHNICAL PAPERS, MAGAZINE ARTICLES, AND NEWSPAPER REFERENCES	170
SELECTED BOOKS ON OLD ARMS, FOREIGN ARMS, ETC.	178
CATALOGUES OF COLLECTIONS OF ANCIENT ARMS	181
BIBLIOGRAPHIES: SPORTING—MILITARY—ENCYCLOPÆDIAS AND TECHNICAL DICTIONARIES	184
INDEX TO AUTHORS	191
SOME RECENT BOOKS AND OMISSIONS UP TO THE END OF 1895	203

INTRODUCTION.

So many books have been written upon guns and shooting that no apology is needed for publishing a guide to them. Incomplete and inadequate as the compilation may be, it is better than none at all; for, if practical utility be the standard by which to measure the value of technical books, few will rank higher in the estimation of students than do bibliographies.

To the book collector this work will be probably of little value: it was compiled for the use of a writer, not a book buyer, and is both conceived and arranged with a view to best serving the needs of the student.

Having departed from the customary method of arrangement, a short explanation is desirable. The classification of books according to the accident of the initial letter of the name of the person writing them entails much additional labour upon all who consult a bibliography in order to identify a book, instead of for information concerning the writer of it; the arrangement of books alphabetically by titles is equally objectionable; and the method of Rumpf, who classed the books in accordance with their size, is worst of all. The classification by authors' names is a survival: in days when authors were few, men of erudition were supposed to know at least the names of all, and doubtless possessed some idea as to the dates at which the various authors wrote. Now authors are numerous, and the persons who most often consult a bibliography, whatever their knowledge of the subject, are rarely well acquainted with the names of the persons who have written upon it. Moreover, in the history of firearms it is the *date*, and in technical matters the *fact*, which is all-important, the personality of the author being frequently of no moment whatever. Learned persons may at once recognise *Walter* in Valturius and *Greaves* in Gravius, but learned persons are not likely to take so much interest in guns and shooting as are class journalists, technical instructors, and gun-makers—persons who are not learned in the dry-as-dust sense. Another trouble with names, particularly foreign names, is to recognise the important designation: *Alenzo Martinez del Espinar* would, in accordance with the British Museum rules of indexing, have to be sought in the catalogue under D, the portion of the name least likely to be remembered. With some double names, particularly those of Austrian writers, it is customary to place the Christian, or added, name after the family name—a process of inversion which human powers of recollection often perform automatically, and after a short time recall Alvarez Perez as Perez Alvarez. In order to save the time of the student, in the alphabetical list of authors some authors have more than one entry, owing to the persistence with which the added name surged up into memory, whilst the correct index name could not be recollected.

Clearly, for the student of history classification by dates is likely to be more convenient. If the student wishes to learn what was known of firearms in the seventeenth century, it is better to turn to a catalogue of the works published at that time than to search through many lists of unknown names, and often, upon choosing a writer, consult the work only to find that it belongs to another period. In the same way the language in which books are written is of minor importance, and the size of the book probably of no account whatever. Therefore, in the *first* part of this bibliography, which is devoted to ancient books —those published between 1450 and 1850—the order is mainly chronological; but the books of the last century are subdivided into English and Foreign, and those of the first half of the present century into English, French, German, Italian, and Spanish.

In dealing with modern books a different classification is advisable. To most it is of the first importance to learn whether the book is written in English—if not, in what language it is written; or to know what technical books exist in any particular language. The subdivisions in this second part therefore deal in the first place with books in English—those relating to arms generally, to particular descriptions of arms, to the technicalities of gun-making, to the proof of guns, to ballistics or gunnery, to the art of shooting with gun and rifle, and, lastly, to sport with the gun at home and abroad. The same method of subdividing is adhered to with French and German books, and, in a minor degree, with those of Italy and Spain.

No bibliography of practical proportions could be produced unless many works were purposely excluded. In this compilation books will be found which at first sight will appear to have no right of entry as long as others are excluded; but there are publications with misleading or too comprehensive titles which need to be specified in order that time may not be wasted by referring to certain books owing to a misconception of their nature. "The Rifle and how to use it," by J. V. Bridgeman, is no indication that the work is a farce, and originally performed at the Haymarket in 1859. A docket to this effect will save the student time and the librarian useless labour.

The exclusion extends in a complete manner to modern military treatises dealing with ordnance, those of a general nature, and those for the most part devoted to the art of war, fortification and military tactics; all such works are enumerated in the military bibliographies, which may be readily consulted. Many sporting works, in which something is said of firearms and shooting, have also had to be passed by, and only a bare hundred out of the many recent works devoted to sport abroad have been selected. Foreign sporting works, of little technical interest, have also been omitted; the reader needing them may advantageously consult the more general bibliography of Souhait. Russian sporting books have been excluded; it must not, however, be inferred that Russia has no literature of this description, only that the typographical difficulties were considerable, and the interest at present taken in Russian books of the class infinitesimal. The bibliographical notices in "Priroda y Ohhota" and in the service periodicals will probably be sufficient for the purposes of the few readers likely to require to consult Russian sporting books.

The appendices contain a short bibliography of works relating to explosives, such works having been selected as likely to prove of the greatest service to the student of the history of guns and shooting; lists of the most noteworthy technical papers read before learned societies; and an index to technical articles in various periodicals. The student of history will find short references to works dealing with the archæology of firearms, a list of catalogues of various collections of arms, and also the titles of various bibliographies, which may be of use in supplementing the one now presented.

The introduction of firearms into Europe preceded the invention of printing by nearly two centuries; but the earliest manuscripts which treated of guns were subsequently printed, or, like those of Cataneo, were lost. As is well known, the first mention of the use of firearms in England, contained in a contemporary record, is found in the indenture of John Starlyng and Helmyng Leget, dated 1338, and referring to the equipment of the King's ships *Bernard de la Tour* and *Christofre de la Tour*; but there are several who wrote of their use in the past tense; as John Barbour, who in 1375 stated of the Scotch that in 1327—

> "Twa noweltys that dai thai saw
> That forouth in Scotland had bene nane
> Tymmris for helmys war the tane,
> That thaim thoucht than off grete bewte
> And alsua wondre for to se.
> The tothyr crakys war off wer
> That thai befor herd nevir er."

The use of firearms seems to have been so widely known in Chaucer's time as to warrant that writer in drawing a simile for great velocity from the flight of a shot, thus:

> "Swift as a pillet out of a gonne
> When fire is in the pouder ronne."

At least a score separate and distinct treatises on firearms, gunpowder or matters incidental to their employment, had been written and published on the Continent before an English work on the subject was produced. To William Bourne, who in 1587 published the "Arte of Shootinge in Great Ordnance" belongs the honour of first place; his little book of 94 pages contained much that was original, and served as a basis for several better known and more pretentious works.

On the Continent the literature of the art of war has always been more extensive than in England; and military science was one of the few subjects which could be treated liberally. True, the works were dedicated to, and that is to say, were not only under the patronage of, but were practically supported by, some strong ruler; and the strong ruler was ordinarily a successful warrior whose achievements were lavishly extolled in the works. To this class must be ascribed the book of Valturius and some of the treatises written by Cataneo, Colliado, and Tartaglia. The more practical among this class of writers gave instructions for the manufacture of cannon, gunpowder, projectiles and military fireworks; for in those days, when it was usual to build a cannon at the place where it was to be used, and to break it up after it had served in the one siege, the science of gun construction was a necessary part of the knowledge of a good commander. Another class of writer was that to which W. Bourne belonged, the practical gunner. Very numerous are the treatises on the art of aiming cannon, and the instruction of the "perfect canoneer" seems to have included always a careful grounding in elementary arithmetic and plane geometry. Thus the historian and philosopher on the one hand repeated the lore of ancient military commanders, with the addition of elementary facts drawn from recent experiences, and sometimes gave indications of the application of natural law to the flight of projectiles; and on the other, master gunners wrote practical instructions for the acquisition of a difficult art and the study of elementary mathematics. It was not until the epoch-marking book of Benjamin Robins appeared, in 1742, that theoretical gunnery received particular attention from the writers of technical books; from that date the works on artillery, instead of containing rule-of-thumb descriptions, like those of Ufano, Saint Julien, Gaya, and Siemenowicz, treated the principles of gunnery more in the modern scientific manner.

With reference to the manufacture of small arms, not so much was written, but more probably than was written of any other industrial art. It is hardly to be expected that any practical art can have a considerable literature;

for what the skilled workman learns by practice he cannot impart by verbal descriptions, even were he so minded. When hand firearms came into general use the trade guilds were already firmly established, and a separate guild, that of gunmakers, was not possible in all centres, because the existing guilds of the smiths and the carpenters divided the work between them, and were jealous of any interference with their privileges. As the "art and mystery" of gunmaking was not recognised until the end of the seventeenth century, and as arms were considered national in the sense that their manufacture could be improved and their form changed without incurring the enmity of manufacturing corporations, firearms developed quickly. Cataneo wrote a treatise informing how the processes of manufacture should be carried on, Bossi told how to improve the principle of construction, and Jacquinet showed how the finished weapon should be ornamented; all before any Gunmakers' Company was chartered in England, and when the Suhl gunmakers were petitioning for incorporation. Not that the inventor's lot was any more happy in the seventeenth century than in the nineteenth. Poor Bossi, who appears to have been a genius and determined upon perfecting the double-barrelled gun, started from his native Rome to try his fortune in Flanders, even then a centre of the firearms industry. His success there appears to have been poor, for he subsequently tried Paris and other centres, and the double gun remained an unappreciated invention.

Quite apart from these writers of treatises upon firearms from the military standpoint, there remain to be considered the champions of the gun as a sporting weapon. Although, as Sidney Smith states, the tenth Muse is courted in this country more assiduously than in any other, and although the earliest known manuscript in the English language is upon a sporting topic, and the first "boke" in our tongue likewise devoted to a princely pastime, there are no English writers upon sport with firearms until late in the seventeenth century. Pablo del Fucar and Erasmo di Valvasone had both treated of the use of firearms for sporting purposes in the sixteenth century; Tamariz de la Escaler and Vita Bonfadini had written treatises on the art of wing shooting long before Blome produced his great tome and taught how to creep within range of jugging partridges and pot them unawares.

The "Maison Rustique" was the precursor of the country encyclopædia, of which Blome's book was a fair specimen, and a variety of which is still with us,—even to-day "British Rural Sports" is on the railway bookstalls,—but these early compilations were far from being the thorough works modern encyclopædias have become, now that each article is contributed by an expert and constitutes not seldom the best monograph extant on the subject treated. The early cyclopædias were put together by the publisher's hack, and the student in search of original facts and reliable information will do well to avoid them and choose some of the less pretentious publications.

The poets have contributed not a few lines to firearms. The epic on the chase was a favourite essay for Italian writers. It was a congenial theme with the much-satirised poet laureate Pye; and though his verse is far from approaching in interest the better known "Chace" of W. Somerville, he is far from being the worst author of metrical lines on shooting. Watts wrote facetiously, and Aldington heavily and seriously; Francis Fawkes and K. McLemon have not made their names immortal by their poems on sport with the gun; but, notwithstanding their example and lack of success, verse on the subject is still being produced.

An important class of authors has been recruited from

the ranks of the gunmakers. Bossi and Jacquinet in the seventeenth, Page and Baker in the eighteenth, Brandeis, Deane, Dougall, and three generations of Greeners in the nineteenth centuries, have each and all had practical experience of the trade, and, taken collectively, may be said to have contributed the greater part of the original matter found in the technical literature of the firearms industry. It is surprising, even to one acquainted with literary plagiarism, to note the persistency with which information on technical and sporting matters was annexed in the "good old days," and palmed off as first-hand authority. The much-extolled Marolles, whose essay of 1784 was translated into English and has been constantly quoted, drew freely upon Vita Bonfadini and Tamariz de la Escaler, less from Spadoni, Juan Mateos, and Martinez del Espinar, leaving the original matter to be gathered by interviewing some Parisian gunmakers and listening to the gossip of sporting friends. Again, what a mine of wealth to the writer on field sports Colonel P. Hawker's "Instructions" has proved!

To another class belong the authors who, at the commencement of this century, were so infatuated with Scottish sports as to create a special literature. Very poor is the quality of much that was produced in the passion of the time. " Unreal in fact and artificial in form " is likely to be the verdict of posterity upon the productions of even the best of the writers; though to state it *now* would probably bring angry retorts from the sportsmen still living to whom the craving for northern field sports was once no imaginary desire.

Better, in the sense of being more practical, than Wilson are the reminiscences of Scrope; better, in the sense of being more natural, are Colquhoun of "Moor and Loch" and Lloyd of "Northern Europe"; but worse, from the literary point of view, are many works even more recently issued. In truth, the ancient fire appears to have almost burnt out, and such light as is shed by the glow of dying embers shows that the love of sport which animated such writers as Scrope and Colquhoun no longer burns within the breast of the modern sportsman-author. Scotch shooting appears more as a fashion, deerstalking a function, and grouse-shooting an exhibition in which the society man, and often the society woman, is expected to share. It would be wrong to attribute the change to the want of skill in the writers; they do but reflect the tendency of the times. Indications are not wanting to show that the special craving, or that stimulus to action which only the sport of shooting can appease, no longer occurs with the frequency it did half a century ago. Shooting is now but a means to an end: the end may be some social excitement among a country house party, or it may be the collection of a wild Thibetan camel for a natural history museum; but the prompting does not arise purely from the love of sport,—as it once did, if our authors are to be believed. To many, a life of adventure is a necessity: when the shooting of large game is also a way of earning money, no wonder men enter into the business as upon any other career; but to large game hunting for commercial purposes an end will quickly come unless game is more efficiently protected than was the American bison. The percentage of sportsmen to whom the agony of a buffalo dropped to their rifle is a sight to remember with pleasure, is small, and to the majority of these a stalk in Chillingham Park would probably be as pleasurable as an expedition to Central Africa. On the other hand, there is a very large and rapidly growing community for whom all things living in a state of nature have a powerful attraction. To many men it would afford more real enjoyment to get close to a herd

Introduction. 11

of deer and observe their habits than to stalk within range for a pot shot. These men, who would hunt with the camera, and prefer to bring back a good negative showing large game sporting in native haunts, rather than an elephant's tail or a tiger's skin, have no sympathy with the sportsmen whose only object is to kill, and who by dissociating themselves from woodcraft and its attractions, have killed their desire for sport, and require only to glut their craving for blood or win approbation for their marksmanship.

Thus it seems probable that, for the purposes of sport as for the purposes of war, the hand firearm is rapidly reaching the close of its day. To those to whom the literature of field sports written half a century ago is familiar, it will seem impossible that the enthusiasm can have died out; and to those to whom the rifleman of the fifties was the hero and saviour the hysterical writing of those times proclaimed him, it would never occur that the man with the gun is to be of quite secondary importance in the wars of the future. It would be idle to argue that shooting will not long continue as a sport with some classes, and that the infantry man will not again do excellent service in guerilla warfare; but the contention deduced from contemporary literature, and not now advanced for the first time, is that the hand firearm, both for purposes of sport and as a military weapon, will not, in the early future, be regarded as possessing the importance attributed to it in the recent past. The delight of sports afield will be more keenly enjoyed by the man in closer harmony with nature than the modern skilled wing shot; and, in the event of war occurring between civilised nations, the machine gun and an endless variety of automatically acting mechanical contrivances to insure the defence of the party attacked will have superseded the infantry man.

But firearms, both sporting and military, at present

engage the attention of the most clever among a generation of able mechanical inventors; in the manufacture of guns there is expended some of the best skilled labour the century has produced, and whatever its future may prove, none can deny the present achievements of a notable industry. To the historian, firearms, of all weapons, will present masterful attraction; the part they have played in the world's history is too great ever to be ignored, even should the part they have yet to play prove to be one of minor importance.

WIRT GERRARE.

July 1st, 1894.

NOTE.

The author added an "Appendix" bringing the work up to the end of 1895.

PART I.
Ancient Books.

BOOKS WRITTEN PRIOR TO 1600.

1.—RE MILITARI. *Robertus Valturius.* In twelve books, of which the tenth deals with artillery *et inventu hominum varius reperitur.* The illustrations to the Paris edition of 1532 are more numerous than in the Verona edition of 1483, and give exact representations of bombards, hand cannon, etc., and show also the manner in which they were used from ox waggons, ships, fortifications, gun carriages, etc. An arrangement of eight cannon, like the spokes of a vertically pivoted wheel, is shown; also the *Turris Tormentaria, et alia mirabilis machīa.* Verona, 1472 and 1483; Paris, 1532. Folio.

2.—ENSALADA Y AVISOS DEL ARCUBUZ. *Alejo de Puelles.* A manuscript dating back to 1500, and cited by D. N. Antonio y Huerta as existing in the library of the Escurial. (Spanish.)

3.—TRATTATO DI ARTIGLIERA. A sixteenth-century manuscript (codice della Riccardiana). Is divided into eight chapters, and has a vocabulary explaining such words as "gragnuola," "balzo," "cespi." (Italian.) Venice (?). 1529-39.

4.—NEUE UND BEWERKE RECEPT. Fisch und Vogel zu fahen. The contents of this book "of all manner of recipes for taking birds, beasts and fishes," are not known to the compiler. (German.) 1530. In 8vo.

5.—ORDNUNG. Nahmen und Zahl aller Büchsen. *v. Preuss.* A list of military troops, arms, and a classification of ordnance. (German.) Strasburg, 1530.

6.—BALLESTAS MOSQUETES Y ARCABUCES. *Pablo del Fucar.* A book on sporting firearms, cited by bibliographers, but not generally known. (Spanish.) Naples, 1535.

7.—ISTRUZIONE DEI BOMBARDIERI. *Gabrielo Busca.* A bibliographical rarity, contains "things useful to know." A soldiers' handbook, frequently quoted; usually appeared in small 4to. (Italian.) Venice, 1545, 1554, 1559. Carmagnola, 1584. Turin, 1598.

8.—QUESITI ET INVENTIONI DIVERSE. *Nicolas Tartaglia.* An incomplete treatise in Latin on the invention and qualities of artillery; first appeared in Venice 1528, according to Ayala. The 1546 edition, usually accredited as the first, is dedicated to Carlo VIII., King of England. See *Journal des Armes Speciales,* June, 1845.

9.—TRATTATO DELLA CACCIA. *Dominico Mazzo Bocca.* Book VIII. has a colophon "which finishes the eighth book of M. D. Bocca Mazzo, in which is narrated the various and diverse things belonging to the chase." (Italian.) Cartolari Perosina. Rome, 1548. 4to.

10.—ORDONNANCE. A Royal Edict forbidding the taking of game or its sale or purchase. Paris, 1549. Small 8vo, 8 pp.

11.—SCLOPETORUM SIVE ARCHIBUSORUM VULNERIBUS. *Alfonso Ferro.* A treatise on the wounds caused by firearms, and one of the earliest on the subject. Rome, 1552.

12.—ORDONNANCES. Edicts of Henry II. of France respecting sporting and forest rights. Paris, 1554. Small 8vo.

13.—MODO DI FER DIVERSE SORTE DI FUOCHI ARTIFICIALE. An Italian sixteenth-century MS. (codice della Magliabechiania classe xix. n. 7), and makes mention of a battery in Brescia in 1564. It is almost entirely taken up with the preparation of saltpetre and its use for military fireworks.

14.—AVVERTAMENTI e essamini intorno a quelle case che richiedemo a un perfetto bombardiero. *Girolamo Cataneo.* This book forms the fifth portion of the author's "Arte Militare." T. Bezola, Brescia, 1567, in 4to, Venetia, 1582; and A. Solicato, Vinegia, 1596, 4to.

15.—ARTE DI FARE LE ARME ET I FUCILI. *G. Cataneo.* One of the first treatises on the art of making firearms. The writer was the author of "Arte Militare," and is usually described as of Novara. This treatise is quoted by Gassendi and Cotty, but is not known to bibliographers, nor is a copy known to exist; it is supposed to have been issued at Brescia about 1577.

16.—BUCHSENMEISTERIE. A treatise on artillery, gunnery, etc., attributed to the Emperor Maximilian I. 1569.

17.—MACHINIS BELLICIS. Heronis mechanici. An edition of Hero, by Francesco Baroccio, Venice. Another work by Bernardino Baldo is more common. Its title is "Heronis Chesibii Belopeeca, hoc est telifactiva, etc." The text in Latin and Greek. This book does not contain any reference to firearms, although translators and annotators occasionally mention them, and attempts have been made to read various references into the text. Venice, 1578.

18.—DISCOURS SUR L'ARTILLERIE. A MS. among the archives of the town of Turin. Attributed to S. A. Duc Charles Emmanuel. Turin, 1580.

19.—PRATICA MANUELE PER L'ARTIGLIERIA. *Luigi Colliado.* A complete treatise on artillery, ancient and modern. The history of the art of war and the engines used therein. Pyrotechny and the making of artificial fireworks, etc., etc. The author was a Spaniard, long settled in Italy, and writing the Tuscan dialect. Various editions of the work appeared; in some the author's name is printed Collado. (Italian.) Dusmelli, Venice, 1586, folio. Bordoni e Locarni, Milan, 1606; Milan, F. Ghisolfi, 1641, in 4to.

20.—ARTE OF SHOOTING in GREAT ORDNANCE. Contayning very necessary matters for all sortes of Seruitores eyther by sea or by lande. Written by *William Bourne*. The first book in English dealing with gunnery. On it, or on foreign works, the better known books of Norton, Moore and Nye were based. It is dedicated to Ambrose Dudley, Earl of Warwick. The introductory preface consists of 5 pp. in italics, then 94 pp. text, in black letter, and 2 pp. table of contents. London; printed by Thomas Dawson for Thomas Woodcocke, 1587.

21.—PATHEWAY OF MILITARY PRACTICE, with a kalender for the ymbattelinge of men. *Barnabie Riche*. A tract on military exercises. Riche, London, 1587.

22.—MACCHINE DIVERSE ET ARTIFIZIORE. *Captain Ramelli*. Paris, 1588.

23.—PATHWAYE OF MILITARYE PRACTISE. Three Bookes of Collequies concerning the Art of Shooting in great and small pieces of artillery, variable randges, etc. This is a translation of the Italian of Nicolas Tartaglia, by Cyprian Lucar, who also augmented the volume. Whether or not this is the same "Pathway" as that published by Riche, the compiler has been unable to discover. London, 1588, folio. Another edition, entitled "Lucar Solace," in four books, 1590, 4to.

24.—BALLAD. Discrybinge the vallure of our Englishe archers and shotte that accompanied the Black Prince of Portugal, their governor, into the fieldes on Tweesdale, the 12 of August, with the welcome into Lyme Streete, by *Master Hugh Offley*. Jones, London, 1589.

25.—BOOKE OF HONOUR AND ARMES, wherein is discoursed the causes of quarrel, and the nature of iniuries with their repulces, with the meanes of satisfaction and pacification. A treatise on duelling. Richard Jones, London, 1589.

26.—MILITARY DISCIPLINE. In Spanish, by *D. S. de Lomdomo*, with one other booke, entitled THE OFFICE OF THE SERGENT MAIOUR. One of several like works on the ordering of troops, etc. J. Woolf, London, 1589.

27.—CERTEN DISCOURSES CONCERNING the great mistakinge of the effectes of diverse sortes of wepons, and chiefly of the musket, calyuer, and long bowe; and of the use of archers. Compiled by *Sir John Smith*. This is the gravest charge brought against the use of firearms for military purposes, by a commander who had much experience in Spain. Mr. Humphrey Barwick took up the case on behalf of the musketeers and bombardiers, and Sir John Smith subsequently modified his views, but remained the staunch champion of the English long-bowmen. See the "British Bowman" for an abstract of the work, which in the original state is very scarce. The MS. is in the Harleian Collection. Rich. Jones, London, 1590.

28.—BREEFE DISCOURSE, concerning the force and effect of all manuall weapons of fire, and the disability of the long bowe or archery in respect of all others now in use. With sundry probable reasons for the verifying thereof; the which I have doone of dutye towards my soveraigne and country, and for the better satisfaction of all such as are doubtfull of the same. Written by *Humfrey Barwick*, gentleman, souldier, and captaine. *Et encor plus oultre*. A continuation of the musket-bow controversy led by Sir J. Smith, this little manual of 42 pp. is a brief for firearms, and was soon answered by Sir J. Smith, who admitted that firearms had their use. See "The English Bowman," 1810. Rich. Olife, 1591, 4to, black letter, 42 pages, with a folding woodcut manual.

29.—TRATADO DE ARTILLERIA. *J. Ferrufino*. A manuscript in the National Library, Madrid. The work of an Italian who left Milan in 1588, for an appointment as Director of Artillery. 1591, 1595.

30.—UNTERRICHT. *Kaspar Burger.* How to shoot from fortifications or in the field, the ordering of ordnance and the loading of arms. (German.) Strassburg, 1591. 4to.

31.—INSTRUZZIONE DE BOMBARDIERI. *Eugenio Gentillini.* A manual for gunners. (Italian.) Venice, 1592. 4to.

32.—MANNER HOW TO HANDLE WEAPONS SAFELY, as well offensive as defensive. *Giacomo de Gresse.* A translation of an inferior Italian treatise. J. Jagger, London, 1593.

33.—CERTEN INSTRUCTIONS, observaconns and orders militarie requisite for all cheeftaines, captaines, and higher and lower men of charge. *Sir John Smithe, Knight.* Another treatise by the chief advocate for the suppression of hand guns in the British Army. Rich. Jones, London, 1594.

34.—ABSOLUTE SOLDIER, or Pollicee of Arms. Ponsonby, London, 1595.

35.—HAWKING, HUNTING, FOWLING, FISHING, with the true measures of blowing. *Will Gryndall.* This book is rarely found: whether or not it treats of shooting is not known by the compiler. London, 1596, folio. [Not in British Museum.]

36.—POLIORCETICON SIVE DE MACHINIIS. *Justus Lipsius.* An account of the artillery of the ancients, in five books, of which the fifth is the only one treating of *Tormentis*, or firearms. The writer was born in 1547, and, according to Scaliger, was venerated almost as a deity in the Netherlands. This book is usually found bound up with other books, commonly with *De Cruce*, published the following year. (Latin.) Antwerp, 1596, folio, 263 pp. plates; included also in complete edition of works, published in 1665.

37.—BUCHSENMEISTEREI. The art of gunnery, and directions for making guns, muskets, powder, projectiles, and fireworks. (German.) Frankfort, 1597.

38.—NOMI DELL' ARTIGLIERIA. An Italian sixteenth-century MS. (codice della Riccardiana). The writer was on board a Venetian vessel in 1597 at Lisbon preparing for the invasion of England. Among other matters dealt with are English usages in comparison with those prevalent in Lisbon and among the Venetians.

39.—THEORIE AND PRACTISE OF MODERN WARS, descoursed in dialogewise. Ponsonby, London, 1597.

40.—CORONA E PALMA MILITARE DI ARTIGLIERA. *Alexandro Capobianco*. A treatise on artillery, measuring instruments, mathematics, and gunnery. Bariletti, Venice, 1598, 1602, 1618, 1647, fol.

41.—DIANA of George of Monte Mayor, done out of the Spanish into English by *Bartholomew Younge*, gent. Geo. Bysshop, London, 9 September, 1598.

42.—ARTE OF GUNNERY, by *Thos. Smythe*, of Barwycke-upon-Tweed, souldyer. London, 1599.

43.—BUCHSENMEISTEREI UND FEUERWERKEREI. *Brechtel*. A treatise on firearms and fireworks. Nurnberg, 1599. 8vo.

44.—MAISON RUSTIQUE, or THE COUNTRIE FARME, compiled in the French Tongue by *Charles Stevens* and *John Liebault*, doctors of physicke, and translated into English by *Richard Surflet*, practitioner in physicke. Also A SHORT COLLECTION OF THE HUNTING OF THE HART, WILDE BORE, HARE, FOXE, GRAY CONIE, OF BIRDS AND FAULCONRIE, the contents whereof are to be seen in the page following. London, printed by Edm. Bollifant for Bonham Norton, 1600.

Another edition MAISON RUSTIQUE, or THE COUNTREY FARME, compiled in the French Tongue by *Charles Stevens* and *John Liebault*, doctors of physicke, and translated into English by *Richard Surflet*; now newly reviewed, corrected, and augmented, with divers large additions, out of the works of Serres, his Agriculture, Vinet, his Maison Chapestre (French); Albyterio in

Spanish, Grilli in Italian, and other authors. And the husbandrie of France, Italy, and Spaine, reconciled and made to agree with ours here in England, by *Gervase Markham*, the whole contents are in the page following (see below). London, by Adam Islip for John Bill, 1616. Illustrations. Folio.

This is the FIRST EDITION edited by *Gervase Markham*. The following is a summary of the contents: "Whatsoever can be required for the building, or good ordering, of a Husbandman's House, or Countrey Farme; as, namely, to foresee the changes and alterations of Times; to know the motions and powers of the Sunne and Moone, upon the things about which Husbandry is occupied: as, to cure the sicke labouring man, to cure Beasts and flying Fowles of all sorts; to DRESSE, PLANT, OR MAKE GARDENS, AS WELL AS FOR THE KITCHIN, AND PHYSICKE USE, AS ALSO IN QUACTERS; WITH MANY FAIRE AND CUNNING PORTRAITURES, TO MAKE COMPARTMENTS OF DIVERS FASHIONS IN EVERIE QUARTER: WITH A LARGE DESCRIPTION OF THE HEARBE NICOTIANA (TOBACCO), OR PETUM (*with a woodcut of the plant*), as also of the root Mechoacan: TO PLANT, GRAFT, AND ORDER ORANGE-TREES, Citron-trees, and such other strange trees: TO ORDER BEES: TO MAKE CONSERVES: TO PRESERVE FRUITES, Flowers, Roots, and Rindes: to make Honey and Wax: TO PLANT AND GRAFT ALL SORTS OF FRUIT TREES: TO MAKE CYDER, PERRIE, DRINKE OF CERVICES, AND OYLES: TO DISTIL WATERS AND OYLES, or Quintessences, of whatsoever the Husbandman's store and encrease, with manie patterns of Limbeckes for the distilling of them: TO FEED AND PRESERVE SILKWORMS: to make and maintaine Medow-groundes: FISHPONDS OF RUNNING OR STANDING WATERS: TO TAKE FISHES: to measure and tyll Corne-ground: TO BAKE BREAD: TO TRIMME VINES: TO MAKE MEDICINABLE WINES; WITH A VERRIE LARGE AND EXCELLENT DISCOURSE TOUCHING THE NATURE AND QUALITIE OF WINE IN GENERAL: AND AFTER THAT, ANOTHER SPECIAL AND PARTICULAR ONE, OF ALL SUCH WINES as grow in Gasconie, Languedoc, Touraine, Orleans, Paris, and other countries of France: to Plant Woods of Timber-trees and Under-growth: to make a warren; TO BREED HERONS: AND TO IMPARKE WILD BEASTS. AS ALSO A LARGE DISCOURSE OF HUNTING THE HART, WILD BORE, HARE, FOX, GRAY CONIE, AND SUCH LIKE: WITH THE ORDERING OF HAWKES, AND ALL SORTS OF BIRDS, and lastly in the end thereof, is briefly shewed the nature, manner of taking, and feeding of the NIGHTINGALE, LINNET, GOLDFINCH, SISKIN, LARKE, AND OTHER SUCH SINGING MELODIOUS BIRDS."

The original French edition appeared in 1566, founded upon L'AGRICULTURE ET MAISON RUSTIQUE of the same author (*Charles Estienne*), published in Paris in 1564, Lyons 1565, and Antwerp 1565, and in Paris 1565. A similar book, PRÆDIUM RUSTICUM, in Latin, appeared in 1554. Other editions of this country encyclopædia are given by *Souhait* as follows Paris, 1567, 1570, 1570 (Geneva imprint), 1572, 1573, 1574, 1576, 1578, 1583, 1586 (two editions), 1589, 1598 (three editions), 1612, 1620, and 1683. Rouen, 1598 (three editions), 1600, 1602 (three editions), 1608 (two editions), 1620 (two editions), 1624, 1625 (three editions), 1629, 1632, 1641, 1646, 1647, 1655, 1656, 1658 (three editions), 1664, 1665, 1666 (three editions), 1668, 1674, 1676 (two editions), 1677, 1685, 1698 (two editions). Lyons, 1578, 1583, 1584, 1586 (two editions), 1590, 1591, 1595, 1597, 1607, 1608, 1610, 1611, 1628, 1637 (two editions), 1645, 1650, 1653, 1654, 1655, 1659, 1667, 1680 (two editions), 1686, 1689, 1698, and 1702. Geneva, 1569. Montluel, 1572. Lunéville, 1577. Cologne, 1695; there was also an edition (unidentified) in 1660. In Italian, as L'AGRICULTURA E CASA DI VILLA, it appeared at Venice, 1581, 1591, 1668, 1677. Turin, 1582, 1583, 1590, 1609, 1623. As BÜCHER VON DEM FELDBAW in German, at Strassburg, 1580 and 1588. In Dutch as HOF-STEDE EN LANDT-HUYS. Dordrecht, 1612. The numerous editions are accounted for by the publication of an appendix, CHASSE AUX LOUPS, almost annually.

SIXTEENTH-CENTURY MANUSCRIPTS.

45.—ARTILLERIE. Graf Solms. A manuscript in the Hesse-Darmstadt Ducal Library.

46.—DUE TRATTI DI ARTIGLIERIA. Two volumes of manuscript in the Parmense collection.

47.—Istruzione intorno al modo di preparare le Artiglierie Militari. A manuscript formerly in the Royal Library, Paris; probably destroyed.

48.—Su' Cannoni. A manuscript in the Vatican collection (389 art. 67).

49.—Manuele. Carlo Giudotti da Mantova. A manual for the bombardier, presumed to have been written or compiled by the Commandant of Artillery of Lecce (Loffredo Lecco). Twenty-three chapters. Vatican MSS.

SEVENTEENTH-CENTURY BOOKS.

101.—Imperatorum Regum atque archiducum . . . quorum Arma in Ambrosianæ arces armamento conspiciuntur. *Jac. Schrenck.* A very rare work on armour, with 129 full-length figures of knights in full suits, and useful as a sidelight upon the arms of the period. A copy is priced by Quaritch at £12 12s. Ænoponti, 1601.

102.—Macchine. *Achille Tarducci.* A treatise on the engines of war used against the Hungarians at Vaccia in 1597, and in the Transylvanian Campaign of 1600. Contains also comparisons of the weapons of the ancients with those used in the seventeenth century. (Italian.) Ciotti, Venice, 1601 and 1631.

103.—A Spedie way for the wynninge of any Breache. Bound up with a tract on the use of "Cole baules" for "fyer" and "some other new and seruisable invensions answerable to the tyme." Short, London, 1602.

104.—Della Caccia. *Erasmo di Valvasone.* A poem in five cantos, written in the sixteenth century, and probably first published at Padova in 1593. The compiler's copy appears to have been printed at Venice in 1602, for F. Bolzetta, of Padova. The title states that the text is "Ricovvetta et di molte stanze ampliata. Con le annotationi di M. Olimpio Marcucci." Several plates, sporting firearms shown, also pictures of shooting with them at boar, deer, etc. 252 pp. text, 40 pp. notes, six plates. Venice, 1602.

105.—ISTRUZZIONI DE BOMBARDIERI. *Orlandi.* Cited by Ayala. Rome, 1602. 4to.

106.—TRATTATO DI SCIENZA D'ARME. *Cornelius Agrippa.* Cited by Rumpf. Venice, 1604.

107.—ELEMENS DE L'ARTILLERIE. *Flurance Rivault.* Watts says this is a rare and curious work. It is mentioned by Rumpf, but does not appear in the catalogues of the chief general or technical libraries. Paris, 1605.

108.—APPAREIL DES MACHINES DE GUERRE. (Also known as "Forge de Vulcain.") *Ch. de Saint Julien.* A curious treatise in which is specified a variety of warlike engines and arms. It treats also of the materials used, and the construction of the machines, their appearance, and the effects caused by their proper use. Guill. de Voys. The Hague, 1606. 8vo.

109.—BRIEFVE INSTRUCTION SUR LE FAICT DE L'ARTILLERIE DE FRANCE. *Daniel Davelcourt.* An account of French cannon and a treatise on gunnery. Paris, 2nd edition, 1608. 8vo.

110.—L'ARCENCAL DE LA MILICE FRANÇAISE. *"Fumée."* Paris, 1608.

111.—MANIEMENT D'ARMES; d'arquebuses, mousquets et piques, en conformité du Prince Maurice d'Orange. *Jacob de Gheyn.* The Hague, 1608. Folio.

112.—ARCENAL ET MAGASIN DE L'ARTILLERIE. *D. Davelcourt.* Contains also the "Brieve Instruction," which see *ante.* Paris, 1610. 8vo.

113.—ISTRUTTIONE D'ARTIGLIERI. *D'ayalo Santo Ajello.* The instructions give the practice usual in the kingdom of Sicily at the time. Palermo, 1610, 8vo; another edition in 4to in 1689.

114.—RECHERCHES ET CONSIDÉRATIONS SUR LE FAICT DE L'ARTILLERIE. *D. Davelcourt.* Also the "Epitome ou abrégée, contenant maximes, etc." A rare treatise on the artillery of the French. Napoleon I. is said to have sought in vain for a copy. An incomplete copy sold at the Laing sale for £7 10s. Quaritch prices a copy at £5 5s. Paris, 1610, 1619, five vols., sometimes bound as one. 12mo.

115.—NOBLE ARTE OF VENERIE. Paris, 1611. 4to.

116.—ARTILLERIA. *Diego Ufano.* This treatise on the artillery used in Flanders has been extensively copied, and served as a basis for the works of *Hancelet, Siemenowicz, Saint Remy,* and some English writers. The first edition appears to have been published at Brussels in 1612 or 1613, a second, also in Spanish, at Brussels in 1617. In 1614 French and German editions were published at Frankfort by *Theo. de Bry,* also Zutphen, 1621, and Rouen, 1628. It was Englished by *Eldred* (*q.v.*), and in 1643 a Polish translation by *J. Deckau* was published at Lesznie. Usually folio in three parts, about 179 pp.

117.—BUCHSENMEISTEREI. *Zuebler.* Geometrical gunnery: a manual of instruction for Artillerymen. Zurich, 1614. 4to.

118.—BUCHSENMEISTEREI-COMPENDIUM. A cyclopædia of gunnery. Strasburg, 1616. 8vo.

119.—LONDON'S ARTILLERY. *R. Niccols.*

120.—RECHERCHES ET CONSIDÉRATIONS SUR LE FAICT DE L'ARTILLERIE. *D. Davelcourt.* A work on experimental and theoretical gunnery. Paris, 1617. In 8vo.

121.—ARCHILEN-KRIEGS KUNST. *V. Wallhausen.* The Art of War (German). Hanau, 1617. Folio.

122.—CACCIA. Poema heroico. *Alessandro Gatti.* An epic poem on the chase. Italian blank verse. Printed in London. (?) Imprint, Gio Billio, London, 1619. 8vo.

123.—GESCHUSS UND FEUERWERK. *Theo. de Bry.* Given by Rumpf; is probably a later edition of Ufano. *V. supra*, anno 1613. Frankfort, 1619.

124.—DISSERTATIO DE BOMBARDIS. Besoldi, 1620. Given by Rumpf.

125.—KRIEGS UND ARCHILLEN KUNST. *Ruscelli.* A translation of "Percetti della Militia Moderna," Part I. (German.) Frankfort, 1620.

126.—WAFFENHANDLUNG DER MUSKETEN UND PIKEN. *Isselburg.* A book of drill and military practice. (German.) Nurnberg, 1620. 4to.

127.—WAFFENHANDLUNG VON DEN ROHREN, MUSKETEN, UND SPIESSEN. *Jacob de Gheyn.* See No. 111, *supra*.

128.—ARTIGLIERIA. *Pietro Sardi.* Italian romance, divided into three books. G. Guerrigli, Venice, 1621. Folio.

128.—EDITS, ETC., AUGMENTES DES ORDONNANCES DU ROI HENRI, SUR LE PORT D'ARQUEBUSES. This compilation was made by *M. Durand.* Cramoisy, Paris, 1621. In 8vo.

130.—OPLOMACHIA. A treatise on the manner of using arms. (Spanish.) Siena, 1621.

131.—TRAITE D'ARTILLERIE. *Diego Ufano.* A translation from the Spanish, published at Zutphen, 1621, Rouen, 1628, and in German, at Frankfort, in 1621. *V. supra*, anno 1613.

132.—ESSAY DES MERVEILLES DE NATURE. *(Etienne Binet) René François.* A cyclopædia of little interest; has a few pages on arms and sports. (French.) Twelve editions published, 1621—1726. Osmont, Rouen, 1622. 4to.

133.—DISCOURS VON DER ARTILLERIE. *Schwachü.* Is said to be a copy of Ufano. Dresden, 1624. 4to

134.—Breve trattato d'alcune inventioni che sono state fatte per rinforzare e raddoppiare el tiri degli archibuigi e moschetti. *Giulano Bossi.* This book, which apparently existed in manuscript in 1616, is one of the most important dealing with ancient gunmaking, giving as it does minute particulars, more especially with reference to double guns. Bossi was an Italian inventor, who resided for some years in the Netherlands, and is believed to have made gun-making his profession. An author of several pamphlets treating of arms. (Italian.) G. Verdussen. Antwerp, 1625. In 12mo.

135.—Kriegs Munitions und Artillerie Buch. *Ammon.* Frankfort, 1625.

136.—Ordonnance et Placcart . . . sur le port des Arquebuzes. (French.) Bruxelles, 1625.

137.—Soldiers' Accidence. *Gervase Markham.* An introduction to military discipline, for Infantrie, Foote Bandes, Cavalry, and Horse Troopes. Bellamy, London, 1625. 4to, 66 pp.

138.—Trattato Cinegetico. *Fr. Birago.* A rare tract on sport. (Italian.) B. Bidelli. Milan, 1626. 18 pp. (one blank).

139.—Halanitro-pyrobolia. *Josephus Furttenbach.* A new art of gunnery, pyrotechny, and treatise on the manufacture of saltpetre. *V. infra,* anno 1643. Ulm, 1627. Folio.

140.—Gunner. *Robert Norton.* Showing the whole practice of artillerie, with all the appurtenances thereunto belonging, together with the making of artificial fireworks. Wrote also "Historie of Queen Elizabeth," and published revised or annotated editions of Stevin's "Disme, or Art of Tenths"; Bourne's "Gunner's Dialogue," 1643; Digge's "Art of Great Artillery," 1624. H. Robinson, London, 1628. Folio.

141.—ORDER. The effect of certain branches of the Statute made in anno 33 Henry VIII., treating the maintenance of artillerie, and the punishment of such as use unlawful games, to be put in execution by order from the King's Majestie. London (black letter), 1621. S. sh. folio.

142.—WHOLE ART OF GUNNERY. *Sir John Smith.* The writer of the *Bow and Musket* controversy. London, 1628. 4to.

143.—TREATISE OF ARTIFICIALL FIREWORKS; both for Warres and Recreation. *Francis Malthus.* A translation from the French. Hawkins, London, 1629. 8vo.

144.—DISSERTATIO DI BELLI FULMINE LANGREANO, QUO PLURES ORDINE ET DISTINCTO INCENDIO, GLOBI EX UNO EODEMAQUE TORMENTO EXPLODUNTUR. An account of a wonderful invention in pyrotechny; a destructive bomb for use with mortars. Bruxelles, 1630. Pamphlet.

145.—MYSTERIES OF NATURE. *John Bate.* A treatise in four parts, of which the second deals with "fyerworkes." T. Harper, for R. Mab. London, 1634 and 1635. 4to.

146.—ORIGEN Y DIGNIDAD DE LA CAZA. *D. Juan Mateos.* A first-class book treating fully of arms for sporting purposes, and illustrated with numerous woodcuts. Is one of the best books for details of the construction of antique sporting guns. (Spanish.) Madrid, 1634. 1 vol. 4to.

147.—PYROTECHNICA, or a discourse in Artificial Fireworks, whereunto is added a treatise of Geometry. *John Babington* (a gunner). In three parts. London, 1635. Folio.

148.—PARALLELA HOROSCOPA, SEU DE DIRECTIONE TORMENTORUM. An anonymous treatise on ballistics and the science of gunnery; the first book on the subject printed in Poland. (Latin.) Vilna, 1636. 4to.

143.—PYROTECHNIE. *Lorrain Hazelet.* The secrets of machines and of artificial fireworks. ———, 1636. 4to.

150.—DISCOURS sur les machines des victoires et conquêtes. *Douet.* Paris, 1637. In 12mo.

151.—DIRECTIONS FOR MUSTERS. Wherein is showed the order of drilling for the musket and pike . . . set forth in pictures, with the words of command and brief instructions for the right use of the same. T. Buck and R. Daniels, Cambridge, 1638. 4to.

152.—MARTYR'D SOULDIER. *Henry Shirley.* A Tragedy in five acts and in verse; edited by I. K. J. Okes, London, 1638. 4to.

153.—COMPLEAT CANNONIERE, or THE GUNNER'S GUIDE, by *John Roberts.* The author of a tract, entitled "Great Yarmouth's exercise, in a very compleat and marshall manner, performed by their Artillerymen," published in 1638, of which this book is apparently an enlargement. The author is described as a gentleman of Bath. J. Okes, London, 1639. 4to.

154.—SCOLARE BOMBARDIERE. *Alex. Chincherni.* A manual of instruction for the gunner. (Italian.) G. Gironi, Ferrara, 1640. In 8vo.

155.—LA CACCIA DELL' ARCOBUZIO. *Cap. Vita Bonfadini.* One of the earliest books on sport with firearms. Marolles drew from it for his "Essai." (Italian.) First appeared at Bologna, 1640. Other editions: Ferrini, Bologna, 1641; Milan, 1647-8; Ferrara, 1652; Bologna, 1672; Venice, 1691; Bologna, 1729; Bologna and Bassano, no date. See No. 175.

156.—ARTE FABRILE. *Ant. Petrini.* A treatise on the useful arts by a Florentine master. Deals particularly with the nature of metals; various inventions relating to arms; the duties of a bombardier. Various editions have different titles. (Italian and Latin.) Florence, 1641, or earlier.

157.—ARTE MILITARE. *Gio. Batt. Colombina.* A manual for the soldier, with particulars of Artillery and instructions for its use. The first edition of this book, from the press of M. Antonio, Trevigi, 1608, is exceedingly rare; a second edition is said to have appeared at Venice in 1617. See "Arte della Guerra." (Italian.) Guinti, Venice, 1641. In 4to.

158.—PRACTICA DI ARTIGLERIA. *E. Gentilini.* See *supra*, No. 31. Venice, 1641.

159.—PRACTYKE DER BOSSCHIETERYE. *Wilhelm Claesz van Utrecht.* A manual in the Netherlands vernacular for the artilleryman. (Dutch.) Rotterdam, 1641; Utrecht, 1659; and Amsterdam, 1695 and 1696.

160.—PRATICA MODERNA DELL' ARTIGLIERIA. *Luigi Collado.* See *ante*, No. 19. (Italian.) Milan, 1641.

161.—MANEGGIO DELL' ARMI MODERNO. *Galezzo Gualdo Priorato.* A small handbook on the use of arms, and manual training for soldiers. (Italian.) Vicenza, 1642. 12mo.

162.—TRADADO DE ARTILLERIA. *Lazaro de la Isla.* Lisbon, 1642.

163.—BUCHSENMEISTERIE SCHULE. *J. Furtenbach.* The School for Gunners, by the author of "Halynitropyrobolia," or Particulars of Gunnery, published at Ulma in 1627. This treatise was published at Frankfort in 1643. (German.)

164.—MILITARY DISCIPLINE, or THE YOUNG ARTILLERYMAN. *Captain W. Barriffe.* London, 1643, 3rd edition. Small 4to.

165.—ARTE DE BALLESTERIA Y MONTERIA. *Alenzo Martinez del Espinar.* The treatise from which Marolles drew his information of gunmaking in Spain. Madrid, 1 vol. 4to, 1644. Last edition 1761.

166.—BALLISTICA ET ANCONTISMOLOGIA IN QUA SAGITTARUM JACULORUM ET ALIORUM MISSILIUM JACTUS ET ROBUR ARCUUM EXPLICATUR. *Merseuni.* A treatise on external ballistics and the science of gunnery. Paris, 1644.

167.—DE MOTU GRAVIUM ET NATURALITER PROJECTORUM. *Torricelli.* Florence, 1644. 4to.

168.—LECCIONES DE ARTILLERIA. *T. de Cerda.* Madrid, 1644.

169.—NOUVELLE FORTIFICATION. *N. Goldman.* A pretty book, illustrated with numerous plates, of no particular value apart from its form. Elzevir, Leyden, 1645.

170.—GUNNER'S GLASSE, set forth by way of dialogue between an experienced gunner and a scholler, with tables of randomes, whereunto is annexed a part of the excellent work of Diago Uffans. *William Eldred.* Practically a translation from the Spanish of Diego Ufano. London, January 16, 1646, O.S. 4to.

171.—ARS MAGNA ARTILLERIA. *Casimir Siemenowicz.* A standard work on the art of war. The contents will be given in the account of the English translation published 1729. Early editions are rare. Folio, with plates, Amsterdam (Latin text), 1650, (French) 1651, (Italian) 1651. A translation by Daniel Elrich into German, published at Frankfort in 1676, and same year and place a translation by Noiset.

172.—COMPLETE BODY OF THE ART MILITARY. *Richard Elton.* 3 parts. London, 1650, fol., and 1654.

173.—POLVORA. *Maria Afflito.* The treatises of this Spanish General are known as "Muniendarum urbium methodus modernus, de munitione et fortificatione, b. 2" (Bib. Magliabechiana, MS. of 1650). The more important is "De igne et ignivomis," 1661 (see *Dormer*): cap. 5 treats of "belico pulvere," cap. 6 "pyrobolis ac bombis." See *infra,* "Breve Trattato," No. 241.

174.—PRATIQUE DE LA GUERRE. *Malthus.* A treatise in French concerning the use of artillery, bombs, mortars, artificial fireworks, petards, mines, bridges, earthworks, etc., etc. Paris, 1650.

175.—CACCIA DELL' ARCOBUGIO. *Captain Vita Bonfadini.* A treatise on the use of firearms for sporting purposes and the art of shooting in the wing, together with a lot of miscellaneous information for the use of sportsmen. A clever little work with wonderful illustrations of arms, showing the various bores and how to gauge them with fingers and thumb, of powder and shot measures, of a pistol candlestick invented by the author for the use of students, and some curious information concerning the manufacture of firearms, gunpowder and shot. Dedicated to Benedetto Macciavelli; has a laudatory poem on the Arqubus, by Mariscotti, and one by Carlo Possenti on the invention of powder. Giuseppe Gironi, Ferrara, 1652. Small 12mo, 102 pp.

176.—TRACTATUS DE ARMIS. *Joh. de Bado Anreo* (Rumpf). Ed. Bessaei. London, 1654.

177.—TRATADO DE LA CAZA DEL BRELO. *Fernando Tamariz de la Escaler.* A treatise on the use of the Arcubus for sporting purposes given in ten chapters, viz.:— I. General rules. II. On the management of the Arcubus. III. On loading the weapon. IV. Loading for special purposes. V. Shot-gun shooting. VI. Rules to be observed in the field. VII. Game seasons. VIII. Habits of game. IX. Hints to shooters. X. Final directions. *Laus Deo*, and an appendix on the setting dog and how to use it. Title, ½-title, 4 pp.; dedication, authorisation, 1 p.; and address to the reader, 4 pp. 31 pp. text. Madrid, 1654. 12mo.

178.—SECRET SHOOTING of the wicked reproved. *James Naylor.* The incoherences of a lunatic Quaker. London, 1655. Folio.

179.—BUCHSENMEISTER DISCOURS. *Schreiber.* A dialogue on the art of gunnery, etc., and a treatise of military fireworks (German). Brieg, 1656. Folio.

180.—OIL DU CANNON, ou la mire Française. *Chevillard.* Paris, 1657.

181.—FORTII MILITARIA, cum imaginibus instrumentorum projectorum. Amsterdam, 1660.

182.—PLUSIEURS MODELS des plus Nouvelles Manières qui sont en usage en l'art d'arquibuzerie. *Jacquinet.* Specimens of firearms and the manner in which they are ornamented, by a Paris artisan. Only one copy known; but see No. 1038, for particulars of Quaritch's reprint. Paris, 1660. Folio, plates.

183.—COMPLEAT CANONEER. *Anonymous.* Showing the principles and grounds of the art of gunnery, as also of fireworks for sea and land. London, 1661.

184.—BUSSCHIETERY KONST. *F. van Zedlitz.* A gunner's manual in the Netherlands vernacular. Amsterdam, 1662. 12mo. The same treatise in German. Frankfort, 1676. 12mo.

185.—REAL CAZA DE VOLATERIA. *Joseph de Xibaja* and *Diego de Morales.* An official publication. Madrid, 1664. Folio, 22 pp.

186.—BERICHT VON GESCHUTZ. Breslau, 1666.

187.—TRAITÉ DES BLESSURES. *Pierre Dailly.* A surgeon's book treating of the nature of wounds caused by firearms. (French.) Paris, 1668.

188.—ARTILLEREN UND ZEUGWARTING. Heidelberg, 1669. Folio.

189.—INSTRUCTION SUR LE FAIT DE L'ARTILLERIE. *Coehorn.* Paris, 1633, 1669. 12mo.

190.—ART OF GUNNERY. *Nathaniel Nye.* This treatise is composed for the help of all such gunners and others that have charge of Artillery, and are not well versed in arithmetick and geometry. Nye was master gunner of the city of Worcester; he gives in his treatise an account of the firearms made at Bromsgrove, of testing coulverines at Deriton, and an illustrated description of a powder tester, very different to the common eprouvette. Also treats of the manufacture of gunpowder and nitre and of artificial fireworks. W. Leak, London, 1647, 1648, 1670. 8vo, plates.

191.—VESTIBULUM PYROBOLIA, SIVE COMPENDIUM ARTILLERIÆ. *Sigismund Kestner.* The author of this treatise on the elements of gunnery was an officer in the Danish Artillery. (Latin.) Frankfort, 1671-9. Folio.

192.—DELICIÆ CRANACHIANÆ. *Ulrich von Cranach.* A description of unique war engines, weapons and devices the invention of the author. (Latin.) Hamburg, 1672. Folio.

193.—HOLLANDTSCKE BURGERY in ruste . . . vervat in een Schuyt-Praetjen tusschen een Domine Politick Militair en Borger. A political rather than a military treatise. Amsterdam, 1672. 4to.

194.—MILITARY AND MARITIME DISCIPLINE. *Captain Thos. Venn.* Book I., Tactics; II., Military Architecture; III., The Compleat Gunner. London, 1672. Folio.

195.—TRATTATO DELL' ARTIGLIERIA. *Moretti.* Venice, 1665. Brescia, 1672.

196.—VENERIE ROYALE. An account of the hunting establishment, etc., of the French Kings. Paris, 1672. 2 vols., 18mo.

197.—CACCIA DEL SCHIOPPO. *Nicola Spadoni.* A treatise on sport with the arqubus, together with descriptions of the various firearms used for sporting purposes and directions for using them, given in 74 letters of instruction, necessary to the making of a valiant and expert shot with the gun. G. Longhi, Bologna, 1673. Small 12mo, 93 pp., and one sheet of illustrations of guns and gun parts. Rare.

198.—GENERAL USE AND EFFECT OF GUNNES. *Robert Anderson.* Contains particulars of experiments and tables of projection, exactly calculated by T. Streete. 2 parts. London, 1674. 4to. See also *infra*, Nos. 226, 229, 232.

199.—TRAITE DES ARMES, DES MACHINES DE GUERRE. *Louis de Gaya.* A short account of the arms used in the French Army, together with a short history of other arms, French, Roman, etc. The author gives precise particulars as to the size of muskets, carbines, etc., the number of rifled arms to others, qualities of matchlocks and firelocks; and states that he saw an air-gun tried in France. The book has 20 plates of illustrations. S. Cramorsey, Paris, 1678, pp. 1-4 and 1-172, in 12mo. For an English edition see *infra*, 205.

200.—ARCHERIE REVW'D, or the Bow-Man's Excellence. An heroick poem. *Robert Shotterel* and *Thos. Durfey.* Exhorting all brave spirits to the banishment of vice, by the use of so noble and healthful an exercise.

"Let Gunners with our Archers now joyn hands.
. . . . .
Our Frontiers guarded well with Guns and Bows,
Whose strong contracted power would dare alarms,
And conquest win, though Hell rose up in Arms."

Roycroft. London, 1676.

201.—HISTORY OF BIRDS. *F. Willoghbœus.* A book on natural history; but there is a rare edition of 1678, having as an appendix a treatise on the "Arts of fowling, falconry, and ordering of fishing birds," by *John Ray.* Several editions in Dutch were published at Amsterdam. The original treatise is in Latin, the edition of 1678 in English.

202.—DIALOGUS DE ARTE ARTILLERIA. *Jes. Dietrich.* Whereby you are taught what a good gunner should know. (Latin.) Nurnberg, 1679. 12mo.

203.—DOPPI ARCHIBUGI A RUOTA. *G. Bossi.* A brief treatise on the double wheel-lock gun, the invention of G. Bossi, of Rome. A small work of 22 pp. (Italian.) Paris, 1679.

204.—WISSENSCHAFT UND VERRICHTUNGEN EINES BUCHSEN-MEISTERS. *Eisenkramer.* Ulm, 1679. 12mo.

205.—TREATISE OF THE ARMS AND ENGINES OF WAR, OF FIREWORKS, ENSIGNS AND MILITARY INSTRUMENTS, both Ancient and Modern, WITH THE MANNER THEY ARE AT PRESENT USED, as well in French Armies as amongst other Nations, enriched with many figures, written originally in French, by Lowis de Gaya, author of the Treatise called the Art of War, translated for Publick Advantage. This is a translation of L. de Gaya's "Traité des Armes"; it is prefaced by a number of instructions (31 pp.) upon the drilling and ordering of troops, and its title is "English Military Discipline, or the way of exercising Horse and Foot according to the practice of the time, with a Treatise, etc." It is generally found bound with "The Art of War." Robert Harford, at the Angel in Cornhill, London, 1680, pp. 1, 31 and 143, 20 plates. 8vo.

206.—COMPLEAT SOLDIER, or expert Artilleryman. The several postures and exercises of the Pike and Musquet. *E. Rawlings.* Treats of drill and military manœuvres, words of command, etc., etc. Sawbridge, London, 1681. 12mo, 240 pp.

207.—BESCHRYWINGE VAN DE ARTILLERIE. *T. Nelson Brinck.* Gravenhaag (The Hague). 1681, 1699. 8vo.

208.—FUNDAMENTUM ET PRAXIS ARTILLERIÆ. *Braun.* In six parts, Dantzig, 1682, 1687. Folio.

209.—THEORIA ET PRAXIS ARTILLERIÆ. *Buchiers.* A treatise on the firearms in actual use. In three parts, Nurnberg, 1682, 1690. Folio.

210.—GENERAL TREATISE ON ARTILLERY. *Sir Jonas More's* translation from the Italian of T. Moretti. An edition appeared in 1689 which was bound up with a work on " Fortification " and Sir A. Dager's " Artificial Fireworks." Neither of the publications are of exceptional value. London, 1683.

211.—MARINER'S MAGAZINE contains the art of Gunnery and Artificial Fireworks, by *Colson.* London, 1684.

212.—ESAME DE BOMBISTI. *Sigismondo Albergetti de Venezia.* By the author of several works on Artillery: see NOVA ARTILLERIA. (Italian.) V. Pinelli, Venice, 1685. In 12mo.

213.—GUNNERY EXPERIMENTS AT WOOLWICH.—*John Greaves* or *Gravius.* A contribution to the Transactions of the Philosophical Society. London, 1685.

214.—HANDBUCHLEIN ÜBER DIE BUCHSENMEISTEREI. — *Eugenii.* (German.) Augsburg, 1685. 12mo.

215.—KOMPENDIUM DER ARTILLERIE. *Winkrat.* Inspruck, 1685. 12mo.

216.—GENTLEMAN'S RECREATION. An encyclopædic work in two divisions: the first treats of Heraldry, Music, Painting, the Fine Arts, etc. ; the second of Horsemanship, Deer, Fox and Hare Hunting, Hawking, Fishing, Fowling and Shooting, Cock Fighting, etc. It is illustrated with numerous plates. This book was one of the first of a long series of " publisher's books " sold on subscription and rarely worth the money asked for them. Bibliographers give Blome a bad character, declare that he derived from other authors and publishers what he published as his own, and that his writings are unreliable and his illustrations coarse and cheap. The chapters on Shooting are short, and their contents insignificant. The plates deserve no praise. The first edition is worth £6 if clean, subsequent editions much less. See also "The Complete Sportsman." Richard Blome, London, 1686, folio; and later under various titles.

217.—DISCOURSE CONCERNING GRAVITY, and its property, its influence on Gunnery. See Transactions Philosophical Society Abridgments, vol. iii., p. 261.

218.—EXPERIMENTS IN SHOOTING. *Nicholas Papin.* A contribution to the Transactions of the Philosophical Society. See their Abridgments, vol. iii., p. 273. London, 1686.

219.—ORDONNANCE DU ROY. Concerning the proofs of powder. (French.) Versailles, 1686.

220.—EXPERIMENT FOR IMPROVING THE ART OF GUNNERY. *Sir R. Moray* (or Murray). See Transactions of the Philosophical Society Abridgments, 1688.

221.—TRAITÉ DE VENERIE. *D'Yauville.* Premier Veneur, et ancient Commandant de la Venerie du Roi. The royal hunts described, nothing to do with shooting. Paris, de l'Imprimerie Royale, 1688, in 4to, 12 and 415 pages, and 41 engraved sheets of music. Reprinted in 1859 by *Journal des Chasseurs.*

222.—CHARACTER OF A GOOD COMMANDER, with an eulogium upon the London Artillery, and an encomium on the Duke of Brandenburgh. *Thos. Plunket.* London, 1689, 4to.

223.—COMPLETE SPORTSMAN, OR COUNTRY GENTLEMAN'S RECREATION. *Thomas Fairfax.* Contains the whole Arts of BREEDING AND MANAGING GAME COCKS, with the BEST METHOD OF FIGHTING THEM, of Rearing and Backing Colts, of Managing Race Horses, Hunters, &c., of HORSE-RACING, of BOWLING, of HARE HUNTING, of FOX HUNTING, of Buck Hunting, of Otter Hunting, of COURSING, of Breeding and Ordering Dogs for the Gun or Chase, &c. ; of ANGLING IN ALL ITS BRANCHES, of Breeding Pigeons, Rabbits, Canary Birds, &c. ; of Finding the Haunts of Partridges, Pheasants, and all Manner of Game ; of Shooting and of Shooting Flying, &c., together with several other equally curious articles too numerous to be mentioned in this Title-page. See *supra*, anno 1686. *J. Cook.* London, n.d. (1689). 8vo, plate.

224.—LIGHT TO THE ART OF GUNNERY. *Bunning.* Wherein is laid down the true weight of powder, both for proof and action ; also the true allowance for wind, with conclusions for the Practice of Gunnery in Sea and Land Service. London, 1689. 4to.

225.—INSTRUCTION POUR LES GENS DE GUERRE. *Gautier.* A treatise on Artillery, bombs, grenades and grenade throwing, &c. (French.) Paris, 1690-92. 12mo.

226.—To HIT A MARK as well upon an ascent and descent as upon the plain of the horizon experimentally and mathematically demonstrated. *Robert Anderson.* London, 1690.

227.—TRAITÉ DE L'ARTILLERIE. (Rumpf.) Lyons, 1690. 12mo.

228.—INSTRUTTIONE DEL BOMBARDIERO. *G. B. Colomberini.* In the form of a dialogue between captain and pupil. A small and unimportant brochure. (Italian.) D. Amadio, Vicenza, 1691. In 4to.

229.—CUT THE RIGGING, and proposals for the improvement of great artillery. *Robert Anderson.* London, 1691. 4to.

230.—NOUVELLE INSTRUCTION pour les gardes des eaux et forêts, chasses et pêches. An old manual for gamekeepers and woodmen. (French.) Charpentier, Paris, 1692, 206 pp.

231.—HANDBUCHLEIN ÜBER DIE BUCHSENMEISTERIE. *Edel.* Augsburg, 1693. 12mo.

232.—MAKING OF ROCKETS, in two parts, experimentally and mathematically demonstrated. *Robert Anderson,* London, 1696. 8vo.

233.—SCHOOL OF RECREATION, or a guide to the most ingenious exercises of Hunting, Riding, Racing, Fireworks, Military Discipline, Science of Defence, Hawking, Tennis, Bowling, Ringing, Singing, Cockfighting, Fowling, Angling. R[obert] [Howlett]. The shooting with the Harqubus is treated in one short paragraph, and the sport is illustrated in one of the six divisions of the plate forming frontispiece. H. Rhodes, London, 1696. 12mo, 182 pp.

234.—GENTLEMAN'S RECREATION. *Nicholas Cox.* Apparently four parts, Hunting, Hawking, Fowling, and Fishing, from Blome's book (see *supra*, No. 216). It was published in 8vo, with plates in 1697, and another edition in 1721.

235.—MÉMOIRES D'ARTILLERIE. *Saint Remy.* Artillery practice on sea and land; a much overrated work, based on Siemenowicz and Valturius. Paris, 2 vols. 4to, 1697—1707. Amsterdam, 1702.

236.—TH' EXPERIENC'D FOWLER. Containing the art of taking fowl with nets, etc. Illustrated. London, 1697. 18mo.

237.—BESCHREIBUNG . . . BUCHSENMEISTERIE. *George Schreiber.* A treatise on a new method of gunnery. (German.) Breslau, no date. 4to.

238.—GRUNDLICHER UNTERRICHT VON DER ARTILLERIE. *Coehorn.* A translation from the Dutch into German. Hamburg, 1699.

239.—NOVA ARTIGLERIA VENETA ICTIBUS PROPELLENS. *S. Alberghetti.* A posthumous work published in 1699 and 1703 in Latin and in Italian at Venice. Codice della Marciana (Class VII., No. DXXII.). "Sigismundus Alb., novæ artilleriæ inventor et ex Anglia redux, obiit MDCCII."

240.—PERFETTO BOMBARDIERO Y ARTILLERO. *Sebas. Ferd. de Medrano.* Bruxelles, 1699. 8vo.

241.—TRATTATO D'ARTIGLIERIA. Treats also of sword blades and the barrels of muskets. Is an Italian MS. of the 17th century (codice della Magliabechiania, classe IX., No. 80).

242.—UNTERRICHT VON DER ARTILLERIE. *Peirander.* Hamburg, 1699.

243.—INTORNO AL FONDERE DELLE ARTIGLIERIE. *Leonardo da Vinci.* A MS. consisting of 108 pp. in 8vo, said to have some illustrations on the margins by the author's hand. Much unintelligible according to Ayala.

EIGHTEENTH-CENTURY ENGLISH BOOKS.

251.—SCHOOL OF RECREATION, or a Guide to the Most Ingenious Exercises of Hunting, Riding, Racing, Fireworks, Military Discipline, the Science of Defence, Hawking, Tennis, Bowling, Ringing, Singing, Cockfighting, Fowling, etc. London, 1710, 1732. 12mo.

252.—FISHING AND HUNTING: The Art and Cunning of Hunting the Hart, Stag, Hare, Fox, Otter, Wild Goat, etc., the Art of Fishing and sundry curious baits, viz., Worms, Flies, Pastes, etc. *T. Bailey.* London, 1720. 8vo, pamphlet.

253.—COUNTRY GENTLEMAN'S VADE MECUM. *Jacob Giles.* A compilation by a well-known "bookmaker." London, 1717, 12mo.

254.—COMPLETE SPORTSMAN.—Another compilation by *J. Giles*, who also published in 1740 a compilation of game laws, and list of statutes relative to game licences, etc. The "Complete Sportsman" appeared in 1718.

255.—POEM. PLERYPLEGIA, or the Art of Shooting Flying. *Abraham Markland, D.D.*, Prebendary of Westminster. London, 1727, 4to.

256.—GREAT ART OF ARTILLERY. *Casimir Simienowicz.* Translated from the French by G. S. Shelvock. The translator states that the book in the original or any Latin edition could not be procured, so he was forced to translate from the French edition (Amsterdam, 1661), which he complains "is now grown very obscure and obsolete . . . it is the most carelessly printed book I ever saw." It was compared with a German edition (Frankfort, 1676). This book was for long the standard work on artillery. It contains: Book I., xiii. ch. on the calibre; Book II., xxxii. ch. concerning pyrotechnics; Book III., x. ch. on rockets; Book IV., pt. 1, iv. ch. on Fire globes or balls, pt. 2, xix. ch. Military fire-balls; Book V., Warlike Firearms, 2 parts, xiii. and x. ch. Tonson, London, 1729. Folio, 404 pp., 23 copper plates. See No. 171.

257.—TREATISE ON GUNNERY. *John Gray, F.R.S.*, of Carthagena. London, 1731, 1781. 8vo.

258.—NEW PRINCIPLES OF GUNNERY. Containing the determination of the force of gunpowder, and an investigation of the difference in the resisting power of the air to swift and slow motions. *Benjamin Robins, F.R.S.* This book is epoch-making, and probably no book dealing with firearms is better known or so frequently quoted; its principles were accepted generally, and the work was recognised as the standard authority for many years. Nourse, London, 1742. 8vo, pp. lvii, 95, 1 plate.

259.—COUNTRY GENTLEMAN'S COMPANION, OR SPORTSMAN'S DICTIONARY. London, 2 vols. 4to, 1744; in 12mo, 1755; an edition in 8vo, Dublin, 1756.

260.—LIGHT TO THE ART OF GUNNERY; or Sea Gunner's Companion. . . . with the most necessary conclusions for the Practice of Gunnery, either in land or sea service. *Captain Thomas Binning*, mariner. London, 1744. Small 4to, 114 pp., 2 plates, tables, diagrams.

261.—DOCTRINE OF PROJECTILES: Demonstrated and applied to the most useful problems in practical gunnery. *William Starrat*. Published by subscription and dedicated to the Fellows of Trinity College, Dublin. Has list of subscribers. Dublin, 1746. 8vo, pp. xii, 176, 4 plates.

262.—ATTACK AND DEFENCE OF FORTIFIED PLACES. *John Muller*. The first of a number of technical books by a "Professor of Artillery and Fortification." London, 1747. 8vo, 3 parts.

263—PRACTICAL SEA-GUNNER'S COMPANION. An introduction to the Art of Gunnery. *William Mountain, F.R.S.* Might be more aptly named a Treatise on Arithmetic and Elementary Mathematics. Is based on Povey and Binning. Rumpf gives date as 1747. London, 1747, 1750, 1781; 127 pp. The 1781 edition has *addenda*, 7 pp., plates and figures.

264.—POEM. COMPLEAT MARKSMAN. *Hon. R. Coote.* On the art of shooting flying. London, 1755. 8vo.

265.—TREATISE ON THE PRACTICAL PART OF FORTIFICATION. *John Muller*. A work written "for the use of the Royal Artillery at Woolwich." London, 1755, 8vo, 28 copper plates.

266.—EASY INTRODUCTION to Practical Gunnery, or the Art of Engineering. *Francis Holliday*. A work on ballistics, by a Professor of Mathematics, the author of numerous works in Arithmetic, Geometry, etc. Innys and Richardson, London, 1756. 8vo, xv and 173 pp., plates.

267.—TREATISE ON ARTILLERY. *John Muller*. Contains: 1, General construction of brass and iron guns used by the sea and land forces, and of their carriages; 2, General construction of mortars, howitzers, their beds and carriages; 3, The dimensions of all kinds of carriages used in the artillery; 4, The exercise of the regiment abroad; 5, March and encampment, ammunition stores and horses; 6, The necessary laboratory work. To which is prefixed a theory of powder applied to firearms. Appeared in 1757. Afterwards published with an appendix or supplement. London, 1757, 1768. 8vo.

268.—ART OF SHOOTING FLYING. *T. Page*. A dialogue between a gunmaker and his pupil; gives some curious particulars of guns and gunmaking, Spanish barrels, loads; practice at moving targets, etc. The later edition has an appendix with long excerpts from and remarks upon the "Principles of Gunnery," by the ingenious Mr. Robins. Crouse, Norwich, 1766, 1782. 8vo.

269.—POEM. Various scenes of Shooting. *John Aldington*. London, 1767. 4to.

270.—POEM. Partridge Shooting. *Francis Fawkes*. "An eclogue to the Hon. C. Yorke." London, 1769.

271.—POEM ON THE CRUELTY OF SHOOTING. *John Aldington*. London, 1769. 8vo.

272.—INTRODUCTION to Marine Fortifications and Gunnery. *Lieut. J. P. Ardesoif, R.N.* Gosport, 1772. 8vo, two parts, plates.

273.—ART OF ENGLISH SHOOTING; with necessary observations for the Young Sportsman when out and returning home. *George Edie.* A treatise inferior to that of T. Page, but on similar lines. Cooke, London, 1777. 8vo, 31 pp., 1 plate.

274.—PRINCIPLES OF GUNNERY, investigated and explained, comprehending Euler's Observations upon the New System of Gunnery, published by Mr. Robins, to which are added many necessary explanations and remarks. *H. Brown.* London, 1777. 4to.

275.—DISCOURSE on the Theory of Gunnery. *Sir John Pringle, Bart., M.D., P.R.S.* London, 1778. 4to, pamphlet.

276.—POEM. THE ART OF WAR. *H. J. Pye.* Translated from the French of the King of Prussia. London, 1778.

277.—THE SPORTSMAN'S DICTIONARY, OR THE GENTLEMAN'S COMPANION, for the Town and Country, containing full and particular instructions for Setting, Hunting, Fowling, Hawking, etc., etc., the Management of Dogs, Gamecocks, Dunghill Fowls, Turkeys, Geese, Ducks, Pigeons, Singing Birds, etc., collected from the Best Authors, with very considerable Additions and Improvements, by Experienced Gentlemen. First edition, London, 1778, 4to, plates, second edition 1782, other editions 1787, 1792, 1800.

278.—RESTITUTION of the Geometrical Treatise of Apollonius Pergæus on "Inclinations." Also, "The Theory of Gunnery." London, 1779. 4to.

279.—DESCRIPTION OF DOUBLE FIREARMS. *Dr. John Aikins.* Believed to be written by an ingenious surgeon, a voluminous writer, who also did much to improve surgical and orthopædic instruments. I have been unable to find a copy. See Watt, "Bib. Brit." London, 1781. 8vo.

280.—DISSERTATION ON THE ERRORS OF MARKSMEN AND GUNMAKERS. *K. McLemon.* London, 1782.

281.—SHOOTING. A Poem. *K. McLemon.* London, 1782.

282.—SHOOTING. A Poem. *Faulder.* London, 1784. 4to.

283.—SHOOTING. A Poem. *H. J. Pye.* Nos. 282-3 are given as distinct publications by Watt. I have been unable to refer to a copy of Pye's poem of this date. London, 1784.

284.—POEM; written during a shooting excursion on the Moors. *W. Greenwood.* R. Crutwell, Bath, 1787. 4to, pp. 25.

285.—ESSAY ON SHOOTING. Anonymous. A translation of Marolles' book, interspersed with a few remarks, and the addition of "The Game of this country as connected with the Amusement of Shooting." In the preface to the first edition the author acknowledges his indebtedness to M. Marolles, but claims to have added much new matter. (The work is practically a literal translation of Marolles.) In the second edition he writes of the "Metaphysics of the Art," and terms gunsmiths "a set of men who have little or nothing to do with the manufacture of the most important part of the instrument." Cadell, London, 1789, 1791. 8vo, 313 pp.

286.—TREATISE ON GUNPOWDER, a treatise on firearms and treatise on the service of artillery in the time of war. Translated from the Italian of A. V. Papacino D'Antoni by *J. Thompson.* London, 1789. 8vo, 374 pp., plates.

287.—AMUSEMENTS. A poetical essay. *H. J. Pye.* Has some lines on shooting, and a denunciation of the practice of slaughtering hand-reared birds. J. Stockdale, London, 1790. 44 pp., 4to.

288.—THE SPORTSMAN'S DICTIONARY. Compiled by *G. Montague.* First edition appeared in 1792. There was a subsequent edition about 1803.

289.—POCKET BOOK. The Sportsman's and Gamekeeper's Pocket Book; or a comprehensive and familiar treatise on the Game Laws, comprising, amongst other matters, all the statutes and resolutions of the courts relating to hares, rabbits, grouse, fish, and other game, together with some general and particular remarks tending to explain their import and facilitate their construction, to which are also added the mode of recovering Penalties under the Game Laws, the Law concerning Trespass in the Pursuit of Game, and the General Law relating to Dogs. *Anonymous.* For "Game Laws" see also *ante*, No. 254. W. Clarke & Son, London, 1794. 58 pp., 12mo.

290.—THE BRITISH SPORTSMAN, or Nobleman, Gentleman, and Farmer's Dictionary of Recreation and Amusement, including a most improved system of Modern Farriery and Anatomical Dissection of the Horse, with concise Rules for Choosing good Horses, and the secrets of Training them with Wind and Vigour for the Course, Field, and Road, particular Instructions for Riding, Racing, Hunting, Coursing, Hawking, Shooting, Setting, etc., etc. *W. A. Osbaldiston.* London, 1795. 4to, plates.

291.—OBSERVATIONS on the English and French Locks, and on one newly constructed by an Officer of the Guards. London, 1799. Privately printed (?).

292.—OBSERVATIONS on the present state of Game in England, and proposal offered for its more effectual preservation. *W. Taplin.* London, 1772. 8vo.

293.—ADVICE to officers of the British Army. *Francis Grose.* A satire. London, 1782, 8vo; 1783, 1787, 12mo. Reprinted 1867 by the Agathynian Club.

294.—TREATISE on Ancient Armour and Weapons. *Francis Grose.* A series of illustrations and descriptions of old arms. Supplement, with distinct pagination and title, published at intervals. London, 1786—1789. 4to, 3 parts, plates.

295.—MILITARY ANTIQUITIES ; respecting the history of the English Army from the Conquest to the present time. *Francis Grose.* This remains the standard work upon the subject of the military equipment of the British army in mediæval times. It was improved in later editions by descriptions and illustrations of the arms and stores in the Tower. The best edition is that of 1812, 4to, 2 vols. T. Egerton, London, 1786-88. 4to. New edition, enlarged, 1801, 1812.

296.—SONGS. *The Royal Sportsman's Delight:* a collection in 8vo, 1765, 1800, 1820. *Sportsman's Delight:* a collection of hunting songs in 12mo, 1790. *Sportsman's Garland:* five new songs. Bristol, 1770.

297.—THE CHASE. *W. Somerville.* A poem descriptive of hunting. With it is often found "Hobnol, or Rural Games" and "Field Sports," a poem. Numerous editions, 1735, 1757, 1767, etc. "Field Sports" published separately by J. Orphoot, Edinburgh, 1809, pp. 87. A good edition of *The Chase* and "Field Sports" annotated by E. Topham, in 12mo, from the Albion Press, 1804, illustrated with plates and woodcuts.

298.—PERIODICAL. *The Sporting Magazine.* This pioneer of sporting periodicals and general repository of all pertaining to field sports was started in 1793, and quickly became famous. The second series, started in 1815, terminated in 1842 ; a third was run from 1843 to 1870. The illustrations, which were particularly good, are highly prized; an index to them has been made by the Hon. F. Lawley. Demy 8vo. 1793—1880.

299.—PRINTS. Too numerous to specify particularly. A set published 1770 by Woollets, after Stubbs, seems to fairly represent shooting at that period.

EIGHTEENTH-CENTURY BOOKS—FOREIGN.

301.—NÄDIGS UNDERRUTTILSE OM ARTILLERIE TIL LANDS OCH SIÖS, etc. *Grundels.* A practical and theoretical treatise on Artillery in Swedish. Stockholm, 1705. 4to.

302.—CURIEUSER KRIEGS- UND FRIEDENS-STERN. *Geisler.* Treatise on military fireworks by one who had nearly half a century of experience in the art. Dresden, 1707. Folio.

303.—PYROPHILI, ARS TORMENTARIA ENUCLEATA. A textbook for gunners. Frankfort, 1703, 1707. 8vo.

304.—ANLEITUNG FÜR ARTILLERIE. *Hasenbank.* Hamburg, 1710. 8vo.

305.—REFUTACAM DOS CANOS, etc. *Bernardino Botelho de Oliveira.* A treatise on Shot Guns, among other things, and the use of them explained, demonstrated and proved. (Portuguese.) A. P. Galvam, Lisbon, 1714, 1 vol., 8vo.

306.—ADELIGES LAND UND FELD LEBEN. *W. H. von Hohberg.* A book of natural history, with chapters on fowling, shooting, hunting, etc. ("Adeliches Land leben," by same author, first appeared in 1682.) Nurnberg, 1716. Folio, plates.

307.—CURIEUSE VOLLKOMMENE ARTILLERIE. *Geisler.* A treatise on cannon. Dresden, 1718. Fol.

308.—ESPINGARDA PERFEITA. *Joao Rodrigues.* About improved firearms, and the rules to be observed in using them. (Portuguese.) A. P. Galvam, Lisbon, 1718. 1 vol. 4to, pp. xxxii, 183.

309.—ESPINGARDA PERFEYTA. *Cesar Fioscono* and *Jordam Guserio.* A treatise on the perfect musket, its use and capabilities. (Portuguese.) A. P. Galvam, Lisbon, 1718. 1 vol., pp. xvii, 183, 4to, with illustrations.

310.—ART DE TOUTE SORTE DE CHASSE ET DE PÊCHE. A compilation, a book of which the brothers Lallemand write, "contains nothing new." Boudet, Lyon, 1719. 2 vols. I., 393 pp.; II., 436 pp.

311.—GRUNDSAETZE DER ARTILLERIE. *Liebnechts.* Frankfort, 1726. 8vo.

312.—ARRET. An act of the Parliament of Toulouse prohibiting the killing of partridges. 1729.

312.—DE JUSTAE TORMENTORUM. *Heinsius.* The construction of cannon on mathematical principles. Leipzig, 1734. 4to.

314.—NACHRICHT VON GEZOGENEN BUCHSEN. *A. Leutmann.* A translation from the Latin of an article in the Comm. Acad. Petropol. Vol. III., St. Petersburg, 1733.

315.—GRUNDLEHREN DER ARTILLERIE. (*Meinigs.*) *Plutonei.* Leipzig, 1734. Folio, 2 parts.

316.—ESSAI de l'application des forces centrales aux effets de la poudre à canon. *Bigot de Morogues.* Experiments upon which to base a correct theory for the construction of mortars. Paris, 1737, pamphlet.

317.—MOYENS DE CONSERVER LE GIBIER. *J. B. Simon.* An amusing treatise written to interest sportswomen. Vve. Prudhomme, Paris, 1738, 1743. 12mo, 84 pp., frontispiece.

318.—UNTERRICHT IN DER ARTILLERIE WISSENSCHAFT. *Heinrich Vogel.* Second edition, Zurich, 1739; 3rd edition, 1756. 8vo.

319.—TRAITÉ DES ARMES. *Girard.* Paris, 1740, 4to.

320.—ANLEDNING TIL SKIUTA, etc. *Ehrenswerd.* A treatise on theoretical and practical gunnery in Swedish. Stockholm, 1741. 8vo; an enlarged edition, 1757.

321.—AMUSEMENTS DE LA CHASSE. A compilation; contains instruction for taking birds, fish, animals, and hints on sport, together with much extraneous matter. Arkslee & Merkus, Amsterdam and Leipzig, 1743. 12mo, 2 vols.

322.—CAZADOR INSTRUIDO. *D. Juan Manuel de Arellanus.* Instructions to sportsmen in the art of shooting with gun, on foot and on horseback, etc. Joseph Gonzalez, Madrid, 1745, 8vo; other editions, Madrid, 1788, Barcelona, no date, Madrid, no date, and Madrid, 1807.

323.—MÉMOIRES D'ARTILLERIE. *Saint Remy.* A new edition, largely augmented by *Le Blond.* Paris, 1745, 1747, 4to, 3 vols. The Hague, 1741. A Russian edition appeared about 1754. See also No. 235, 1697.

324.—CHASSE. A well-written article of 32 pages, illustrated with 23 plates, by Prevost and Defehrt, appears in Diderot and Alembert's Encyclopædie du XVIII. Siècle, 1751-72.

325.—SCHUTZE UND JAGER. (Partly written by J. F. Stahl.) A manual of instruction for shooters and hunters, with directions for target shooting. Various editions. Frankfort, 1752, 1760; Stuttgart, later. Price 5 sgr.

326.—ABHANDLUNG VON DER BAHN DER GESCHUTZ KUGELN. Three treatises with this title were published at Rostock in 1754: one by *Friedrich,* one by *Count Graevenitz,* and one by *Karsten.* There were many other treatises, elementary or otherwise, dealing with gunnery, trajectories, shell firing, etc., etc. Published in German, Swedish and Dutch. They are enumerated in Rumpf, and later ones in Pohler. See *Bibliographies.*

327.—COMPENDIO DE ARTILLERIA. A treatise on naval gunnery; a service publication, cited by Rumpf, but not given in Almirante. Cadiz, 1754. 4to.

328.—SILVA VENATORIA. *Don Augusterio Calvo Pinto y Velarde.* The methods of hunting all kinds of birds and beasts. Gordeguela. Madrid, 1754. 8vo, pp. xvi. and 303.

329.—KRIEGS BIBLIOTHEK. A series of works, some relating to gunnery and muskets. The first series was edited by *Gröben* and published in 10 vols. 4to, at Breslau. Translations in various languages in 8vo, 1755-72. Another edition, 1772-80. Another "Kriegs Bibliothek," published at Leipzig, in 5 vols. 8vo, in 1815-17.

330.—L'ARTILLERIE NOUVELLE. *Tronson de Coudray.* An examination of the modifications made in cannon. There were also some anonymous letters published in between 1756 and 1770. Amsterdam, 1772, 8vo; Amsterdam in 1773. They are attributed to the same author.

331.—POLVERE DA FUOCO. *Francesco Vandelli.* A work in Latin by a professor of military architecture at the Bologna Institute. Is of a controversial character, and the author propounds his own theory of the qualities of explosives. May be found in the "Commentarii Bolognesi," vol. iv., B. V., part II. Bologna, 1757.

332.—LECION DE ARTILLERIA. *Tomas Cerda.* A treatise by a Jesuit priest, the author of several mathematical works, cited by Rumpf and Almirante. Spanish. Barcelona, 1764. 4to.

333.—MÉMOIRE SUR LA DESTRUCTION DES LOUPS. An official order printed at the Royal Press, Paris, in 1770. 4to, 4 pp.

334.—PRINCIPES NOUVEAUX D'ARTILLERIE. This treatise is founded on Robins, with Wilson's additions, and was translated by Dupuys. Grenoble, 1771. 8vo, 2 vols.

335.—MANUEL DU CHASSEUR. *De Chaugrain.* A treatise on the chase, hawking, etc., previously published as the "Almanach du Chasseur." First edition, 1773. Also in 1780 by Saugrain, Paris. 12mo. Frontispiece by Choffard.

336.—COLLECTION DE MÉMOIRES AUTHENTIQUES. Expressions of different opinions on cannon and gunnery, by Gribeauval and S. Auban. Also another volume on the same subject, entitled, "Observations and Experiences." Alethopolis, 1774. 8vo.

337.—CONSIDÉRATIONS SUR LA RÉFORME DES ARMES. An account of the proceedings of the Council at the Invalides, Paris. Paris, 1774, fr.

338.—MÉMOIRES DE PHYSIQUE. *Grignon.* Contains an article on the manufacture of cannon, forging barrels, etc. Paris, 1775. 4to.

339.—GEWEHR-RECHTE JAGER. *J. F. Stahl.* A treatise on the art of shooting with the shot gun for sporting purposes. Metzler, Stuttgart, 1776. 8vo.

340.—MÉMOIRES D'ARTILLERIE, containing also "New Artillery," by *Scheel.* Copenhagen, 1777. 4to. Paris, 1798.

341.—RECEUIL de piéces sur un nouveau fusil. *D'Arcy.* Paris, 1777. 8vo pamphlet.

342.—AVICEPTOLOGIE FRANÇAISE. *Bulliard.* Natural history of game birds, etc. This book was in reality produced by a gunmaker and sporting goods dealer of Paris, named Krezné, *q.v.* Didot le Jeune. Paris, 1778. 12mo, 34 plates. Twelve editions have appeared.

343.—EXPLICACION DE LAS PIEZAS, etc. *Nadal y Mora.* A vocabulary of the component parts of firearms, muskets, carbines, pistols, etc. Madrid, 1779. 8vo.

344.—LETTRES SUR UNE ARME À FEU. Relates to a new infantry arm, and adduces evidence to show that musketry fire was not appreciated at its proper value. Contains also particulars respecting a new pattern Prussian rifle. Avignon, 1780. 8vo.

345.—CHASSE AU FUSIL. *Magnè de Marolles.* This book is very frequently quoted by writers on firearms and gunmaking. The author was born at Tourouvre (Orne), France, and employed in the King's Household. He died at Paris when about sixty years of age, in the year 1792. The first edition of his book had six plates illustrating arms—(1) the marks of barrel-makers; and (2) plans. Tables of contents, xvi and 582 pp. The 1836 edition has ten plates, xvi and 494 pp. Paris, 1788, 1836.

346.—ANFANGS GRUNDE DER GESCHUETZ KUNST. *Fuchs.* An elementary treatise on artillery shooting. Gotha, 1790. 8vo.

347.—VERSUCH ÜBER DIE GEWEHRFABRIKEN. *G. E. L. von Timaeus.* This treatise on gunmaking, the art of shooting, and sport with the gun, appears to be a compilation by a well-known publisher, and is said to have been derived from English sources. I have been unable to examine a copy. Reinecke, Leipzig, 1792. 8vo, 8 plates.

348.—RESUMEN SACADO, etc. *D. Ig. Ahadia.* An account of the arms in the Royal Armoury, Madrid. (Spanish.) Madrid, 1793. 8vo.

349.—COMPENDIO HISTORICO de los Arcabuecros de Madrid. *Isidoro Soler.* A compendious history of the gunmakers of Madrid, with the marks they use and the current counterfeits of them. Aznar, Madrid, 1795. 1 vol. 4to.

350.—Dictionnaire de Toutes Espèces de Chasses. *Fr. Lacombe.* A compilation published with the same illustrations as used in L'Encyclopædie du XVIII. Siècle, of which it forms the 19th part. Agasse, Paris, 1795. 1 vol. and atlas of 32 plates. 4to.

[Note.—The compiler has not included in the foregoing list of eighteenth-century books several works which treat of gunnery, the use of artillery, etc., incidentally, as part of the general scheme of works devoted to such subjects as fortification, military architecture, tactics, discipline, or naval matters; particulars of such books are readily ascertained upon reference to military bibliographies. In the same manner some books of minor interest have been omitted. In the following short list are given titles of books, MSS. and articles, chiefly of Italian origin, the dates and some other particulars of which the compiler has been unable to verify.]

351.—Esercizio d'Artigliera e maneggio del Fucile. *Ant. Sorra.* A treatise on artillery and musketry drill. Venice, 1703. 4to.

352.—La Nobilità e Virtu, che ha in se la virtuosissima professione del vera archisbusiere, composta per suo divertimento, etc. *Cartello de Lari.* This is a manuscript, *circa* 1714, praising the soldiers' calling, and is said to be written facetiously. Codice della Maricelliana ccclxxv.

353.—Dissegni d'ogni sorta de cannoni et mortari. Particulars of the various kinds of cannon, mortars, construction, weight, loads, ranges, etc., with directions. A manuscript of the Salluziana collection, date 1732.

354.—Sentimento sopra la prova delle polvere. A MS. treating of gunpowder tests, etc. Now in the Turin library, date 1745.

355.—Sperienze intorno alla carica, etc. Experiments relating to loads, ranges, possible weights of cannon, etc., cited by Balbo in his "Life of Papacino." Supposed to have been written at Valetta, Malta, 1747. *Marandone* of Turin supposed author.

356.—SPERIENZE SU LA LUNGHEZZA DE TIRI. Experiment to ascertain the range of cannon. *D. Vincenti.* Turin, 1754.

358.—ARTIGLERIA VENETA. *Domenico Gasperoni.* A rare book treating of Venetian artillery, and the author promised another dealing with ancient arms, but this does not appear to have been written. "Artigleria" has 20 engraved plates. Venice, 1779.

359.—REGOLAMENTO, respecting dimensions of the barrel, bayonet, lock, etc., of the infantry musket, 1788 model. Naples, 1793.

360.—POLVORA. *D. Pedro Castro.* A paper in which proofs are set out that gunpowder was used in Italy prior to 1380. MS. now in the library of the Acad. de la Hist., Madrid; written about 1767.

361.—POLVORA. *Espicion de Castro.* A MS. treating of the sale of gunpowder; gives also some particulars concerning the use of the arqubus and artillery, and a history of firearms generally. (Ayala.) Bib. de F. San Roman. Sig. xvi, folio 43.

362.—ESAMINE DELLA POLVERE. *D. Antonio, P. A. de Villafranca.* Published at Turin, 1763. 8vo.

363.—MACHINA. *G. Casale.* An account of a special machine designed in order to prove certain theories of ballistics. The description is included in Vol. V., COMMENTARII, 1767.

364.—ARTE FABRILE. *Petrini Antonio da Firenze.* This treatise has some particulars of the manufacturing arts of possible interest to gunmakers. See No. 156.

365.—DISSERTATIO ARTIGLIERIA. Various MSS. with this title are among the MSS. Salluziana.

366.—STATO DELL' ARTIGLERIA. A MS. in the Parmense collection.

ENGLISH BOOKS, 1800—1850.

401.—REMARKS ON RIFLE GUNS. *Ezekiel Baker.* The full title to the 11th edition is: "Remarks on Rifle Guns; being the result of sixty years' practice and observation, with specific remarks on fowling-pieces, the percussion lock, and firearms in general. To which are subjoined descriptions of a new bullet mould and clipper, various improvements in gun and door locks, spring bolts; a description of firearms deposited in the Royal Arsenal at Woolwich, including all the improvements and inventions for which three silver medals have been awarded by the Society of Arts, together with tables of balls, descriptive plates, etc., by Ezekiel Baker, Gun and Rifle Maker to His Majesty, the Honourable Board of Ordnance, and the Honourable East India Co." The author's work as an inventor will be found recorded in the Society of Arts Transactions. This book has an etching by Barlow, some curious plates, and strictures on Birmingham-made military guns. Smith, Elder & Co., London, 1800 (1798?), 1804. Eight other editions before 1835. (11th edition), 8vo, pp. 268, half-title and plates.

402.—CAUTIONS TO YOUNG SPORTSMEN. *Sir Thos. Frankland.* London, 1801 (2nd edition, with additions). 8vo.

403.—ENGLISH BOWMAN. *T. Roberts.* This is the most easily obtained book containing the Musket and Bow Controversy between Sir J. Smith and H. Barwick and others in the 16th century. Printed for author by C. Roworth, Strand, London, 1801; second edition 1804. Plates, including one folding of cross-bows. 8vo, pp. 300.

404.—RURAL SPORTS.—*William Barker Daniels.* An inferior Sporting Cyclopædia, redeemed by some fine plates due to J. Scott. Sometimes found in three vols. London 1801-2. 2 vols. 8vo. A Supplement in 1813; another edition in 3 vols. 1812.

405.—SPORTING DICTIONARY and Rural Repository of general information upon every subject pertaining to Sports of the Field. *Wm. Taplin.* There is a stable directory, a sort of veterinary handbook, by the same compiler, which is sometimes confounded with the above. London, 1803. 8vo.

406.—SPORTSMAN'S CABINET. Songs. 1803. 4to.

407.—SHOOTING DIRECTORY. *R. B. Thornhill.* London, 1804. 4to; price 31s. 6d.

408.—SPORTSMAN'S DICTIONARY. Improved and enlarged by *H. J. Pye.* Fifth edition, 17 plates. See No. 288. London, 1807. 4to.

409.—ORIENTAL FIELD SPORTS. *Thomas Williamson.* A complete description of the wild sports of the East. Drawings of Animals by S. Howitt. London, 1807. Folio.

410.—ORMES' COLLECTION OF BRITISH FIELD SPORTS, with 20 engravings from designs by S[amuel] H[owitt]. London, 1807. 4to, oblong. These must not be confounded with a series of copper-plate engravings often bound together with this title, but without letterpress, and which originally appeared in oblong folio about 1650, at Leipzig (?).

411.—SCLOPPETARIA. *Captain Beaufoy.* "Considerations on the nature and use of rifled barrel guns with reference to their forming the basis of a permanent system of national defence agreeable to the genius of the country." On the formation of rifle corps, and arms for their use, plates of gun parts, butts, diagrams, etc., tables and index. Egerton, London, 1808; 2nd edition, 1812; pp. 251, 10 plates and frontispiece.

412.—GROUP OF ANIMALS FROM LIFE. *S. Howitt.* No text. London, 1811. 4to.

413.—BRITISH SPORTSMAN. *Samuel Howitt.* A book descriptive of Field Sports, and illustrated with 70 coloured plates. Ed. Orme, London, 1812. 4to, plates.

414.—FOREIGN FIELD SPORTS, with supplement of New South Wales. The supplement has separate title, and issued apart. Illustrations by S. Howitt, Atkinson Clark, Maus Kirch, etc. The original was produced in sumptuous style—green morocco, extra bound, sporting tools on back and broad borders, gilt edges. It contained 50 plates. Present value £3 to £4. London, 1814. 4to.

415.—INSTRUCTIONS TO YOUNG SPORTSMEN in all that relates to Guns and Shooting. *Peter Hawker.* Probably the best known book on the subject. It was written, the author states, "at the particular request of some sporting friends of the author, who had recourse to the press in order to present each of them with a legible copy. A few supplementary impressions also were provided for the amusement and instruction of the inexperienced sportsman"; and eleven editions were published between 1814 and 1859. The first is very rare, the third is the best early edition, the ninth the most full. Subsequent to the author's death, his son, P. W. L. Hawker, edited the work, and the contents were abridged. The third edition is 8vo, has 470 pp., 10 lithographed plates, 4 coloured, a list of London gunmakers, remarks on the Game Laws, and some natural history notes; but the chief value of the book arises from the practical information given, the results of original experiments, particulars of "timely inventions," and the opinions of gunmakers. There is very little superfluous anecdote, and not so much argumentative writing as in sporting books of the time. Printed by Charles Wood, Poppin's Court, Fleet Street, for Longman, Hurst, Rees, Orme, Brown and Green. 1814, 8vo; 1816, 1824, 1825, 1826, 1830 corrected, 1844, 1854, edited by P. W. L. Hawker,

1859. A supplement containing the additions to the fourth edition was published in 1825, and an Abridgment of the Game Laws, with suggestions, being an Appendix to the sixth edition, was published in 1831. The book is not rare, and is worth about 10s.

416.—NOTICES to all Sportsmen, and particularly to Farmers and Gamekeepers. *Colonel George Hanger.* This is a medley of recipes, including remarks on "fowling-pieces, rifle-guns; and muskets rifle-shooting; How to keep all arms loaded for two or three years so as to fire more sure than if fresh loaded; methods of netting partridges, to prevent poaching, to stalk red deer, to shoot wild fowl, remarks on the rifle-breach, etc., etc.; to which is added, A plan for training and developing a corps such as never yet has appeared in any army of Europe, armed with a peculiar gun which will shoot with the precision of a rifle one-third farther than any rifle hitherto used on service, and can also be loaded with cartridges and fired as quick as a common musket." This book gives much information respecting small-bore American rifles, from which the "express" principle is supposed to have been developed. J. J. Stockdale, London, 1814. 8vo, 226 pp.; price 12s.

417.—REPORT: *Manton* v. *Parker.* The case for Joseph Manton's improved gun lock, heard at Westminster July 6th, 1814, relates to the formation of the hammer, which allows the air to escape when loading, but stops egress of powder. The judge said, "It seems to me that the utility of this invention and the purpose of the patent wholly fail." W. Clarke & Sons, London, 1814. 8vo, 65 pp., and plate of gun hammers.

418.—THIRTY YEARS' PRACTICE IN HORSES AND DOGS; with REMARKS ON FOWLING-PIECES, RIFLES, etc., together with plan for training a corps armed with a peculiar gun. *Colonel G. H. Hanger.* London, 1814, 1816. 8vo.

419.—LETTERS ON SHOOTING. *Robert Lascelles.* One of three parts of a treatise called "Angling, Shooting, Coursing." London, 1815. 8vo.

420.—THOMAS'S SHOOTERS' GUIDE, or complete Sportsman's Companion. (*T. B. Johnson.*) London, 1816. Post 8vo, frontispiece.

421.—COMPLETE SPORTSMAN; containing a compendious view of the Ancient and Modern Chase, etc. *T. H. Needham* (*i.e.* T. B. Johnson). Simpkin & Marshall, London, 1817. 12mo, 312 pp.

422.—BRITISH FIELD SPORTS. *W. H. Scott.* Embracing Practical Instructions in Shooting, Hunting, Coursing, Racing, Cocking, Fishing, etc., with Observations on the Breaking and Training of Dogs and Horses, also the Management of Fowling-Pieces and other Sporting Implements. Thirty-four engravings by J. Scott, after Berenger, etc., and woodcut vignettes and tailpieces by Bewick. London, 1818. 8vo.

423.—SHOOTER'S COMPANION; or Directions for the Breeding, Training and Management of Setters and Pointers, with an Historical Description of Winged Game. The fowling-piece considered, particularly as to the use of Percussion Powder; the various methods of making Percussion Powder, and the best pointed out. Of scent . . . shooting illustrated; and the art of shooting flying simplified and clearly laid down. The Game Laws familiarly explained . . . as well as every information connected with the use of the Fowling Piece. *T. B. Johnson,* author of "Thomas's Guide and Needham's Companion." The sub-title too fully indicates the scope of this small book. It is inferior to others of earlier date. Edwards & Knibb, London, 1819. 12mo, 156 pp., 3 etchings by Charles Towne.

424.—SHOOTERS' GUIDE, or Complete Sportsman. *B. Thomas* [T. B. Johnson]. London, 1820. 12mo, 1 plate.

425.—NATIONAL SPORTS OF GREAT BRITAIN. *John Lawrence* and *Henry Alken*. Descriptions in English and French of a series of coloured illustrations. London, 1821. Folio.

426.—SPORTSMAN'S PROGRESS, a poem descriptive of the pleasures derived from field sports. Represented from 2nd edition of Scott's "British Field Sports." London, 1820.

427.—SHOOTING ON THE THAMES. *J. Hassell.* This is contained in a scarce little book called "Excursions of Pleasure and Sports on the Thames." A series of aqua-tint illustrations. Simpkin, London, 1823. 12mo, pp. iii, 191 ; coloured engravings.

428.—SHOOTING. *Henry Alken.* Coloured Plates caricaturing the sport. Oblong folio. McClean, Haymarket, London, 1824 (re-issue ?).

429.—SPORTSMAN'S COMPANION. Songs. J. Pitts, London, 1825. S. sh., folio.

430.—SPORTSMAN'S COMPANION or Gamekeeper's Account Book. Chelmsford, 1827. 8vo.

431.—OBSERVATIONS, on the manufacture of Firearms for military purposes, on the number supplied from Birmingham to the British Government during the late War, on the proof to which barrels are subjected, and on the Proof House, together with some remarks upon the inexpediency of the Ordnance Department fabricating small arms, and upon the obstacles to the free export of arms. [*S. King.*] An anonymous publication, evidently the work of a Birmingham firearms merchant, full of statistics relative to the firearms trade of this country. Longman, London. J. Drake, Birmingham, 1829. 8vo, pamphlet, 3 parts.

432.—ADVENTURES IN RIFLE BRIGADE in the Peninsula, France, and Netherlands, from 1809 to 1815. *John*

Kincaid. A record of soldiering; later, wrote some "Random Shots of Rifleman" (1835). London, 1830, 12mo; 1838 (12mo).

433.—DICTIONARY OF MILITARY SCIENCE. *E. S. N. Campbell.* London, 1830. 8vo.

434.—FIELD SPORTS IN THE NORTH. *L. Lloyd.* "Comprised in a personal narration of a residence in Sweden and Norway in the years 1827, 1828." Illustrated. London, 1830. 8vo, 2 vols. Enlarged edition. Simpkin & Marshall, Glasgow. Printed 1885. 8vo, 416 pp. Swedish edition, Stockholm, 1830.

435.—SPORTSMAN'S SHOOTING JOURNAL and Game Account Book. On an improved plan, embracing the advantages of the Holkam Game Book. London, 1830. 8vo. An annual.

436.—THE SPORTSMAN'S VOCAL CABINET. *C. Armiger.* Lyrics. London, 1830. 12mo.

437.—SPORTSMAN'S CYCLOPÆDIA. "Being an elucidation of the science and practice of the field . . . etc." *T. B. Johnson.* London, Liverpool printed, 1831. 8vo, frontispiece.

438.—WILD SPORTS OF THE WEST. *W. H. Maxwell.* With Legendary Tales, by a writer of fiction. London, 1832, 4to; 1833, 12mo; 1839, 8vo; 1850, 8vo; 1882, 8vo; pp. 158.

439.—HINTS to Grown Sportsmen. Longmans, London, 1832. 12mo.

440.—THE FIELD BOOK. *W. H. Maxwell.* "Sports and Pastimes of the United Kingdom, by the author of 'Wild Sports of the West'; being Sports and Adventures in the Highlands and Islands of Scotland," and numerous other similar books. London, 1833. 8vo, woodcuts.

441.—TWENTY-FIVE YEARS IN RIFLE BRIGADE. *William Surtees.* Edited by J. Surtees. Edinburgh, 1833. 8vo.

442.—METHODS USED IN POINTING GUNS AT SEA. *Captain J. H. Stevens.* A brochure on naval gunnery. J. Murray, London, 1834. 8vo, 45 pp., and plates.

443.—THE GUN; or, a Treatise on the various descriptions of Small Firearms. *William Greener.* The first of Mr. Greener's books, and the most original work on the subject published this century. Colonel G. Hawker considered it "by far the best work ever wrote on the subject." The author had much difficulty in procuring correct illustrations, and the publication was in consequence long delayed. In apologising for the delay in the preface he adds "Should it be objected that the book is too thin for the price, he has only to say that had it been half the thickness, he would not have thought of charging it one farthing less; the immensely expensive scale upon which his experiments have been conducted have, in a great measure, been ruinous to himself." The book was written in Newcastle about 1832, and printed in Sunderland in 1834. Dedicated to the Duke of Wellington. Longman & Co., London; Cadell, Edinburgh, 1835. 8vo, 240 pp., 4 plates, and woodcuts in text. Price 15s.

444.—REMARKS ON SHOOTING. *W. Watt.* Instructions on shooting, and part of the Game Laws done into "familiar verse," by a facetious and much quoted sportsman, who lived at Islington. Sherwood & Co., London, 1835, 8vo; enlarged edition, 1839, 8vo. 96 pp., plate.

445.—OAKLEIGH SHOOTING CODE. By *Thos. Oakleigh* (*i.e.* James Wilson), "containing 220 chapters of information relative to shooting, with numerous notes." London, 1836. 12mo.

446.—HUNTERS OF THE PRAIRIE; or, The Hawk Chief. *J. T. Irving.* A Tale. London, 1837. 12mo.

447.—THE ART OF DEERSTALKING; illustrated by a narrative of a few days' sport in the forest of Athole. *William Scrope.* This excellent book was republished as "Days of Deerstalking," by Hamilton, Adams & Co., 1883, with illustrations by Sir E. and C. Landseer. London, 1838, 8vo; new edition, 1883, 8vo. 324 pp.

448.—MAXIMS and Hints on Shooting. *Richard Penn.* A book of instructions for all sports. J. Murray, 1839 (?), 8vo, 7s. 6d.; 1855, 12mo, 1s.

449.—NARRATIVE of Expedition to South Africa . . . during the years 1836-37. *Sir W. C. Harris.* Illustrated. Bombay, 1838. 8vo.

450.—SNOBSON'S SEASONS. Annals of Cockney Sports. *R. B. Peake*; the 92 illustrations by *R. Seymour.* A much-sought, facetious work. A good copy is worth £12. London, 1838, 1841. Royal 8vo, cloth.

451.—SPORTING. Embellished by large engravings and vignettes illustrative of Field Sports, with literary contributions by various writers. By "Nimrod" (*i.e. C. Apperley*). London, 1838. 4to.

452.—WILD SCENES IN FOREST AND PRAIRIE. *C. F. Hoffman.* London, 1839. 8vo. 2 vols.

453.—WILD SPORTS OF SOUTH AFRICA. *Sir W. C. Harris.* London, 1839, 1840, 1841.

454.—ENCYCLOPÆDIA OF RURAL SPORTS. Edited by *D. P. Blaine.* This is a work of mediocre performance, essentially a publisher's book. London, 1840, 8vo; 1852, large 8vo, revised by "Harry Hieover"; and the best edition, having plates and 600 woodcuts, 1858, revised by *R. Braunston*, has plates by Leech. An edition partly rewritten and brought up to date was printed in Edinburgh 1870, and published by Mackenzie, London.

455.—MOOR AND LOCH. *John Colquhoun.* "Containing practical hints on most of the Highland Sports; and notices of the habits of the different creatures of game and prey in the mountainous districts of Scotland." Edinburgh, 1840, 8vo; London, 1851. Fourth edition enlarged, 2 vols, 1878; Fifth, 1880, 1884.

456.—PORTRAITS OF GAME. *Sir W. C. Harris.* The sketches of African Field Sports drawn by F. Howard, the animals "delineated from life in their native haunts." London, 1840. Folio.

457.—RIFLE AND ITS EXERCISE. Contained in "Defensive Exercises." Edited by *D. Walker.* London, 1840. 8vo.

458.—MS.—Account of Gun-making in Birmingham. *Hawkes Smith.* Written about 1840. Quoted by S. Timmins in "Industrial History of Birmingham."

459.—ROD AND GUN. *James Wilson.* The Angling and Shooting articles from the "Encyclopædia Britannica." Black, Edinburgh, 1840, 1841, etc. 8vo, with engravings and a frontispiece.

460.—GUIDE TO THE TOWER. *John Hewitt.* Some descriptions of the Armour and Weapons in the Tower of London. First published in 1841.

461.—ENGINES OF WAR; or historical and experimental observations on ancient and modern warlike machines and implements; including the manufacture of guns, gunpowder, and swords, with remarks on bronze, iron, steel, etc. *Henry Wilkinson, M.R.A.S.* A readable treatise by the eminent sword manufacturer and gunmaker of Pall Mall. It is based on a paper read before the Royal Institution, and its theory of the discovery of gunpowder is most ingenious. The descriptions of manufacturing processes are not accurate, and the author was led into a serious error as to the "composition of explosives." W. Greener exposed the error in his "Science of Gunnery," and a note correcting the mistake was inserted in copies issued after. There seems to have been a charge of plagiarism made by Wilkinson, for Greener retorts: "I have already shown that Mr. Wilkinson is wrong in a many of his conclusions, but in none can he be more so than in imagining I had borrowed from him. Impossible! He has nothing to lend, and, of course, nothing worth borrowing." Longman & Co., London, 1841. 8vo, 268 pp.

462.—SCIENCE OF GUNNERY, as applied to the use and construction of Firearms. *William Greener*. This book embodies "The Gun," and has additional chapters on "Ancient Arms, Gunpowder, Shot, etc., together with much matter of controversial nature, and examinations of the theories of Robins, Hutton, etc." A vigorously written and interesting book, and having as frontispiece an excellent engraving by Nicholson, representing the author shooting the wild white cattle of Britain in Chillingham Park. The preliminary "advertisement" is incorrectly dated 1831; should be 1841. Dedicated to Prince Albert; engraved title. Longman & Co., London, 1841. 8vo, 324 pp., 8 plates. New edition, Woking, 1846.

463.—SPORTSMAN IN FRANCE. *F. Tolfrey*. Account of a sporting ramble through Picardy and Normandy, with particulars of boar shooting in Lower Brittany. London, 1841. 12mo, 2 vols., 12 illustrations.

464.—MODERN SHOOTER. *Captain R. Lacy*. "Containing practical instructions and directions for every description of inland and coast shooting." Was reviewed by P. Hawker, in the preface to the ninth edition of "Instructions," and did not reach a second edition; it is nevertheless well worth possessing, and if not containing much that is new, is fairly illustrated, and a happy specimen of the facetious style of writing then the fashion. Whittaker & Co., London, 1842. 8vo, 548 pp., engraved title by Landells, frontispiece by T. A. Priors, woodcuts.

465.—THE OLD FOREST RANGER; or, Wild Sports of India, on the Neilgherry Hills, in the Jungles and on the Plains. *Walter Campbell.* London, 1842, 8vo; third edition, 1852; American edition, 1853.

466.—SHOOTER'S HANDBOOK; being the treatise on shooting from the "Rod and Gun." By *J. Wilson.* Edinburgh, 1842. 12mo.

467.—SCENES AND SPORTS IN FOREIGN LANDS. *E. H. D. E. Napier.* London, 1842. 12mo, 2 vols. WILD SPORTS IN EUROPE, ASIA, AFRICA. *E. H. D. E. Napier.* London, 1844. 8vo, 2 vols.

468.—HYDE MARSTON; or, a Sportsman's Life. "*Craven*" (i.e. *W. Carleton*). London, 1844. 8vo, 3 vols.

469.—HIGHLANDS OF ÆTHIOPIA. *Sir W. C. Harris.* A book of African Sport. London, 1844. 8vo, 3 vols. Second edition same year.

470.—THE SHOOTER'S PRECEPTOR. *T. B. Johnson.* Certain practical instructions in the choice and management of dogs used in shooting. The fowling-piece fully considered. The art of shooting flying simplified, etc. London, 1844. 12mo.

471.—SPORTSMAN'S DIRECTORY and Park and Game Keeper's Companion. *John Mayer.* Illustrated. London, 1845. 8vo.

472.—SPORTING EXCURSION TO NIAGARA AND THE CANADIAN LAKES. By *Saron.* Three Articles from *The New Sporting Magazine.* Two cuts added. 8vo, half calf. London, 1845.

473.—SPORTSMAN IN CANADA. *F. Tolfrey.* London, 1845. 2 vols. 12mo.

474.—RECREATIONS IN SHOOTING. "*Craven*" (i.e. *John William Carleton*). A pleasantly written and well illustrated book on the favourite field sport, with some account of the game of the British Islands. London, 1846. 8vo. Added to Bohn's Illustrated Library, with engravings on wood by Branston and on steel after A. Cooper, 1849.

475.—THE SPORTSMAN'S LIBRARY. *J. Mills.* A compilation by a novelist; P. Hawker and others are laid under heavy contribution for the matter. Edinburgh, 1845. 8vo.

476.—HIGHLAND SPORTS and Highland Quarters. *H. B. Hall.* H. Hurst. London, 1847. 2 vols. 8vo, 21s.

477.—INSTRUCTIONS TO YOUNG MARKSMEN. *John R. Chapman.* Treats of the general construction, practical manipulation, causes and liability to error in making accurate performances, and the theoretic principles upon which such accurate performances are founded, as exhibited in the improved American Rifle. Has some interesting notes on rifle manufacture in America. Appleton, New York, 1840. 160 pp., litho. plates, woodcuts.

478.—NATURAL HISTORY OF IRELAND. —*Thompson.* This work has a chapter on punt guns, punts, and some notes on wildfowling. Reeve & Co., London, 1849.

479.—WALKER'S MANLY EXERCISES. The ninth edition, edited by "Craven," has more about gun handling than others. London, 1849. 8vo.

480.—THE SHOOTERS' POCKET COMPANION. *"Trigger."* A manual for sportsmen. Field, London, 184-. 12mo, 2s. 6d.

481.—SHOOTERS' HANDBOOK. A treatise on shooting. Simpkin, London, 184-. Post 8vo, 6s.

482.—SPORTSMAN AND HIS DOG; or, Hints on Sporting. By the Author of "Scottish Sports and Pastimes." London, 1850. 12mo.

483.—THE SPORTING ADVENTURES of *T. S. Haubuck.* Facetious. Longman, London, 1847.

484.—INTRODUCTION to the Field Sports of France. *R. O'Connor.* Murray, London, 1846. 8vo, 6s.

485.—BRITISH AND FOREIGN SPORTS. Spiers, London. 2 vols., 4to, 16s. each.

486.—THE ENGLISH COUNTRY GENTLEMAN, his Sports and Pastimes. — *Lloyd.* A poem. Longman, London, 1849. 8vo, 2s.

487.—SPORTING EXCURSION in the Rocky Mountains. *J. K. Townshend.* Colburn, London, 1839. 2 vols. 8vo, 18s.

488.—FIELD SPORTS IN AMERICA. *H. W. Herbert.* The English edition of "Frank Forester." Bentley, London, 1848. 2 vols., post 8vo, 21s.

489.—YOUNG SPORTSMAN'S MANUAL. Chapman & Hall, London, 1849. Post 8vo, 7s. 6d.

490.—EXMOOR; or, Footsteps of St. Hubert in the West. *H. B. Hall.* Of little sporting interest. Newby, London, 1849. 2 vols., 8vo.

491.—SPORTSMAN AND HIS DOG; or, Hints on Shooting. *H. B. Hall.* Darling, 1850. 12mo, 2s. 6d.

492.—THIRTY-SIX HINTS TO SPORTSMEN. Okehampton, 1850. 4to, 18 pp.

FRENCH BOOKS, 1800—1850.

501.—THÉORIE GÉNÉRALE de toutes les Chasses. This book appeared under various titles; as *Aviceptologie* it is attributed to Ball⸱rd. It appears to have been compiled by Kre⸱ a manufacturer of sporting accessories, and the work was again added to by Cussac. It is a compilation with 36 illustrations, the literary contents drawn chiefly from Marolles, Desgraviers, Buffon, and the Encyclopædia. See also No. 342.

502.—DICTIONNAIRE THÉORIQUE et Pratique de Chasse et de Pêche. *D. de Sales.* The author was born at Lyons 1743, died 1816. He wrote numerous books. This one came under the ban of the censor and was suppressed, only to reappear under other titles.

503.—FABRICATION DES ARMES PORTATIVES. *M. Cotty.* A treatise on the manufacture of small arms for military purposes, by an artillery officer, and the inventor of the Cotty flint lock. Magimel, Paris, 1806. In 8vo.

504.—INSTRUCTION SUR LES ARMES À FEU. A text-book of drill, etc. Magimel, Paris, 1806. In 8vo.

505.—MÉMOIRE sur la Fabrication des Armes portatives de Guerre. *H. Cotty.* An exact account of the methods followed in producing the various types of firearms. Magimel, Paris, 1806. 8vo, 230 pp. and table.

506.—MANUEL DES CHASSEURS. *Chevalier Blanc-St.-Bonnet.* A shooting code; manual for sportsmen and a bibliography of 5 pp. Eymery, Paris, 1820. 12mo. Another edition in 8vo; an enlarged edition in 1821.

507.—FUSILS DE CHASSE. *Henri Roux.* Devoted chiefly to the percussion gun invented by Pauly, but with some remarks on the manufacture of firearms generally, on shooting, on gunpowder, and its effects. Delaunay, Paris, 1822. 8vo, 82 pp.

508.—PRÉCIS DES ÉPREUVES. An account of the comparative test made in 1820 and 1821, with cannon of different kinds. Baron Field-Marshal C——. Paris, 1822.

509.—ALBUM DU CHASSEUR. *Doneaud du Plan.* Has a small bibliography. Lefual, Paris, 1823. In 18mo, five illustrations.

510.—TARIF DES PRIX DE REPARATIONS. Authorised charges for repairing small arms. Verronais, Metz, 1823. Folio.

511.—PROJET DE LÉGISLATION. *C. de Girardin.* A project made in 1817, and printed at the Royal Press in 1824.

512.—VADE MECUM DU CHASSEUR. An old sportsman's hints on kennel management, etc. Paris, 1827. Three illustrations. Five francs.

513.—ÉCOLE PRATIQUE DE CHASSE. Prospectus of a shooting school. Belin, Paris, 1829. In 4to, 16pp.

514.—CHASSE ET PÊCHE, suivies de poesies diverses. *Comte de Chevigne.* Small edition, printed for the author. Odes, stories, etc. Reims, 1832, 265 pp.

515.—DES EFFETS DE LA POUDRE. *Comte de Bouchage.* Published in 1834, this book is of little use now; it gives the effect of powder in sporting arms, and upon various projectiles.

516.—VIEUX CHASSEUR. *Theoph. Deyeux.* Reminiscences. Houdouille, Paris, 1835, in 8vo. Fifty-one litho. illustrations. Other editions 1836, 1837, in 18mo; 1844, in 12mo. In 1851, by Aubry, with fifty illustrations, also by Peon, 1854-55. New edition, with preface. Dentu, 1868, 1873, and one or more later without date.

517.—MÉMOIRE sur le Fusil de Guerre, 1836. *M. Heurteloup.* A descriptive text-book for the 1836 pattern musket.

518.—MANUEL. Nouveau manuel du Chasseur. *M. Thierry.* This book is further described as being a complete treatise on hunting with gun and hound. Huzard, Paris, no date (1838). In 18mo, frontispiece, engraved title, 6 plates, 252 pp.

519.—MUSÉE DU CHASSEUR. *Victor Adam.* A collection of every description of fur and feathered game, with an account of their habits, haunts, etc. Arm. Robin., Paris, 1838. Two parts in one volume. Large 8vo. Coloured lithographs by V. Adam. Italian edition also published. Part I. contains: Animals, pp. viii, 224. Part II.: Birds, pp. xvi, 227. Seventy-two illustrations, coloured or black.

520.—MANUEL DU CHASSEUR. *M. Champeonniere.* A treatise on sporting rights and game laws. Videcoq, Paris, 1844. 16mo.

521.—MANUFACTURES ROYALES D'ARMES. An order repecting the French Government arms factories. Imp. Royale, Paris, 1845. Folio.

522.—USAGE DES ARMES À FEU. *Marquis de Saint Auban.* A translation from the Italian of Papacino d' Antonio.

523.—MAISON RUSTIQUE DU XIX c. *Bixio Bailly and Malpeyre.* A country cyclopædia, in the fourth volume of which are some remarks on field sports and the use of firearms. (*Vide* No. 44.) Dusacq, Paris, no date. 4to.

524.—TRAITÉS DE TOUTES SORTES DE CHASSE ET DE PÊCHE. An imitation of "Ruses Innocentes." The ninety plates of illustrations taken from "Amusements de la Pêche." Vol. I., xvi et 343 pp., II., vi et 271, table of contents and alphabetical glossary of sporting terms.

525.—TRAITÉ GÉNÉRAL DES CHASSES À COURRE ET À TIR. A compilation. Vol. I., xiii et 311 pp., 12 pp. music; Vol. II., 323 pp. The book is much sought by collectors.

526.—CHASSES ET PÊCHES ANGLAISES. This is the same work as "La Chasse et la Pêche en Angleterre et sur le Continent," which see.

527.—TRAITÉ DE LA CHASSE, au silicer à poil. A compilation from articles in the "Encyclopédie Méthodique," Marolles, etc. Bulliard appears to be the compiler. A modification of a "Traité de la Chasse aux Oiseaux." Paris, no date, 223 pp., seven plates (from the "Encyc.")

528.—MÉNAGE DES CHAMPS. Another of Liger's compilations, and apparently often confounded with other books of similar titles.

529.—ÉCOLE DU CHASSEUR. A compilation, chiefly extracted from Diderot's encyclopædia and the Essai of M. de Marolles. Paris, no date, 402 pp., ten illustrations, the latter not new.

GERMAN BOOKS, 1800—1850.

601.—SCHIESSEN MIT DER SCHROT FLINTE. A manual on the art of shooting with the shot gun; for sportsmen. From the English. Baumgärtner, Leipzig, 1802. In 8vo.

602.— ERFAHRUNG GEGRUNDETER UNTERRICHT FÜR BUCHSENSCHUTZEN. *F. B. G. Grasshoff.* A guide to the art of shooting with the rifle (purschbuchse or Stutze). W. B. Korn, Breslau, 1803, and 1813. 8vo.

603.—GEWEHRFABRIK IN SUHL. *Heinrich Anschutz.* The foundation, history, and present position of the industry and the methods followed in the manufacture of both sporting and military firearms. Arnold, Dresden, 1811, 8vo. Two plates. Price 26½ n. groschen.

604.—ANLEITUNG. *Carl Fr. von Sponek.* How to take Red, Fallow, and Roe Deer. Groos, Heidelberg, 1812, 1819, 1825, 1827; also Leipzig, 1819.

605.—HULFSBUCHLEIN fur Jagdliebhaber scheibenschutzen. A manual for the sportsman and marksman with the art of shooting with the gun. (Steinacker, Leipzig), Gotha, 1817. 8vo, 7½ n.g.

606.—GEWEHRKENNER. *J. W. Roux.* A theoretical and practical treatise on the sporting gun and rifle. Steinacker, Leipzig, 1822. 8vo, price 15 n. gr.

76   *Ancient Books.*

607.—SCHIESSKUNST. *C. F. E. Thon.* A treatise on the
  art of shooting with the rifle, shot gun and pistol,
  as well at the target as in the field and on service.
  Eight editions. Sonderhausen, 1822, 1824, subsequently issued at Weimar. 8vo, two parts, price 1. 10.

608.—SCHIESSPULVER. *C. F. Saltzer.* A treatise on the
  history, manufacture and qualities of gunpowder.
  Müller, Carlsruhe, 1824. 26½ groschen.

609.—ANWEISUNG. *Gunther Schild.* The full title is
  " Deutl. Anweisung über den richt, und zweckmassig.
  Gebr. d. Jagd-Flinte, mit praktischen beispielen
  erlautert." A treatise on shooting. Nordhausen,
  Leipzig, 1824. 8vo.

610.—ERKLARUNG üb. d. Bestandtheile d. Feuergewehrs.
  How to use firearms, and particulars respecting some
  varieties. Neukirch, Basel, 1824. 8vo, one woodcut,
  price 4 groschen.

611.—PRAKT-JAGERSCHULE. *Gunther Schild.* A treatise
  on the art of shooting, etc. Dorffling, Leipzig, 1824,
  1837. 8vo.

612.—FEUER UND SEITEN GEWEHRE. *Beroald-Bianchini.* A
  general treatise on small arms. Gerold, Vienna, 1829.
  2 vols. 4to, 38 illustrations, price 8 r. thalers.

613.—ENGLISCHE BUCHSENMACHER, oder gruendliche Anweisung alle Arten von Gewehren, Buchsen und
  pistolen, nebst Percussions, Sicherheitsschlosern und
  übrigem zubehor, nach den neuesten-Erfurdungen und
  Verberserungen zu verfertigen nebst. Belehrungen
  über die verschiedenen Arsen des Schiers- und Knall-
  pulvers, Nachrichten über die bedeutensten Gewehrfabriken Europa's und dgl. mehr. Für Buchsenmacher
  und Buchsenschafter. *George Christ. Alison.* Nach
  dem Englischen bearbeitet und mit mehreren franzo-
  sischen und deutschen Erfindungen und Verlusser-
  ungen vermehrt, mit 103 Abbildungen in Steindruck.

Gottfr. Basse, Quedlinburg & Leipzig, 1832. This book of 84 pp. and three plates of drawings somewhat belies its title. It consists for the most part of descriptions of new inventions, translations of newspaper articles and excerpts from technical papers. It has an illustrated description of a double-barrelled breech-loading fowling-piece furnished with a safety lock. Also a description of an intercepting safety bolt working from a lever on the hand of the gun-stock, for which invention we are informed that Dr. Romershaufen received the Civil-Verdienst-orden from his Majesty. The book contains interesting details of improvements in gun-locks, the manufacture of detonating balls, fulminating powder, and copper caps; also of thread-wound shot cartridges, experiments with wire cartridges, the oval bore, etc. The gun factories at Tulle and Votka (Viatka) are described in detail; but with the exception of recipes for browning gun-barrels the technical instruction is wanting.

614.—JAGERSCHULE. *Chr. F. E. Thon.* An instruction-book for sportsmen and foresters, with a vocabulary of technical words. Various editions (published annually with calendar). Ilmenau, 1834. 8vo, 25 illustrations. 6 lithographed plates. Subsequently issued by Voigt, Weimar. Price 2 th. 10 ngr.

615.—KUNST auf der Jagd gut zu Schiessen. *E. Eichenlaub.* A practical treatise on the art of shooting with the shot gun and sporting rifle; the various kinds of game and methods to be used in aiming, etc., described. Contains also a glossary of sporting and technical words. Various editions published, some with lithographed illustrations. Furst, Nordhausen, 1834-41. 16mo.

616.—VOLKOMMENE JAGER. *L. Hoffman.* The art of expert shooting. According to Souhait, first edition appeared in 1811. Tender & Schaefer, Vienna, 1834. 3rd edition.

617.—HULFSBUCH FÜR JEDEN GEWEHRBESITZER. *A. Sponeman.* Manual for all who have guns. Brasse, Quedlinburg, 1839, 1840. 8vo.

618.—WALDSCHNEPPE. *C. Diezel.* Leipzig, 1839; also in 1842.

619.—SCHIESS FÜR SCHIESS. *W. K. Chrestman.* Shot upon shot. A treatise for sportsmen, game shots, etc. Forderer, Villingen, 1843. 12mo. 1 litho. plate.

620.—VOLKOMMENDE JAGD UND SCHEIBEN SCHUTZE. *Ch. Fr. G. Thon.* Instructions for becoming speedily a correct shot at game or at target. Voigt, Weimar, 1843, 1852. 12mo.

621.—HANDBUCH der Gewehr und Schiesskunde. *M. F. Elrichs.* A guide to the art of shooting, instructions for handling guns, written for sportsmen, riflemen and military. With illustrations. Brugmann, Leipzig, 1844, 1849. 8vo.

622.—BEHANDLUNG der percussionsirten Jagd- und Schützengewehre. *M. F. Elrichs.* Full instructions for the use of percussion, field and target guns. A handbook for the rifleman and the sportsman, with illustrations. Furst, Nordhausen, 1846. 12mo.

623.—ZEITUNG FÜR BUCHSENMACHER und Gewehr fabrikanten. The *Gunmaker's Journal*, edited by E. O. Schmidt, illustrated. Published by Voigt, Weimar, 1844, etc. This was the first technical periodical for the firearms manufacturers, and nominally appeared quarterly, really at irregular intervals. The compiler's set shows that six numbers were issued to each volume, and that publication ceased with the fifth number of the 3rd volume, issued in 1855. Large quarto, lithographed plates with each issue.

624.—PRAKTISCHER JAGD-BETRIEB. *L. Allich.* Treatise on game shooting and trapping. Landherr, Heilbronn, 1846. 12mo.

625.—VOLLST. ANWEISUNG AUFSCHEIBEN und bei Jagden gut schiessen zu lernen. *L. Allich.* Treatise on art of target shooting, and use of the gun for sport, culled from the most trustworthy sources, with practical directions for the acquirement of a difficult art. Landherr, Heilbronn, 1846. 12mo.

626.—PRAKTISCHES HANDBUCH DES GEWEHR-FABRIKANTEN UND BUCHSENMACHERS. *Eduard Oscar Schmidt.* A treatise on gunmaking, including directions for all branches, and the preparation of the necessary material. It is really only a small pamphlet in a paper wrapper compiled by a voluminous producer of trade and technical handbooks. [The first portion of the book is devoted to practical directions for barrel making, browning, smith's work, hardening and tempering; the second to the fitting of the patent breech, lock-making, sight-filing, and particulars of the percussion system. The illustrations consist of twelve 8vo pages of lithographs of gun parts, furniture, etc., and are not of special interest. The book is of the kind from which the intelligent artisan of half a century ago might obtain useful hints and designs.] Gottfried Basse, Quedlinburg and Leipzig, 1848. 8vo, paper wrapper, 68 pp., 12 plates.

627.—GEWEHR KENNER. *Joh. W. Roux.* Practical and theoretical treatise on sporting firearms, their use and expert handling.

ITALIAN BOOKS, 1800—1850.

701.—STRUTTURA E GOVERNO DEL FUCILE DE FANTERIA. *Seb. Maurizio Bordino.* A small book approved by the Royal Military Academy. Chirio e Mini, Turin, 1820. In 8vo.

702.—ARTE DI FARE LE SCIABOLE DI DAMASCO. *Antonio Crivelli.* This brochure is reprinted from the Proceedings of the Institute of Science, Letters and Art, and is divided into numerous short chapters, the whole in 73 pp. It relates to the manufacture of Damascus iron, swords, etc. Royal Press, Milan, 1821. In 8vo, 73 pp.

703.—FUCILE DI FANTERIA CON ESCA FULMINANTE. *S. M. Bordino.* A work on the percussion gun, which had the honour of a French translation. The author was Director of the Royal Arms Factory. Fodratti, Turin, 1839. In 8vo. French edition, 1841. Government Print.

704.—MOUVEMENT des projectiles appliqué aux armes à feu. *P. A. Arena.* A treatise on external ballistics, the force of explosives and initial velocities. Turin, 1839.

705.—MUSEO DEL CACCIATORE. See Musée du Chasseur, of which it is a translation. In large 8vo, 72 lithographed illustrations. Venezia, 1844.

SPANISH BOOKS, 1800—1850.

801.—RESUMO HISTORICO das armas de fogo Portatiles. *Ant. Huet. de Bacellar.* Short account of the history and development of hand firearms. Written specially for the instruction of military cadets. Imp. Reg., Lisbon, 1816. Un foll. 8vo, 75 pp.

802.—CONSTRUCCION DE UNA LLAVE DE FUSIL. *D. Joaquin de Loresecha.* Published in the *Mem. Artill.*, 1844. Valencia, 1831. 19 pp., 2 plates.

803.—ARTE para aprender a tuar la escope de dos Canones. A treatise on the art of shooting the double gun; a curious work. V. Myar. Madrid, 1834. 8vo.

804.—TRATADO DEL PERFECTO TIRADOR. *D. Juan Codies.* A manual for marksmen. F. Pascual. Madrid, 1834. 1 vol. 8vo, 3 plates.

805.—TIR DU FUSIL. *D. J. Gonzalez y Arcaina.* A treatise written in French for A. des Bordeliers. Madrid, 1842. Un foll., 48 pp.

806.—FABRICATION de armas de fuego Portatiles. A paper on the manufacture of military rifles, written by *D. F. A. de Elorza* in collaboration with *D. F. S. Meneses,* and appearing in the *Mem. Artilleria,* 1846.

807.—APUNTES HISTORICOS, etc. *D. J. Almirante.* Historical notes relative to the introduction of gunpowder and the early use of firearms. This paper was inserted in the *Memoirs of the Artillery* for 1847. Pamphlet, 8vo.

808.—FUSIL DE PISTON. *D. Victor Duro.* A paper on the percussion system, inserted in the *Rev. Mil.,* 1847, t. i.

809.—FABRICA DE ARMAS. *D. Esteban Guillelmi.* An account of the arms factory at Seville. Chiefly relating to cannon. Appeared in the *Mem. de Artill.,* 1849.

810.—TUBOS DE TIROS de M. Delvigne. *D. Pedro de La Llave.* A description and criticism of the well-known invention of M. Delvigne, to enable soldiers to become expert marksmen without actual rifle practice. See *Mem. de Artilleria,* 1 series, 7 vol., 461 pp.

PART II.
Modern Books.

MODERN ENGLISH BOOKS.

GUNS AND SHOOTING—GUNMAKING—GUN TRADE—PROOF OF GUNS.

1001.—GUN CLEANING, LOADING, etc.; being practical hints to young sportsmen. *G. Webb.* A handbook of instructions. Simpkin, 1857. 12mo, 2s. 6d.

1002.—GUNNERY in 1858. *W. Greener.* The last of the late Mr. W. Greener's books. It is a compendious treatise of rifles, cannon and sporting arms, the science of gunnery and criticisms of new inventions; full of controversial matter; and although embodying "The Gun," is inferior in point of originality to previous works of the same author. Smith, Elder & Co., London, 1858. 8vo, 440 pp., 5 plates, 37 woodcuts, 15s. Out of print.

1003.—MANUAL OF THE HISTORY AND SCIENCE OF FIREARMS. *J. Deane.* A good comprehensive treatise, but containing little original matter. Longmans, London, 1858. 8vo, pp. ix, 292, 3 folding plates, woodcuts.

1004.—OUR ENGINES OF WAR, and how we got to make them. *J. W. Jervis.* This is a popular account of the introduction of firearms into Europe, their early use in Italy, and their adoption by Great Britain, and development. It is illustrated with facsimiles from

Valturius, etc., and gives a mass of information in too concise form to be absolutely accurate as a guide. Chapman, 1859. 8vo, 115 pp., illustrations and appendices, folding frontispiece.

1005.—THE SHOT GUN AND SPORTING RIFLE. By "*Stonehenge*" (i.e. *J. H. Walsh*). When the author of "British Rural Sports" undertook the editorship of the *Field* in 1857, he found it necessary to inaugurate two gun trials, to settle the breechloader and muzzleloader controversy; and being thereby thrown into close intimacy with gunmakers, the author determined to set forth from the sportsman's point of view all respecting guns and shooting. The contents are: "The Theory of Gunnery"; "The Shot Gun" and "The Sporting Rifle"; "Game, the Animals used in the Pursuit of it"; "Methods of Preserving;" "Present Game Laws." The book is not of equal value to the later works of the writer; it is less technical, more popular in style, and less dogmatic, and is of course quite out of date as a practical sporting guide, and inferior to other books of the same period as a technical work of reference to arms. Routledge, Warne & Co., London, 1859. 8vo, 448 pp., woodcuts, n.e. 1862.

1006.—THE GUN; and How to Use it. *T. B. Johnson*. A sportsman's manual. Houlston, 1860. Fcap. 8vo, 1*s*. 6*d*.

1007.—STORY OF THE GUNS. *J. Emerson Tennent*. Treats of the Whitworth invention and rifled ordnance. Longmans, London, 1864. 8vo, 364 pp., woodcuts.

1008.—ANOTHER STORY OF THE GUNS. A reply to J. E. Tennent. Macmillan, London, 1864. 8vo, 2*s*.

1009.—SHOOTING. *Robert Blakey*. "A manual of practical information." This little book had a large sale, and continued in demand until a couple of years ago, although it contains very little of interest to users of breechloaders, or relating to shooting in the modern manner. G. Routledge & Sons, London. Crown 8vo,

1865, 183 pp. New edition illustrated with drawings by Harrison Weir.

1010.—SHOOTING HANDBOOK. By "*Newtonensis*." Illustrated. Routledge, 1861, 6*d*.; 1868, 6*d*.

1011.—SHOOTING HANDBOOK. Cassell's, 1866. 6*d*.

1012.—MODERN BREECHLOADERS, Sporting and Military. *W. W. Greener*. The first of a numerous series of technical books by the Birmingham gunmaker, who was son of and "successor to William Greener, C.E., author of 'The Gun,' etc." *The Field*, in its second notice of this work, said: "The whole book is useful without being pretentious, at the same time giving full information up to the latest date on all questions connected with guns and rifles." The book was very successful, and the best of its kind at that date, although inferior to some of Mr. Greener's later books. It has 135 illustrations of breechloading mechanisms and parts. Cassell, London, 1871. Crown 8vo, 242 pp., cloth, 7*s*. 6*d*.; second edition, 1874, reprint with appendix.

1013.—THE BREECHLOADER. "*Gloan*." A sportsman's manual, which had a large sale. Woodward, New York, $2.

1014.—SHOOTING: its Appliances, Practice, and Purpose. *J. D. Dougall*. This is the best edition of "Shooting Simplified," and embodies all the later experience of a painstaking experimentalist and indefatigable student. The illustrations are inadequate, the notes profuse, and the style often discursive; but the book contains too much original information to be undervalued. Sampson Low, 1875. 8vo, 358 pp., 10*s*. 6*d*.; new edition, 7*s*. 6*d*.

1015.—CHOKE-BORE GUNS. *W. W. Greener*. "The object of this work is to bring into one focus the leading features and present position of one of the greatest improvements ever made in the shooting of sporting guns." Contains full information respecting shot guns of the description introduced by the author in 1874, with instructions for loading them and using to best advantage; many reports of trials, tests, etc.; but the history of the invention is inferior to that subsequently given with fuller descriptions. Cassell & Co., London, 1876. 8vo, 215 pp., woodcuts and numerous folding diagrams, tables, etc., detached facsimile targets in pockets of cover, 7s. 6d.

1016.—THE GUN AND ITS DEVELOPMENT, with Notes on Shooting. *W. W. Greener*. This is the standard work for all that relates to the history of hand firearms, their varieties, manufacture, capabilities. It is a compilation by a well-known Birmingham gunmaker, but contains a large amount of original matter. The book has had a larger sale than all other gun books put together: of the first edition alone three thousand copies were issued, and five editions were quickly exhausted. The contents include a history of firearms, descriptions and illustrations of the chief types of ancient and modern arms, methods of manufacture, proof of arms, ballistics of rifles and of shot guns, gun trials, theories, experiments; gunpowder, explosives, cartridges, shot, targets, etc., etc.; the work being in fact a cyclopædia of all relating to guns and shooting. The "notes" consist of instructions in the art of shooting at the target, at game, and of wing and trap shooting, and a gazetteer of the shooting grounds and game resorts of both hemispheres. Cassell & Co., London, 1881. Extra fcap. 4to, 675 pp., 400 woodcuts, cloth, gilt, 21s.; now scarce. Second edition, 1884, 740 pp., cloth, plain. Third edition, 1885, 768 pp. Fourth edition, 1889, 768 pp., reprint of third edition. Fifth edition, 1892, 742 pp. Sixth edition, announced, 1894, 700 pp., 10s. 6d. The third edition is probably the best. French and Russian translations have been published. See Nos. 1506, 1922.

1017.—MODERN SPORTSMAN'S GUN AND RIFLE. *J. H. Walsh.*
Vol. I.: "Game and Wildfowl Guns." This is a
comprehensive work on sporting guns; contains full
descriptions of many varieties, most being well illustrated with carefully executed woodcuts. The theoretical portion is cleverly written, and the value of the
results obtained at the various gun and explosives
trials promoted by the author is well stated. There
is no history of guns. The chief contents are:
"Requirements of the Sportsman's Gun for his various
purposes," "Trials of the Gun," "Construction of the
Gun," "The Hammered Breechloader," "The Hammerless," "Explosives, Shot, Cartridges and Loading."
Book II., "Punt Guns." There is also a Glossary,
Appendices on "Siemens' Steel for Gun-barrels" and
"Choke-boring by Compression," and a capital Index.
The excellent woodcuts are the feature of the work.
(For Vol. II. see No. 1102.) Horace Cox, London,
1882. Demy 8vo, 460 pp. text and 72 pp. advts.

1018.— SOME WEAPONS OF WAR, as improved by recent
American inventors. *Wallace A. Bartlett.* A compilation from patent specifications, about fifty pages
devoted to small firearms. Republican Press, Washington, D.C., 1883. 8vo, 98 pp., zincograph illustrations.

1019.—SPORTING FIREARMS, for Bush and Jungle. *F. F. R. Burgess.* "Hints to intending griffs and colonists on
the purchase, care and use of firearms, with useful
notes on sporting rifles, etc." Some commonplace remarks, rather superfluous advice, and poor illustrations
drawn by the author. The last chapter, treating of
Indian experiences, is the best. W. H. Allen, London,
1884. 8vo, 136 pp., 7 plates.

1020.—SHOOTING. *Lord Walsingham* and *Sir R. P. Gallwey.*
These two volumes of the Badminton Series consist
of Vol. I.—"Field and Covert." A short history of
game shooting, hints for beginners, short history of
gunmaking, prices of guns, choice of guns, shooters,

partridge shooting, pheasant shooting, rearing, rabbit shooting, vermin, keepers, poachers and poaching, dogs and dog breaking, pigeon shooting from traps; index. The chapter on trap shooting is the best in the volume, which is, however, a readable compilation, well illustrated and carefully indexed. Vol. II.—" Moor and Marsh." Contains grouse, black game, deer stalking, deer forests, woodcock, snipe, wildfowl, surface-feeding ducks, diving ducks, waders, rails and cranes, shore shooting, punting, fowling punts, swivel guns, a little plain law for game preservers, index. There is also a short bibliography of wildfowling; but, on the whole, the volume is inferior to the former; it is cleverly illustrated. Longmans, London, 1886. 8vo; vol. i., 358 pp.; vol. ii., 348 pp.; price 10s. 6d. each vol.

1021.—TREATISE ON MILITARY SMALL ARMS. *Lieut.-Col. H. Bond.* 1884, 8vo. Military textbook (official).

1022.—PRACTICAL HINTS ON SHOOTING. By " 20-*Bore* " (i.e. *Basil Tozer*). An ambitious work by a young sportsman. Kegan Paul, 1887, 8vo. 472 pp., 55 illustrations.

1023.—MODERN SHOT GUNS. *W. W. Greener.* The sporting gun treated historically, descriptively, analytically, technically, specifically, critically, and practically. Additional chapters on ammunition and trap shooting. This is by far the most scientific of Mr. Greener's books, and the best written; it contains in a small compass all that sportsmen wish to know of the varieties of sporting weapons and of their capabilities. Cassell & Co., London, 1888. Large 8vo, 192 pp., woodcuts and diagrams, cloth, 5s. Another edition, 1891, 202 pp., additional illustrations, 5s.; also editions in German, Spanish and Italian. The English editions are not now easily obtainable.

1024.—LETTERS TO YOUNG SHOOTERS. *Sir Ralph Payne-Gallwey, Bart.* First series, " on the choice and use of a gun," contains much controversial matter, and some of the statements gave offence to particular gunmakers when the letters appeared as a serial in *The Field*. The second series on theories, experiments, and comparisons. Both volumes are well illustrated, have a capital index, and fulfil the object with which they were written. Longmans, 1890. 8vo; vol. i., 263 pp.; vol. ii., 274 pp.; Appendices; woodcuts, diagrams, etc. n.e. 1893 (Third edition); price 7s. 6d. each vol.

1025.—SOMETHING ABOUT GUNS AND SHOOTING. "*Purple Heather.*" A chatty book of reminiscences; hints to sportsmen and comments upon sporting doings and equipment. Alexander & Shepheard, 1890, 1891. 8vo, 150 pp., cloth, 1s.

1026.—A FEW PRACTICAL REMARKS ON GAME SHOOTING AND ITS ACCESSORIES. "*Purple Heather.*" A short treatise on the art of shooting, with hints on sporting equipment, etc. Alexander & Shepheard, London, 1893. 8vo, 1s., paper cover.

1027.—THE BREECH-LOADER, AND HOW TO USE IT. *W. W. Greener.* "Written for that numerous class of sportsmen who delight in a day's shooting, but have neither the time nor the means to make the sport a life's study." Not so technical as most of Mr. Greener's books; consists of nine chapters descriptive of guns, instructions for their use, shooting etiquette, art of shooting on wing, trap shooting, etc., etc. The price is nominal, as the work is well printed in large type and on good paper. Cassell & Co., London, 1892. 8vo, 288 pp., woodcuts, paper boards. Second edition, 1894. 2s. 6d.

1028.—BIG GAME SHOOTING. *C. Phillips-Wolley.* Two volumes of the Badminton Library. The first, contributed to by Sir G. Baker, W. C. Oswell, F. F. Jackson, Warburton Pike, and F. C. Selous, deals with African sport and the big game of North America, and its 450 pages contain more sporting information than is found in all books of African travel put together, and is a capital volume. The second is not so good, and is more general; but the Indian section, by R. H. Percy, is very well done and as fully as could be expected. Arctic Hunting, by Arnold Pike, is capital, and so are the chapters on the Caucasian Aurochs, the Ovis Argali of Mongolia and the Ovis Poli of the Pamir, by S. G. Littledale. Scandinavian elk shooting, by Sir H. Pottinger, is comprehensive, and the chapters on the Caucasus, camp transport, etc., by C. Phillips-Wolley, are in his best style. The remaining sections are devoted to Chamois, the Stag of the Alps, by W. Baillie-Grohman; European Big Game, by A. H. Percy and the Earl of Kilmorey; The Large Game of Spain and Portugal, by A. Chapman and W. J. Buck; Taxidermy; and Notes on Rifles and Ammunition. These volumes are not a cyclopædia of large game shooting, but they treat of the most popular hunting grounds in an admirable manner. The books are well illustrated, and have both indices and a short bibliography. The natural history notes might have been omitted, and sport in the Malay Peninsula, Java, Borneo, etc., substituted with advantage. Longmans, 1894. 8vo; vol. i., 453 pp.; vol. ii., 443 pp.; 10s. 6d. each, and large-paper edition also issued.

1029.—MODERN AMERICAN PISTOL AND REVOLVER. *A. C. Gould.* Contains a description of modern pistols and revolvers of American make; ammunition used in these arms; results accomplished; and the shooting rules followed by American marksmen. A useful little book. In addition to illustrations of pistols and diagrams, has portraits of noted shots and the positions they assume in aiming. A. C. Gould & Co., Boston, Mass., 1888. 8vo, 138 pp.

1030.—DIGEST OF PATENTS relating to B/L. and Magazine Small Arms (except revolvers) granted in the United States from 1836 to 1873 inclusive, classified and arranged according to the movement of the principal parts for opening and closing the breech. By *V. D. Stockbridge*, Examiner United States Patent Office in charge of firearms, etc. Washington, D.C., 1875. 4to, 172 pp., of which one half consists of illustrations. Index to names of patentees, etc.

1031.—PATENTS: ABRIDGMENTS OF SPECIFICATIONS. *Firearms and other weapons, ammunition and accoutrements.* Part I., 1588—1858, small 8vo, 1s. 4d. Part IA., 1858 —1866, 12mo, 2s. 2d.

1032.—PATENTS: *Firearms, Ammunition, etc.* Division I., *Weapons*, Part II., 1867—1876. 12mo, 4s. 6d.

1033.—PATENTS: *Firearms, Ammunition.* Division II., *Ammunition*, Part II., 1867—1876. 8vo, 2s. 6d.

1034.—NEW SERIES ABRIDGMENTS. Division I., *Firearms*, Part III., 1877—1883. 8vo, 3s.

1035.—NEW SERIES ABRIDGMENTS. Division II. *Ammunition*, Part III., 1877—1883. 8vo, 2s.

1036.—MSS. MANUFACTURE OF FIREARMS. *Richard Prosser, C.E.* Deals with methods current in Birmingham about 1850. Patent Office Library, London, No. 10954 137K, 14ff, and press notices of R. Prosser.

1037.—GUN ORNAMENTATION. A series of forty-five to fifty sheets of lithographed designs suited for models for the ornamentation of sporting firearms, revolvers, etc. Was issued at Leipzig and Antwerp, 1860. A complete set is not now readily obtainable. See also an illustrated article by W. O. Greener in *The Magazine of Art*, February 1891.

1038.—GUN ORNAMENTATION. Plusieurs modèles des plus nouvelles manières qui sont en usage en l'art d'arquibuzerie. A series of engravings by *Jacquinet*, preceded by some quaint plates illustrating the gunmaker at work. Bernard Quaritch, London, 1892, facsimile reprint from the 1660 edition. Oblong folio, plates, 15s.

1039.—GUNMAKING BY MACHINERY. An article in the *Journal of the Society of Arts*, vol. xix., p. 423.

1040.—GUNMAKING IN THE UNITED STATES. *Rogers Birnie.* This is a monograph on ordnance construction issued by the Public Service Publishing Co., New York, 1888. Demy 8vo, 123 pp., plates and diagrams.

1041.—REPORT. On the Manufacture of Firearms and Ammunition in the United States. *C. H. Fitch.* This is an extra Census Bulletin compiled by a special agent, and contains accurate and well illustrated descriptions of the methods of making rifles, guns, revolvers, and metallic ammunition by machinery, as practised in New England and at the Springfield Factory. Washington, D. C., 1882. 4to, 38 pp., woodcuts.

1042.—GUNSMITH'S MANUAL. *J. P. Stelle* and *W. B. Harrison.* Described as a "Complete Handbook for the American Gunsmith, being a practical guide to all branches of the trade." This book is really a collection of workshop recipes and hints, and is designed to furnish such information as shall be of most use as a guide to the everyday conduct of the shop, and for such demands or emergencies as are liable to challenge the skill of the workmen. It does not assume to guide the skilled manufacturer in the management of a large factory; it is intended rather as a guide to the workman in acquiring, first, a practical knowledge in every branch of his calling; and, secondly, in the proper conduct of his business when he is established in a shop of his own. The work covers descriptions of guns and pistols, gun-stocks, gun-barrels, tools for breeching guns, tools for chambering breechloading barrels; gun-ribs, thimbles, rifling guns, gun-locks, fitting gun-hammers, nipples or cones, springs, rods, bullet moulds, screw-making tools, and in fact everything necessary to the instruction of the working gunsmith in his handicraft. Jesse Haney & Co., New York, 1883. 8vo, 376 pp., 3 folding plates, woodcuts, etc., in text; price $2.

1043.—SIGHT-MAKING MACHINERY. An introductory account of Messrs. Muir & Co.'s improved machinery for the manufacture of rifle sights. By *C. F. Partington*. London, 1857. Printed for private circulation. 8vo, 40 pp., woodcuts.

1044.—BULLET-MAKING MACHINE. Illustrated descriptions of Ward's bullet machine, shell-moulding machine, and self-centering railway turn-table. London, 1863. Demy 8vo, 12 pp., plates.

1045.—GUN TRADE. London Gunmakers' Company. The best account of this Company, its charter, its history, its powers, its revenue, and its work, is given in the Report of the Royal Commission on the City Companies, vol. iii., 1884.

1046.—GUN TRADE. THE CASE OF THE GUNMAKERS. A petition by the London Gunmakers' Company asking that the importation of weapons may be discontinued and the sale of foreign-made small arms prohibited. Single sheet folio, 1680 (Brit. Mus. Collection).

1047.—GUN TRADE. THE CASE OF THE COMPANY OF GUNMAKERS OF LONDON. This petition refers to the one presented in 1680, and complains that arms were bought and paid for in cash in Holland; that English arms were not ordered, and for those ordered and delivered payment could not be obtained, £30,000 being then due to the Company from the Government. Single sheet folio, 1710 (Brit. Mus. Collection).

1048.—GUN TRADE, BIRMINGHAM. The best account of the introduction of the firearms trade into Birmingham, and its progress, is contained in an article contributed by F. Godwin, F.S.A., to *The Gentleman's Magazine* of February 1869.

1049.—GUN TRADE. The Gunsmiths' Queries. This is a political tract rehearsing the facts given in the petitions of 1706 and 1710, and still further complaining of the support given to foreign manufacturers, and the want of work at home. Single sheet folio. Printed 1710.

1050.—GUN TRADE. *Pamphlets.* A number of pamphlets, reprints of newspaper articles, correspondence, etc., relating to the firearms trade of Birmingham, *circa* 1860, are conserved in the Birmingham Reference Library. Catalogue No. 60394.

1051.—GUN TRADE. The Firearms Industry of Birmingham. An article contributed by J. D. Goodman to the Handbook of Birmingham Manufactures, edited by S. Timmins, 1866. 8vo.

1052.—GUNMAKER OF MOSCOW. *S. Cobb.* A Novel. New York. 16mo, $1.

1053.—GUNMAKER OF MOSCOW. This is the title of a costume play, *temp.* Peter the Great, in French's Acting Edition. Several musical pieces bear the same title.

1054.—PROOF ACTS. The Acts of Parliament relating to the proving of firearms are private acts, not public statutes; and the only complete copies known to the compiler are conserved in the Reference Library at Birmingham. They are: the Acts of 1813 and 1815, Catalogue No. 17720; the Act of 1855, Cat. No. 17904; the Act of 1867, Cat. No. 34964; the Act of 1868, Cat. No. 17953. Under the heading of "Gun Trade" in the same catalogue there will be found a reference to the "New Rules of Proof" adopted in 1888, and to copies of the Proof House Annual Reports since 1888. See also under "Gun Trade," and numerous articles in *The Sporting Goods Review*, vols. i.—vi.

1055.—PROOF HOUSE. The present proof company the bane of the Gun Trade: a letter addressed to the masters and journeymen gunmakers of the kingdom. By *William Greener*, Ass. Inst. C.E. A pamphlet indicting the wardens of the Proof House. It was owing to the publication of this letter that the Gun Barrel Proof Act of 1855 was promoted. Guest, Birmingham, 1845. 8vo, 12 pp.

1056.—NOTES ON THE PROOF OF GUNS. *J. H. Walsh.* (?) Comments on the new rules and scales of proof passed in 1888, with various letters, etc., reprinted from the *Field*. Mr. Walsh died whilst this brochure was at press; it was really produced in order to prove that the course taken by the *Field* in demanding a better proof test was justified. Horace Cox, London, 1888. 8vo, 54 pp., 1s. See also Nos. 1535-42.

RIFLES.—THE VOLUNTEER MOVEMENT.—MONOGRAPHS OF SPECIAL ARMS.

1101.—MODERN AMERICAN RIFLES. "*Ralph Greenwood*" (*J. C. Gould*). Contains descriptions of processes of manufacturing; appliances used by riflemen for hunting and target shooting; directions for bullet making and reloading cartridges; positions adopted in various styles of shooting; trajectories of rifles; a record of inventions, improvements, and work accomplished with American rifles. A fairly written and comprehensive monograph of American target rifles, with some excellent criticism of their qualities as sporting arms. Bradlee Whidden, Boston, 1893. 8vo, 338 pp., woodcuts and diagrams; 2 dollars 50 cents.

1102.—MODERN SPORTSMAN'S GUN AND RIFLE. *J. H. Walsh.* Vol. II.—"The Sporting Rifle, Match Rifle, and Revolver." The chief contents of this volume are: "Definition of Terms used in reference to the Rifle itself," "Rifling Machines," "Theory of Projectiles by

'T.'" "The Mechanical Construction of the Sporting Rifle and its Ammunition," "Modern Rifled Pistols," "Match or Target Rifle and its Ammunition." This book contains by far the best introduction to scientific gunnery; its fault is that it is too technical and elaborate for the firearms maker, and quite beyond the understanding of the general reader. Copious extracts are made from the "Proceedings of the Royal Society," and the work of Professor Bashforth is utilised. The author acknowledges the assistance received from the late Mr. F. Osborne, and there are numerous contributions from gunmakers and others embodied in the work, which can be regarded as the best compilation of its kind, and affording the readiest reference to the multitudinous technical subjects of which it treats. H. Cox, 1884. Demy 8vo, 544 pp. and 72 pp. advts., woodcuts and diagrams.

1103.—THE RIFLE; its effects on the War; on National Military Organisation and preparation for Defence. *J. Le Conteur.* A brochure written by "one of the rejected," and evidently inspired by the Crimean campaign. Contains a folding plate of target shield. Parker, Furnival, & Parker, London, 1855. 8vo, 132 pp., cloth limp.

1104.—THE RIFLEMAN. *Captain Rafter.* A book of adventures. Routledge, 1858. 1s. 6d.

1105.—RIFLE and Revolver Clubs. *P. E. Dove.* Longmans, 1858. 3s. 6d.

1106.—PROSE AND POETRY about Rifle Clubs. *M. F. Tupper.* Routledge, 1859. 6d.

1107.—RIFLE CLUBS and Volunteer Corps. *W. H. Russell.* Routledge, 1859. 1s. 6d.

1108.—RIFLE VOLUNTEER'S HANDY BOOK. *W. G. Hartley* Saunders, 1859. 7s. 6d.

1109.—MANUAL for Rifle Volunteers. *J. Boucher.* Mitchell, 1859. 5s.

1110.—RIFLE AND VOLUNTEER CORPS. *L. Jewitt.* Ward & Lock, 1860. 1s.

1111.—STORIES about Riflemen and Rifles. *N. Thornton.* A compilation. Whittaker, 1860. 1s.

1112.—RIFLEMAN'S Book of Jokes. Abingdon, 1861. 6d.

1113.—RIFLEMAN'S RECORD of Target Practice. *R. Pinkney.* A score-book. Whittaker, 1860.

1114.—RIFLEMAN'S REGISTER. *R. Brewin.* A score-book. Leicester, 1861. 2s. 6d.

1115.—BURY REGISTER of Rifle Practice. Virtue, 1863. 12mo. 2s.

1116.—DARBY REGISTER of Rifle Practice. Hamilton, 1861. 1s.

1117.—SCORING BOOK. New and Improved Rifle Shot's Register. Gale and Polden, Woolwich, 1894. 16mo, 1s.

1118.—SCORING BOOK. Andrews, Woolwich. 1s.

1119.—SCORING BOOK. Parker, Birmingham. 1s.

1120.—SCORING BOOK. Shooting Register. Spiers & Son. 2s. 6d.

1121.—RIFLE SIMPLIFIED. *J. D. Dougall.* A familiar treatise on an important weapon, and on its efficiency for national defence. A. Hall, Glasgow, 1859. 8vo, 1s.

1122.—RIFLES; and Rifle Practice. *C. M. Wilcox.* New York, 1860.

1123.—LECTURES on the Rifle. *E. C. Walford.* Marlborough, 1860. 2s.

1124.—RIFLE IN THEORY AND PRACTICE. *A. Walker.* Longmans, 1865. 8vo, 5s.

1125.—RIFLE; its Theory and Practice. Judd, New York, n.d. 50 c.

1126.—BREECHLOADING RIFLES. *V. D. Majendie* and *C. O. Browne*. Detailed notes on the Snider and Martini rifles and Boxer ammunition. 4 pts. Woolwich, and Simpkin, London, 1869. 8vo, 3s. 6d.

1127.—THE ENFIELD-PRITCHETT RIFLE. 1854. 8vo. New edition, 1859. 2s.

1128.—SNIDER RIFLE; its construction. Simpkin, 1871. 8vo, 1s.

1129.—RIFLE RANGERS. *Captain Mayne Reid*. Fiction. Chapman, 1873, and numerous editions.

1130.—CRITICAL DISCUSSION of Systems of Rifling and Projectiles. *J. S. Butler*. Van Nostrand, New York, 1875. $7.50.

1131.—MAGAZINE AND SMALL BORE RIFLES. Report by *C. G. Slade* (official). Harrison & Sons, etc., 1888. 2 parts, 12 pp., foolscap folio.

1132.—NEEDLE GUN. *M. U. Sears*. A full descriptive specification of the Sears' breechloader, adapted for military and sporting use. M. U. Sears, London, 1851. Demy 8vo, 24 pp. and folding plate.

1133.—HENRY BREECHLOADER. A series of reprints from various periodicals, *temp.* 1868, descriptive circulars, etc., collected into one volume, are in the London Patent Library.

1134.—THE WHITWORTH RIFLE. *Sir J. Whitworth*. "Rifled Small Arms" is one of a series of papers on mechanical subjects by Sir J. Whitworth, and contains some controversial matter, and is an important contribution to the Enfield Controversy. E. and F. N. Spon, London, 1852. 4to, 42 pp.

1135.—MACHINE GUNS. Most of the machine guns, the Gatling, the Hotchkiss, the Nordenfeldt, and the quick-firing Driggs Schroeder are described and illustrated in quarto volumes, privately printed and published by the inventors, patentees or manufacturers. Some are published by Simpkin, and in the case of the Nordenfeldt the price is fixed at 30s.

GUNNERY, BALLISTICS, FIELD TRIALS, ART OF RIFLE SHOOTING.

1151.—QUESTIONS AND ANSWERS, on Gunnery, etc., for the use of officers of the Auxiliary Forces at Woolwich and Shoeburyness. *F. W. Panzera.* Clowes, 1882. 8vo, 76 pp.; third edition, 1892, pp. xvi, 146.

1152.—TREATISE ON FIREARMS. *F. C. Simons.* Dalton, 1857. Post 8vo, 2s. 6d.

1153.—GUNNERY MANUAL, for the Fleet. Official text-book. Harrison, 1873. 2s.

1154.—GUNNERY INSTRUCTOR. *E. Barret.* An American service manual. New York, 1862. 7s. 6d.

1155.—POPULAR INTRODUCTION TO RIFLED ORDNANCE. Simpkin, London, 1871. 1s.

1156.—GUNNER'S POCKET BOOK. *T. W. Bridges.* This is a treatise for the artilleryman. Spur, 1871. 8vo, 1s.

1157.—GUNNERY CATECHISM. *J. D. Brandt.* A service book. (American.) Trübner, London, 1864. 18mo, 7s. 6d.

1158.—ELEMENTS OF GUNNERY. *J. T. Hyde.* London, Allen, 1861. 8vo. 12s.

1159.—SCIENCE OF GUNNERY. *T. A. Blakely.* Ridgway, London, 1867. 1s.

1160.—LEADING PRINCIPLES OF GUNNERY. *F. L. Simons.*
Particularly those parts of it relating to rotatory
motion; the Minié, Jacobian, and other practical facts
examined. Thacker, Calcutta, 1859. 8vo, 4s. 6d.

1161.—TRAJECTORIES OF AMERICAN HUNTING RIFLES. A
series of tests made by the *Forest and Stream*, at the
Creedmoor Range, Sept. 26th to Oct. 19th, 1885.
Office of *Forest and Stream*, New York, 1885. Paper,
96 pp., folding table. Illustrated. 50 cents.

1162.—REPORTS on Experiments made with the Bashforth
Chronograph, to determine the resistance of the Air
to the motion of Projectiles, 1865-70. W. Clowes &
Son, London, 84/B/1941. Demy 8vo, 170 pp., tables,
folding plates of trajectories, etc.

1163.—TABLES of remaining Velocity, Time of Flight and
Energy of various Projectiles, calculated from the
Results of Experiments made with the Bashforth
Chronograph, 1865-70. London, 1871.

1164.—MATHEMATICAL TREATISE on the Motion of Projectiles,
founded chiefly on the results of experiments made
with the Bashforth Chronograph. Asher & Co.,
London, 1873. Demy 8vo, 132 pp., 82 pp. tables,
frontispiece illustrating chronograph.

1165.—Supplement to No. 1162. Same publishers, London,
1881.

1166.—REPORT on Experiments made with the Bashforth
Chronograph to determine the resistance of the Air to
the motion of Elongated Projectiles (Part II.), 1878-9.
Printed for the Stationery Office, 84/B/2853, 1879.

1167.—FINAL REPORT on Experiments made with the
Bashforth Chronograph to determine the resistance of
the Air to the motion of Elongated Projectiles. 1878-80.
W. Clowes & Sons, etc., London, 1881.

1168.—BASHFORTH CHRONOGRAPH. *Francis Bashforth.* "A revised account of experiments made with the Bashforth Chronograph, to find the resistance of the air to the motion of projectiles, with the application of the results to the calculation of trajectories according to J. Bernoule's method." Also calculated tables. University Press, Cambridge, 1890. Demy 8vo, 318 pp.

1169.—REPORT. The *Field* Trial of Explosives. A full account of the results obtained at the *Field* trial of explosives in choke-bore and cylinder shot guns. H. Cox, *Field* office, 1878. Demy 4to pamphlet.

1170.—REPORT. The *Field* Trial of Large and Small Bores. A full account of the results obtained at the *Field* trials instituted in 1879 to determine the relative values of 12, 16, and 20 bores for sporting purposes. H. Cox, *Field* office, 1879. Demy 4to pamphlet, with illustrations of the *Field* rest and "force gauge."

1171.—TABLE OF CALCULATIONS for use with the *Field* Force Gauge. *J. H. Walsh.* H. Cox, London, 1882. 4to.

1172.—REPORT.—The *Field* Gun Trials of 1875. This is the report of the committee of sportsmen appointed by the proprietors of the *Field* to watch the trials carried out under the superintendence of the Editor, J. H. Walsh, to determine which of the makes of guns submitted for trial gave the best shooting. The trials, which will be found fully reported in the *Field* of May 1875, proved the superiority of the choke-bore guns in general, and of W. W. Greener's make in particular; from them may be dated the modern era of gunmaking. Horace Cox, *Field* Office, 1875. Demy 8vo, illustration of prize cup, tables, etc. Pamphlet.

1173.—PRACTICAL HINTS on Rifle Practice with military arms. Orange Judd Co., New York, 1883. 12mo, 36 pp.

1174.—RIFLE SHOOTING POSITIONS; On the Hythe School of Musketry Instruction in Rifle Shooting. *J. MacGregor.* A reprint from the *Journal of the Society of Arts* of May 17th, 1861. It has some illustrations of old-fashioned positions in shooting. The Orderly Room of the London Scottish Rifle Volunteers, 1861. 4to, ten pages, 1*d*.

1175.—THE RIFLE AND HOW TO USE IT. *J. V. Bridgeman.* This is the title of a one-act farce in Lacy's collection. First performed at the Theatre Royal, Haymarket, September 20th, 1859. French, Strand, London. 6*d*.

1176.—CRACK SHOT.—*E. C. Barber.* The young rifleman's guide: a treatise on the use of the rifle, with rudimentary and finishing lessons; including a full description of the latest improved breechloading weapons, illustrated with numerous engravings; rules and regulations for target practice; directions for hunting game found in the United States and British provinces, etc., etc. The hunting notes are very short; the book is useful as showing the state of arms manufacture in the United States after the war. W. A. Townsend Adams, New York, 1868. 8vo, 342 pp., appendix and advertisements, woodcuts of guns, parts, and diagrams. Price $1 75 c.

1177.—PRACTICE OF RIFLE FIRING. *Captain Thackeray.* The substance of three lectures delivered at Bath, with a description of prismatic telometer. Parker & Co., London, 1853. 8vo, 44 pp. and litho. plates.

1178.—HINTS TO RIFLEMEN. *H. W. S. Cleveland.* Appleton, New York, 1864. $1 50 c.

1179.—HANDBOOK FOR RIFLEMEN. *G. O. Starr.* One of the *Forest and Stream* manuals. Ford, New York, 1876. 50 c.

1180.—INSTRUCTION in Rifle and Carbine Firing. *S. E Blunt.* Scribner's Sons, New York, 1885. $2 net.

1181 —MANUAL OF RIFLE PRACTICE. *G. W. Wingate.* This work includes a complete guide to instruction in the use and care of the modern breechloader. W. T. and T. P. Church, New York, 1872. 16mo, 186 pp., illustrated. $1 50 c.

1182.—MATCH SHOOTING with the Enfield Rifle. Newcastle and London, 1866. 1s.

1183.—RIFLE SHOOTING. *Heaton.* Longmans, 186–; new edition, 1865. 2s. 6d.

1184.—RUDIMENTS OF RIFLE PRACTICE. *C. H. Fenton.* Simpkin, *circa* 1865. 8vo. 1s. 6d.

1185.—COMPANION to the Rifle Musket. *Sir B. Browne.* Allen, 1859. 2s.

1186.—RIFLE PRACTICE. *J. Jacob.* Smith, Elder & Co., 1856, 1858. 2s.

1187.—MANUAL OF TARGET PRACTICE FOR UNITED STATES ARMY. *G. L. Willan.* Claxton; Lippincott, New York, 1862. 75 c.

1188.—SYSTEM OF TARGET PRACTICE. *H. Heth.* Van Nostrand, New York, 1862. 75 c.

1189.—ON SOLDIERS SHOOTING. *H. de B. Hovell.* Being vol. xxxvii. of Gale and Polden's Military Series. Gale and Polden, and Simpkin, London, 1888. Post 8vo, pp. 37. 1s. 6d.

1190.—HINTS ON RIFLE SHOOTING. A pamphlet issued from the office of *Land and Water,* attributed to *Sir Henry Halford,* Bart. 1889. 8vo, 1s.

CURRENT ENGLISH SPORTING BOOKS.

LADIES AND FIELD SPORTS—SPORTS GENERALLY—BIOGRAPHIES—TALES—MISCELLANEOUS.

1201.—SPORTING SKETCHES. "*Diane Chasseresse.*" A series of cleverly written and interesting reminiscences of a sportswoman with the gun. Macmillan, 1890. 8vo, illustrations, 6*s*.

1202.—GENTLEWOMAN'S BOOK OF SPORTS. A volume of the Victoria Library, edited by *Lady Beatrice Violet Greville.* The shooting department is from the pen of "Diane Chasseresse." London, 1892. 8vo.

1203.—LADIES IN THE FIELD. A compilation on outdoor sports for ladies, edited by *Lady B. V. Greville.* The shooting portion contributed by "Diane Chasseresse" and Miss Leale. Ward & Downey, London, 1893. Crown 8vo.

1204.—MERRIE ENGLAND; its Sports and Pastimes. *Lord W. Lennox.* Of little sporting interest. Newby, 1857. 12*s*.

1205.—PICTURES OF SPORTING LIFE. *Lord W. Lennox.* Hurst & Blackett, 1859. 2 vols., post 8vo., 21*s*.

1206.—RECREATIONS OF A SPORTSMAN. *Lord W. Lennox.* Hurst & Blackett, 1862. 2 vols., post 8vo, 21*s*.

1207.—MERRIE ENGLAND IN THE OLDEN TIME. By *George Daniel,* with etchings and other illustrations by John Leech and G. Cruikshank. Of no shooting interest. London, 1842; new edition 1869. 8vo, 2 vols.

1208.—OLD ENGLISH SPORTS; Pastimes and Customs. *Peter Hampson-Ditchfield.* Methuen & Co., 1891. 8vo, pp. xii, 132.

1209.—MODERN ENGLISH SPORTS. *F. Gale.* Sampson Low, 1885. 8vo, 6s.

1210.—COUNTRY SPORTS. There is a chapter on shooting in this compilation. Ward & Lock, 1882. Post 8vo, 1s.

1211.—SPORTS AND RECREATIONS IN TOWN AND COUNTRY. Sonnenschein, 1888. 8vo, 2s.

1212.—SPORTING ANECDOTES, Annals, Descriptions, Tales and Incidents. Hamilton, London, 188-. 8vo.

1213.—RECOLLECTIONS OF OLD COUNTRY LIFE. *J. K. Fowler.* Social, Political, Agricultural, and some Sporting Reminiscences. Longmans, London, 1894. 8vo, 256 pp., 10s. 6d.

1214.—FORTY-FIVE YEARS' SPORT. *J. H. Corballis.* Edited by *A. T. Fisher.* Bentley & Son, 1891. 8vo, pp. x, 502.

1215.—OLD SPORTS AND SPORTSMEN. *J. Randall.* An account of the Willey Country, Biographical Anecdotes of Hunting, etc. Virtue, 1873, 1875. 8vo, 7s. 6d., 5s.

1216.—THE LIFE OF A SPORTSMAN (J. Mytton). "*Nimrod*" (i.e. *C. J. Apperley*). This book is much sought after, possibly on account of its 35 coloured illustrations by Alken. London. Royal 8vo, plates. Value £1 10s.

1217.—BROOKLANDS. A sporting biography. *H. B. Hall.* Newby, 1852. 2 vols., post 8vo, 21s.

1218.—AUTOBIOGRAPHY OF A GAMEKEEPER. *John Wilkins* of Stanstead, Essex. A book of interesting reminiscences. Fisher Unwin, 1892. 8vo, illustrated, 6s.

1219.—MR. SPONGE'S SPORTING TOUR. Illustrated by *Leech.* Caricatures. Bradbury, 1852. 8vo, 14s.

1220.—TOMMIBEG SHOOTINGS. *T. Jeans.* A facetious work. London, 1860. 8vo.

1221.—A Shooting Adventure. *Talberg.* A tale without words. Simpkin, 1889. Square 16mo, 6*d.*

1222.—Tales for Sportsmen. "*Dragon.*" Illustrated by G. Bowers. Simpkin, 1885, 1887. 8vo, 10*s.* 6*d.*; 2*s.* 6*d.*

1223.—The Gun Runner. *Bertram Mitford.* A romance of Zululand. Chatto & Windus, London, 1893. 8vo, frontispiece by S. L. Wood.

1224.—Sport and its Pleasures. *E. C. Grenville-Murray.* London, 1859. 8vo.

1225.—Sport and its Pleasures. An essay in "Palatable Essays." *Lucullus Hall.*

1226.—Horns and Hoofs. *R. Lydekker.* A book on hoofed animals; wild oxen, pigs, sheep, goats, Asian and African antelopes, the deer of Asia and South America, ancient and modern rhinoceroses. With illustrations. H. Cox, 1893. 8vo, pp. xv, 411. 30*s.*

1227.—Notes on Game Shooting. *J. J. Manley.* Reprinted from *The Country.* J. U. Gill, 1880. 8vo, 389 pp., illustrated.

1231.—Handbook of the Game Laws. *G. C. Okes.* The legal digest of Acts relating to game-preserving and the prevention of poaching. Butterworths, 1881, 3 e.p. 8vo, 16*s.* Supplement separate, 2*s.* 6*d.*

1232.—Curiosities of the Game Laws. *Hugh Barclay.* A reprint of an article in *Journal of Jurisprudence,* with additions. Glasgow, 1864. 8vo.

1233.—Practical Game-preserving. *W. Carnegie.* A guide to the preservation and propagation of winged game and the destruction of vermin. *Bazaar* office, 1884. 21*s.*

1234.—A Few Hints on Game-preserving. *E. J. F.* London (privately printed?), 1894.

1235.—Law of Field Sports. *G. P. Smith.* Judd, New York, 1886. $1.

1236.—GAME LAWS. A Compendium of the Laws relating to Game and Game Fish. Revised to date, and edited by *Charles B. Reynolds*. The scope of the work embraces all the laws relating to game and game fish of every State and Territory in the Union and British Provinces. The better to insure accuracy, all the important sections are given in their full text, as they appear on the statute-books. *Forest and Stream* Co., New York. 8vo pamphlet. Price 50 cents.

1237.—GAME LAWS IN BRIEF. Laws of the United States and Canada relating to Game and Fish Seasons. For the guidance of sportsmen and anglers. Compiled by *Charles B. Reynolds*. *Forest and Stream* Co., New York. 8vo pamphlet, price 25 cents.

1238.—GAME LAWS FOR GAME KEEPERS. *H. Neville.*

ART OF SHOOTING — GAME SHOOTING — WILDFOWLING — BRITISH SHOOTING.

1251.—THE ART OF WING SHOOTING. *Charles Lancaster.* "An illustrated treatise, with extracts from the best authorities." This is an attempt to teach by giving pictorial representations, from instantaneous and other photographs, of actual practice by experts. There is very little theory, the explanations of the sketches made by James Temple are succinct, sometimes meagre, and the author too often advances the opinions of diverse authorities when his own views would be more intelligible and instructive. It is the fullest work on the subject. The author, 151, New Bond Street, London, 1889, 1891, 1893, etc. Demy 8vo, 212 pp., 51 full-page illustrations and numerous cuts in text, 7*s.* 6*d.* net.

1252.—FIELD COVER AND TRAP SHOOTING. *Adam H. Bogardus.* Contains hints for skilled marksmen, instructions for young sportsmen, and a chapter on trap and pigeon shooting. The book was edited by

C. H. Foster. It contains a lifelike portrait of the author engraved by Perine. J. B. Ford & Co., New York, 1874. 8vo, 343 pp.

1253.—SHOOTING SIMPLIFIED. *J. D. Dougall.* A concise treatise of the Art of Shooting. One of the best appreciated books on this subject. A. Hall, Glasgow. 1857. 8vo. New edition, rewritten and enlarged, with a special chapter on breechloaders. London, 1865. 8vo.

1254.—DEAD SHOT. "*Marksman.*" A book of instructions in the art of shooting, and manual to the sport generally. London, ———— 1889. 8vo, illustrated.

1255.—PLAIN DIRECTIONS FOR ACQUIRING THE ART OF SHOOTING ON THE WING. Industrial Publishing Co., New York, 1873. 75 cents.

1256.—WING AND GLASS BALL SHOOTING. *H. C. Bliss.* Shooting with the rifle; instructions for beginners in snap-shooting, and exposure of some of the popular fallacies in regard to it. New York, 1884 (?). 8vo, 50 cents.

1257.—SHOOTING ON THE WING.—Plain directions for acquiring the art of shooting on the wing; with useful hints concerning all that relates to guns and shooting, and particularly in regard to the art of loading so as to kill. To which have been added several valuable and hitherto secret recipes of great importance to the sportsman. By "*An Old Gamekeeper.*" This is a popular little manual of instruction, which treats of the gun, how to load, clean, carry and handle it; how to learn to shoot; and gives besides many useful hints and recipes, which contribute to one's success and comfort afield. New York. 8vo, 75 cents.

1258.—ON THE WING. A book for sportsmen. *J. Bumstead.* Happy, New York, 1869. $1 50c.

1259.—THE GUN, and How to Use it to kill every wing shot. *Gwynne Price.* A pamphlet on the art of shooting, more particularly trap shooting. New York, 1876 (?). 8vo, pamphlet, picture cover.

1260.—A SHORT ACCOUNT OF INANIMATE BIRD SHOOTING, and Hints on the Formation and Management of Clubs. *F. C. Borer* and *W. Keep.* Reprinted from the *Shooting Times,* 1894. 8vo pamphlet.

1261.—RULES OF PIGEON SHOOTING. These are included in most shooting books, and the Hurlingham and Gun Club Rules published under the one cover, price 6*d.*, by H. Cox. Various editions, 32mo.

1262.—MANUAL OF BRITISH RURAL SPORTS. "*Stonehenge*" (i.e. *J. H. Walsh*). A cyclopædia of field sports, etc. Routledge, London, 1856, 1859, 1867, 1871, 1875, 1878, etc. 8vo, pp. xvi, 720.

1263.—HINTS ON SHOOTING, FISHING, etc. "*Christopher Idle.*" Longman, 1855. 12mo, 5*s.*

1264.—GAMEKEEPERS' DIRECTORY. *T. B. Johnson.* A book of hints on destroying vermin, etc., for gamekeepers. Paper, 1851, 12mo, 5*s.* An edition also published by Sherwood. See No. 470.

1265.—TREATISE ON THE GUN AND DOG. *R. B. Fellows.* Groombridge, 1857. 12mo, 2*s.* 6*d.*

1266.—DOG AND GUN. *J. J. Hooper.* Judd, New York. 60 cents; 30 cents.

1267.—KNAPSACK MANUAL FOR SPORTSMEN. *Edward Ward.* Bradbury & Evans, London, 1866, 1872. 8vo.

1268.—SHOOTING AND TROUT FISHING. *W. Barry.* Tinsleys, 1871. 8vo, 7*s.* 6*d.*

1269.—SHOOTING ADVENTURES. Canine lore and Sea-fishing trips. Chapman & Hall, 1878. Post 8vo, 2 vols., 21*s.*

1270.—SPORTING SKETCHES. *G. F. Mason.* Kent, 1879. Folio, 10s. 6d.

1271.—THE WILDFOWLER: a treatise on Ancient and Modern Wildfowling. *Henry Colman Folkard.* The best treatise on the subject, whether for historical or practical purposes. Longmans, London, 1859. 8vo. Third edition, 1875.

1272.—HINTS ON SHORE SHOOTING; with a chapter on Skinning and Preserving Birds. *J. G. Harting.* London, 1871. 8vo.

1273.—SHOOTING AND FISHING TRIPS. *Lewis Clement.* Second Series. Sketches contributed by "*Wildfowler*" to *Bell's Life*, and by "*Snapshot*" to the *Country*. London, 1876, 1877. 4 vols. 8vo.

1274.—PUBLIC SHOOTING QUARTERS. "*Wildfowler*" (i.e. *Lewis Clement*). This is a descriptive gazetteer of localities where wildfowl and other shooting can be obtained. *Field* Office, 1881. 8vo, pp. iv, 193.

1275.—MODERN WILDFOWLING. By "*Wildfowler*" (i.e. *Lewis Clement*). A guide to the sport—a *vade mecum* for the wildfowler. H. Cox. Demy 8vo, plates and woodcuts, 10s. 6d.

1276.—THE BOOK OF DUCK DECOYS, their Construction, Management, and History. *Sir R. Payne Gallwey.* J. van Voorst, London, 1886. 4to, pp. x, 214.

1277.—THE FOWLER IN IRELAND; or, Notes on the Habits and Haunts of Wildfowl and Seafowl, including instructions in the art of shooting and capturing them. *Sir R. Payne Gallwey.* With illustrations. Van Voorst, London, 1882. 8vo, pp. xiii, 503.

1278.—SPORTING SKETCHES WITH PEN AND PENCIL. *Francis Francis* and *A. W. Cooper.* A series of twelve sketches, of which five relate to shooting, the others to fishing. The sketches are portraits of sporting men. H. Cox. Demy 4to, 12 illustrations, 24 vignettes, 10s. 6d.

1279.—NEW BOOK OF SPORTS. Essay reprinted from the *Saturday Review*. Bentley, 1885. Crown 8vo, 6s.

1280.—IN THE GUN ROOM. *H. Knight Horsfield*. Shooting sketches, stories reprinted from sporting periodicals, interspersed with original verse. Eden, Remington & Co., 1892. 8vo, 245 pp., 2s. 6d.

1281.—ROUGH SHOOTING. *T. E. Kebbel*. Sonnenschein & Co., 1889. 8vo, 90 pp., illustrations.

1282.—SPORT AND NATURE. *T. E. Kebbel*. Contains "My First Grouse" and other memories. Sonnenschein & Co., 1893. 8vo, 94 pp., illustrations.

1283.—SHOOTING AND SALMON FISHING; Hints and Recollections. *Augustus Grimble*. A book of reminiscences, of no great interest, but readable. The drawings are far from being good. Chapman, Hall & Co., London, 1892. 4to, pp. xi, 259, photogravures.

1284.—TOUR AND SPORT IN SUTHERLANDSHIRE. *Charles St. John*. John Murray, 1849. 2 vols., post 8vo, 18s.

1285.—WILD SPORTS OF THE HIGHLANDS. *Charles St. John*. John Murray, 1846. Post 8vo, 6s.; 1860, 12mo, 3s. 6d.

1286.—WILD SPORTS IN THE HIGHLANDS. *W. H. Maxwell*. Baily, 1843. 2 vols. 8vo, 24s.; Routledge, 12mo, 1s. 6d.

1287.—STRAY SHOTS. *J. Colquhoun*. Published with "Salmon Casts." Edinburgh, 1858. 8vo. And later as "Sporting Days," 1866. 8vo.

1288.—WILD SPORTS OF THE WEST. *W. H. Maxwell*. Routledge, 1849, 2 vols. 8vo, 21s.; 12mo, 3s. 6d ; 1860, 1s. 6d.

1289.—SPORTS AND PASTIMES OF SCOTLAND. *Robt. S. Fittis*. A short history with illustrations. A. Gardner, Paisley, 1891. 8vo, 212 pp.

1290.—SCOTTISH FIELD SPORTS. *J. D. Dougall.* "A volume of mingled gossip and instruction," and a very well written book. A. Hall, Glasgow, 1861. Foolscap 8vo, 3*s.* 6*d.*

1291.—HIGHLANDS AND LOWLANDS OF SCOTLAND WITH ROD AND GUN. *T. Speedy.* Blackwoods, 1884-6. 8vo, 15*s.*; new edition, 15*s.*

1292.—OUTDOOR SPORTS IN SCOTLAND. "*Ellangowan*" (i.e. *W. H. Allen*). New edition, 1890. Post 8vo, 3*s.* 6*d.*

1293.—TWENTY-SIX YEARS' REMINISCENCES OF SCOTCH GROUSE MOORS. *W. A. Adams.* A book of interesting experiences from 1863 to 1888, containing much useful information and some clever illustrations by Charles Whymper and Douglas Adams. Cox, 18—. Crown 8vo, coloured wrapper, 1*s.*

1294.—MOORS. Return of Game registered each season on Grouse Moors. A guide for renters of shooting. Issued from *Land and Water* Office, 58, Pall Mall, London, 1892, etc.

1295.—HOW I BECAME A SPORTSMAN; being early reminiscences of a veteran. "*Avon.*" With illustrations. Chapman & Hall, 1882. 8vo, pp. xii, 208.

1296.—SPORT: Fox Hunting, Covert Shooting, Deer Stalking, etc. *W. Bromley Davenport.* Edited by *A. B. Davenport,* and illustrated by *H. H. Crealocke.* Chapman & Hall, 1885. 4to, large paper, 215 pp.; also 8vo.

1297.—ESSAY ON SPORT AND NATURAL HISTORY. *J. G. Harting.* Contains chapters on Shooting, Lark mirrors, Seals, Wild Swans: altogether thirty-eight essays, with practical hints on Bird-preserving, for the use of travellers and collectors. H. Cox, 18—. 8vo, 463 pp., 32 illustrations, 10*s.* 6*d.*

1298.—GAME BIRDS AND SHOOTING SKETCHES. Coloured plates by *Millais.* Sotheran, 1892. 4to, 105*s.*

1299.—THE PARTRIDGE. A book of the Fur and Feather series, which will provide handbooks to the principal game birds from the zoological, sporting, and gastronomical points of view. Lord Walsingham is responsible for that portion of this volume which treats of shooting. Longmans, London, 1893. 8vo.

SELECTED ENGLISH BOOKS ON FOREIGN SPORT.

FOREIGN SPORT GENERALLY—IN EUROPE, ASIA, AFRICA, AMERICA AND AUSTRALASIA.

1301.—SHIFTS AND EXPEDIENTS OF CAMP LIFE, TRAVEL AND EXPLORATION. *W. B. Lord* and *T. Baines.* A practical handbook for the explorer and hunter, and the very best book of its kind. H. Cox, new edition, 18—. 8vo, 704 pp., xxiii. ch., 400 woodcuts, etc., 15*s*.

1302.—TEN YEARS' WILD SPORT IN FOREIGN LANDS. *H. W. Seton-Karr.* Chapman. 6*s*.

1303.—SPORT AND ANECDOTE. *C. T. S. B. Reynardson.* Scribner & Br. New York, 1887. $4 50 c.

1304.—SPORT WITH GUN, etc. *A. M. Mayer.* Century Co., New York, 1885. New edition. $5.

1305.—SPORTING ADVENTURES IN MANY LANDS. *J. D'Ewes.* Routledge, 1857. 8vo, 5*s*.; 1862, 2*s*.

1306.—LEAVES FROM A SPORTSMAN'S DIARY. *Parker Gillmore.* Sports, adventure, reminiscences. W. H. Allen. 8vo, pp. vii, 341, 6*s*.

1307.—ADVENTURES AFLOAT AND ASHORE. *Parker Gillmore.* 1873. 8vo, 2 vols

1308.—ADVENTURES IN MANY LANDS. *Parker Gillmore.*
Has illustrations by S. P. Hall. Marcus Ward,
Belfast and London, 1879. 8vo.

1309.—ALL ROUND THE WORLD. *Parker Gillmore.* A
story of travel, with illustrations by S. P. Hall. Marcus
Ward, London, 1871. 8vo.

1310.—ACCESSIBLE FIELD SPORTS. *Parker Gillmore.* Some
sporting experiences in North America. London,
1869. 8vo.

1311.—PRAIRIE AND FOREST. *Parker Gillmore.* W. H.
Allen. New edition, illustrated. 1874. Cr. 8vo,
pp. x, 383, 3s. 6d.

1312.—GUN, ROD AND SADDLE. *Parker Gillmore.* Some
records of personal experiences. W. H. Allen, 1869,
1893. Cr. 8vo, pp. viii, 341. 6s.

1314.—ENCOUNTERS WITH WILD BEASTS. *Parker Gillmore.*
W. H. Allen, 1881. Cr. 8vo, pp. 305, illustrated,
3s. 6d.

1315.—HUNTING GROUNDS OF THE WORLD. *Victor Meunier,*
with 32 full-page illustrations. Sampson Low, ——.
Small 8vo, cloth, 5s. ; new edition, 2s. 6d.

1316.—WILD ADVENTURES IN WILD PLACES. *W. Gordon
Stables.* A boys' book. Cassell & Co., 1881. 8vo,
176 pp., illustrations.

1317.—WILD BEASTS AND THEIR WAYS. *Sir S. W. Baker.*
An excellent treatise on large game shooting. Macmillan, 1830. 8vo, 2 vols. ; 1891, 8vo, 1 vol.

1317a.—SHORT STALKS. *E. N. Buxton.* E. Stanford, 1892,
n.e. 1893. 8vo, pp. xiii, 405, illustrated.

EUROPE.

1318.—WOLF HUNTING AND WILD SPORT IN LOWER
BRITTANY. *H. H. Crealocke.* Illustrated, 1875. 8vo.

1319.—SPORTING RAMBLES IN GERMANY, FRANCE, etc. *Hon. F. St. John.* Longman, 1853. Post 8vo, 9s. 6d.

1320.—CHAMOIS HUNTING IN BAVARIA. *C. Boner.* An interesting account of a little-known sport. Coloured illustrations. 1860, 8vo, 10s. ; 1865, 8vo, 5s.

1321.—NOTES ON SPORT AND ORNITHOLOGY. *Prince Rudolph of Austria.* Translated by G. Danford. Gurney & Jackson, 1889. 8vo, illustrated, 18s.

ASIA.

1322.—SKETCHES OF FIELD SPORTS AS FOLLOWED BY THE NATIVES OF INDIA, with Observations on the Animals, etc. *Daniel Johnson.* The second edition contains "Boar Hunting." London (Torrington), 1822. 8vo. New edition, 1827.

1323.—RIFLE AND HOUND IN CEYLON. *Sir Samuel White Baker.* A practical treatise, but not now of much use as a guide to the shooting obtainable in the Island. 1854, 1857, 1874. 8vo, 2s.

1324.—EIGHT YEARS' WANDERINGS IN CEYLON. *Sir S. W. Baker.* London, 1855, 1874. 8vo.

1325.—SHOOTING SCENES IN THE HIMALAYA. *F. Markham.* Bentley, 1856. Royal 8vo, 21s. ; 1860, 10s. 6d.

1326.—RIFLE IN CASHMERE. *Arthur Brinckman.* A narrative of shooting expeditions in Ladak, Cashmere, Punjaub; with advice on travelling, shooting, etc., with notes on Army Reform and Indian Politics. 1862, cr. 8vo, 2 illustrations. New edition, 1865.

1327.—SPEAR AND RIFLE. *H. A. Leveson.* Recollections of Sport in India. 1860. 8vo.

1328.—SPORT IN MANY LANDS. A memoir of Major H. A. Leveson ("Old Shikari"), by *H. F.*, with illustrations. Chapman & Hall (1876), 1879. Two vols. 8vo.

1329.—HUNTING GROUNDS OF THE OLD WORLD. *H. A. Leveson.* London, 1860, 1865. 8vo.

1330.—CAMP LIFE AND ITS ACQUIREMENT, for soldiers, travellers, and sportsmen. By *H. A. L(eveson)*, the "Old Shikaree." 1872. 8vo.

1331.—WRINKLES: or Hints to Sportsmen and Travellers. *H. A. L.* 1874. 8vo.

1332.—THE HIGHLANDS OF TIBET. Large Game Shooting in Thibet and the North-west. *A. A. Kinloch.* Illustrated with photographs of trophies, etc. London, 1869, 1876. 4to, Series 1 and 2. A similar book, illustrated with photogravures, published by Thacker, Spink & Co., Calcutta, 1885. 4to, pp. vi, 237.

1333.—FROM PALL MALL TO PUNJAUB, or With the Prince in India. *J. Drew Gay.* London, 1876. 8vo.

1335.—SPORT IN BRITISH BURMAH, ASSAM, etc. *Lieut.-Col. Pollock.* Chapman, 1879. 8vo, 2 vols.

1336.—THIRTEEN YEARS AMONG THE WILD BEASTS OF INDIA; their Haunts and Habits, from Personal Observation. With an account of the Modes of Capturing and Taming Wild Elephants. *G. P. Sanderson.* The author was the officer in charge of the Government elephant keddahs, Dacca, and his book is the best work ever written on elephant hunting, the weapons, etc., necessary, and is indispensable to hunters of large game, whether in India or elsewhere. There

is a coloured frontispiece, and twenty other fine plates
of spirited hunting scenes. W. H. Allen, 1879 (?)
Four editions, fcap. 4to, maps, plates, 12s.

1337.—EVERY TRUE SPORTSMAN'S FRIEND. A compilation
made from the newspapers by the "*Old Shikaree.*"
P. M. Jones, Serampore, 1880. 8vo, 19 pp.

1338.—REMINISCENCES OF SPORT IN INDIA. *E. F. Burton.*
1885. 8vo, illustrated, 18s.

1339.—TENT LIFE IN TIGER LAND. *Hon. J. Inglis.* This
is included in "Sport and Work" (*q.v.*), but also published separately by Sampson Low & Co. Royal 8vo,
8s

1340.—SPORT AND WORK ON THE NEPAUL FRONTIER. *Hon.
Jas. Inglis* ("*Maori*"). Sporting reminiscences of a
pioneer planter in an Indian Frontier district, with
22 illustrations in chromolithography. Sampson Low
& Co., 1878, pp. xv, 366; 1888, 8vo, 21s.; Macmillan,
1880, pp. xiv, 466. 8vo.

1341.—SPORT IN THE FAR EAST. *C. Cradock.* A guide
illustrated with maps, etc. Griffith, 1889. 8vo, 6s.

1342.—SPORTSMAN'S VADE MECUM FOR THE HIMALAYAS.
K. C. A. J. A book of shooting notes, hints on camp
life, etc., and stories. Contains: Guns and Rifles,
Ammunition, Useful Articles, Dress, Camp Equip-
ments, Stores, Medicines, Writing Materials, Maps,
etc.; Summary of Kit, etc.; Removing and Drying
Skins, General Notes. SPORTING YARNS: Black
Buck, Oorial, Chinkarah, Bustard, Coolun, Markhor
Ibex, Gooral, Barasingh, Thar, Musk Deer, Bears.
H. Cox, 1891. Demy 8vo, 2s.

1343.—RECORDS OF SPORT IN SOUTHERN INDIA. *Douglas
Hamilton.* From journals written between 1844 and
1870, with notes on Singapore, Java, and Labuan.
Illustrated from sketches by the author, and portrait.
R. H. Porter, 1892. 4to, pp. xlviii, 284, 30s. net.

1344.—GOLD, COFFEE, AND SPORT IN MYSORE. *R. H. Elliott.*
Every-day life and red-letter days in the career of
a planter, by the author of "Experiences of a
Planter." A. Constable & Co., London, 1893. Crown
8vo, map.

1345.—WILD BEASTS AND THEIR WAYS. *J. L. Kipling.*
Contains some interesting natural history notes,
exciting adventures and sporting reminiscences of
practical value. Must not be confounded with "The
Jungle Book," by *Rudyard Kipling*, a volume of
fantastic stories. Macmillan, 1891. 8vo, pp. xii, 401.

1346.—SEONEE; Camp Life on the Satpura Range, a
tale of Indian adventure. *Robert Armitage Sterndale.*
Illustrated by the author, with map, etc. Sampson
Low & Co. 8vo, 21s.

AFRICA.

1347.—SPORTING SCENES AMONG THE KAFFIRS. *A. W.
Drayson.* Illustrations by Harrison Weir. This book
was translated into Russian in 1867. The author
wrote several tales of South African life, the first
being "Hans Sterk." Routledge, 1858, 1862.

1348.—ALBERT NYANZA. *Sir S. W. Baker.* An account
of the famous explorer's discoveries in Africa. A
French translation, "Haut Nil," by Decouvert, was
published in 1868 and 1880; and a German edition
has appeared. London, 1866. 8vo, 2 vols.

1349.—ISMAILA. *Sir S. W. Baker.* Contains information
respecting sport in Upper Egypt. London, 1874. 8vo.

1350.—WILD TRIBES OF THE SOUDAN. *Sir S. W. Baker.*
Contains much information respecting game in northern
Central Africa. 1884. 8vo.

1351.—THROUGH GASA LAND. *Parker Gillmore.* Harrison, 1890. 8vo, pp. xii, 349.

1352.—THE GREAT THIRST LAND (*i.e.* Kalahari Desert). *Parker Gillmore.* Sampson Low, 1878. 8vo.

1353.—UNKNOWN HORN OF AFRICA. *F. L. James.* An account of an exploration from Berbera to the Leopard river. With additions by G. J. Thrupp. Illustrations by Rose Hake, and of the fauna by K. Keuleman. The author also wrote of the "Wild Tribes of the Soudan" and on the routes from Wady Halfa to Berber. G. Philip & Son, London, 1888. 4to, pp. 344, illustrations.

1354.—SPORTSMAN IN SOUTH AFRICA. *J. A. Nicolls.* Brit. & Col. Pub. Co., 1892. 8vo, 10s. net.

1355.—FIVE MONTHS' SPORT IN SOMALILAND. *Lord Wolverton.* An account of a trip of a hundred miles across a desert into a poor game country, and so unhealthy that 2000 three-grain quinine pills proved an inadequate supply. The book is not carefully written, but is fairly illustrated from photographs by Col. Paget, and is furnished with a good map. Chapman & Hall, 1894. 8vo, 108 pp.

1356.—HUNTER'S WANDERINGS IN AFRICA. *F. C. Selous.* A narrative of nine years amongst the big game in the far interior of South Africa. Bentley & Son, London, 1881. 8vo, pp. xvii, 455, illustrations by E. Whymper. 2nd ed., 1890.

1357.—TRAVEL AND ADVENTURE IN SOUTH AFRICA. *F. C. Selous.* The best account of game hunting. R. Ward & Co., London, 1893. 8vo, pp. xvii, 503, photographic illustrations.

1358.—TRAVEL AND ADVENTURES IN THE CONGO FREE STATE, and its big game shooting. By "*Boula N'Zau*" (*i.e.* "Elephant Smasher"). *H. Bailey.* A four years' record of sport, etc. Chapman, London, 1894. 8vo, 320 pp., illustrations from Author's sketches, map, 14s.

1359.—CAMP LIFE AND SPORT IN SOUTH AFRICA. *T. J. Lucas.* Chapman, 1878. Demy 8vo, 258 pp., with plates.

1360.—MOSS FROM A ROLLING STONE. *C. A. Payton* ("Sarcelle"). Shooting in Morocco, etc. Cox, 1879. 8vo, illustrated.

AMERICA.

1361.—AMERICAN SPORTSMAN. *E. J. Lewis.* Lippincott, Philadelphia, 1855. 8vo, illustrated.

1362.—SPORTING ADVENTURES IN THE NEW WORLD. *C. Hardy.* Hurst & Blackett, 1855. 2 vols., post 8vo, 21s.

1363.—WILD SPORTS IN THE FAR WEST. *F. Gerstæcker.* (Fictitious.) Routledge, 1856. 12mo, 1s. 6d.; illustrated edition, 3s. 6d.

1364.—SHOOTING AND FISHING IN NORTH AMERICA. *B. H. Revoil.* Tinsleys, 1865. 2 vols., 8vo, 21s.

1365.—HUNTER'S AND TRAPPER'S GUIDE. *S. J. Hunter.* An illustrated handbook. Hunter, New York, 1869. $1; $1.50.

1366.—SHOOTING, BOATING, FISHING. *T. R. Warren.* Scribner, New York, 1871. $1.

1367.—HUNTER AND TRAPPER. *H. Thrasher.* Judd, New York, n.d., $1.

1368.—LIFE IN THE BACKWOODS. *F. M. Reed.* A trapper's guide and manual. (?) New York, 1874. 20 c.

1369.—GUN, ROD, AND SADDLE. *I. Mast.* Meth. Epis., New York, 1876. $1.25.

1370.—ART OF HUNTING, TRAPPING, FISHING, etc., made easy. Hurst. 25 cents.

1371.—HUNTER'S GUIDE AND TRAPPER'S COMPANION. *H. E. Hunter.* Hunter, New York, 1876. 50 cents; 25 cents.

1372.—SPORT AND TRAVEL, Men and Manners in two Americas. *Sir R. L. Price.* Longmans, 1876-77. 8vo, 18s.; new edition, 18s.

1373.—FIFTY YEARS WITH THE GUN AND ROD. *D. W. Cross.* Cleveland, Ohio. 16mo, 7s. 6d.

1374.—SPORTSMAN'S GAZETTEER AND GENERAL GUIDE. The game, animals, birds, and fishes of North America; together with a directory to the principal game resorts of the country. Illustrated with maps. *C. Hallock.* Revised and enlarged edition. Orange Judd Co., New York, 1877-83. 8vo, 2 parts, maps.

1375.—CAMP LIFE IN FLORIDA. *C. Hallock.* A handbook for sportsmen and settlers. New York, 1876. 12mo.

1376.—OUR NEW ALASKA. *C. Hallock.* The Seward purchase vindicated. *Forest and Stream* Co., New York, 1886. 80 pp., 209 illustrations.

1377.—HUNTER'S HANDBOOK. *B. Straton.* Lee & S. N. G., 1885. 50 cents.

1378.—RANCH LIFE AND THE HUNTING TRAIL. *Th. Roosevelt.* Century Co., New York, 1888. $5.

1379.—THE STILL-HUNTER. A Practical Treatise on Deer-Stalking. By *Theo. S. Van Dyke.* "The Still-Hunter" is a work devoted entirely to the subject on which it professes to give instruction. The author is a man familiar with the habits of deer, and his treatise is the best on the subject. New York, 1888. 8vo, 390 pp., $2.

1380.—SPORTSMAN'S PARADISE. *B. A. Watson.* The lake lands of Canada. With illustrations by W. C. and H. Beard. First appeared at Philadelphia. Second edition, 1888. J. Bumpus, London, 1889. 8vo, pp. xii, 390.

1381.—SPORTSMAN'S GUIDE. *W. C. Harris.* A sporting gazetteer to the hunting and fishing grounds of the United States and Canada. Angler's Publishing Co., New York, 1889. $1.

1382.—CRUISINGS IN THE CASCADES. *G. O. Shields.* A narrative of travel, exploration, hunting, amateur photography, and fishing, with special chapters on hunting the grizzly bear, the buffalo, elk, antelope, etc., also on trouting in the Rocky Mountains, life among the Cow Boys, etc. Rand, McNally & Co., Chicago, 1889. 8vo, 339 pp., illustrated. English edition, Low. 10s. 6d.

1383.—RUSTLINGS IN THE ROCKIES. *G. O. Shields.* A narrative of hunting and fishing experiences. Belford, Clarke & Co., Chicago, 1883. 8vo, pp. xv, 306.

1384.—BIG GAME OF NORTH AMERICA. *G. O. Shields.* "Habitat, haunts, habits and characteristics of the big game of the North American continent: how, where, and when to hunt it." Rand, McNally & Co., Chicago, 1890. 8vo, 581 pp., illustrated.

1385.—HINTS AND POINTS FOR SPORTSMEN. "*Seneca.*" This compilation comprises six hundred and odd hints, helps, kinks, wrinkles, points and suggestions for the shooter, etc., about threescore hints on firearms and their use in the field. *Forest and Stream* Co., New York, 1890. 8vo, 610 pp., $1.50.

1386.—SPORT; or Fishing and Shooting. Edited by *A. C. Gould.* Chiefly sought for its illustrations of mallard, antelope, deer, turkey, moose, and wapiti shooting, after water colours by Denton, Remington, Zogbaum, Frost, and Sandham. Bradlee Whidden, Boston, Mass., 1890-93. Five sections, 18 × 24, each three plates. $10 each part, complete half Roxburgh, $55.

1387.—SHOOTING ON UPLAND, MARSH, AND STREAM. Edited by *W. B. Leffingwell* ("*Horace*"). Contains articles by prominent sportsmen on hunting the upland birds of America; their flights, habits, resorts, etc.; the scientific methods of shooting ducks, prairie chickens, grouse, wild turkeys, geese, pigeons, snipe, quail, woodcock, and plovers. The book is, in effect, a collection of monographs on North American game birds, supplemented by accounts of the pursuit of them; and this, even, is humanely considered. Sampson Low, 1890. 8vo, 473 pp., illustrated, 18s. Another edition, 8vo, 10s. 6d.

1387.—WILDFOWL SHOOTING. *W. B. Leffingwell.* Containing scientific and practical descriptions of wildfowl; their resorts, habits, flights, and the most successful method of hunting them; of guns for wildfowl shooting; how to load, aim, and to use them; decoys, blinds, boats, etc. New York, 1890, 1892. 8vo, illustrated, 373 pp., $2.50.

1389.—AMERICAN BIG GAME HUNTING. *Theo. Roosevelt* and *Geo. B. Grinnell.* Contains "A Buffalo Story" (G. S. Anderson), "The White Goat and his Country" (O. Wister), "A Day with the Elk" (W. Chanler), "Old Times in the Black Hills" (R. D. Williams), "Big Game in the Rockies" (A. Rogers), "Coursing the Prongbuck" (T. Roosevelt), "After Wapiti in Wyoming" (F. C. Crocker), "In Buffalo Days" (G. B. Grinnell), "Nights with the Grizzlies" (W. D. Pickett), "The Yellowstone Park as a Game Preserve" (A. Hague), "A Mountain Fraud" (Dean Sage), "Blacktails in the Bad Lands" (B. Rumsey), "Photographing Big Game" (W. B. Devereux), "Literature of American Big Game Hunting," "Our Forest Reservations," etc. *Forest and Stream* Co., New York, 1893. 8vo, 16 full-page plates, 345 pp., $2.50.

1390.—GOLD IN CARIBOO. *C. P. Wolley.* A story of adventures in British Columbia. Blackie & Son, 1894. 8vo, 288 pp. "Sportsman's Eden," another book by the same author, also treats of British Columbia; the

"Trottings of a Tenderfoot to Columbian fiords and Spitzbergen" was published by Bentley in 1884, 8vo, 350 pp.; and the author's other book, "Savage Svanetia" also. First edition, 1883. Two vols. 8vo.

1391.—THE WILDERNESS HUNTER. By *Hon. Theodore Roosevelt.* This work records the experiences of the author with all kinds of game found in the United States, and gives as well many interesting and exciting incidents of cowboy life on the plains. *Forest and Stream* Pub. Co., New York. 8vo, $3.50.

1392.—RIFLE, ROD AND GUN IN CALIFORNIA. Flirtation Camp; or, The Rifle, Rod and Gun in California. A Sporting Romance. By *Theodore S. Van Dyke.* Cloth, 300 pp., $1.50.

1393.—HUNTING TRIPS OF A RANCHMAN. Sketches of Sport on the Northern Cattle Plains. By *Theodore Roosevelt.* Illustrated with 26 full-page illustrations. Cloth, 350 pp. Price $3.00.

1394.—WOODCRAFT. By *Nessmuk.* A book written for the instruction and guidance of those who go for pleasure to the woods. Its author, having had great experience in camp life, has put the wisdom so acquired into intelligible English. *Forest and Stream* Co., New York, 1889. 8vo, cloth, 160 pp., illustrated, $1.

1395.—CAMPING AND CRUISING IN FLORIDA. *Jas. A. Henshall.* A narrative of yachting, fishing and hunting adventure in the Southern peninsula. The volume embraces the narrative of two distinct cruises, the one undertaken in the *Blue Wing* and the other in the *Rambler*, in the course of which the author saw enough to write a vast deal of information on the soil, climate and natural productions of Florida, and on its fish, game, and people. *Forest and Stream* Co., New York, 189-. 8vo, 250 pp., 84 illustrations, list of fauna, maps, $1.50.

1396.—THE BOYS' BOOK OF OUTDOOR SPORTS. Edited by *Maurice Thompson*. Discusses shooting, fishing, archery, boats and boating, etc., etc. *Forest and Stream* Co., New York, 188-. 8vo, illustrated, 350 pp., $2.50.

1397.—AMERICAN GAME BIRD SHOOTING. *J. M. Murphy*. New York, 188-. $12.0.

1397a.—AMERICAN WILDFOWL SHOOTING. *J. W. Long*. Contains also notes for a theory of the action of Choke-boring on a load of shot. Orange Judd & Co., New York, 1879. 8vo, 330 pp., woodcuts.

1398.—CHIPLOQUORGAN. *Captain Dashwood*. A treatise on moose hunting, etc., in Canada. Dublin, 1871. 8vo, 293 pp., illustrated.

1399.—GAME OF THE NORTH-WEST. *J. Hubbard*. A paper on the hunting grounds of the Far West, prepared for the Natural History exhibit of Manitoba at the London Colonial Exhibition. 8vo pamphlet.

1399a.—THE WILD NORTH LAND. *Sir W. F. Butler*, the author of "The Great Lone Land." Both works relate rather to travel and adventure than to sport. W. H. Allen, 1873. 8vo, 18s.; crown 8vo, 7s. 6d.

1399b.—SPORTING SKETCHES IN SOUTH AMERICA. *Admiral Kennedy*. Porter. Post 8vo, illustrated, 6s.

1399c.—WANDERINGS OF A NATURALIST IN NICARAGUA. A privately printed anonymous book, full of information respecting the large and small game of Central America. London, 187-. 8vo.

1399d.—WILD SPORTS ON THE FRONTIER. *J. S. Campion*. Some excellent reminiscences. Chapman, 1877. 8vo 16s.; 1878, new edition, 16s.

AUSTRALASIA.

1399*e.*—OUR AUSTRALIAN COUSINS. *Hon. Jas. Inglis.*
Contains a fair account of sport in the bush. Macmillan, 1880. 8vo, pp. xiv, 466.

1399*f.*—OUR NEW ZEALAND COUSINS. *Hon. J. Inglis.*
Gives particulars of some New Zealand sports. Sampson Low, 1887. 8vo, pp. xii, 311.

1399*g.*—WANDERINGS IN A WILD COUNTRY. *W. B. Powell.*
An account of three years' wanderings amongst the cannibals of New Britain, etc. Sampson Low, 1883. 8vo, pp. vii, 283.

FRENCH BOOKS.

CURRENT WORKS ON SHOOTING.

1401.—DICTIONNAIRE DES CHASSES. *A. Pairault.* A vocabulary of sporting terms ancient and modern. Has an introduction by M. de Cherville, and is dedicated to the Duchess d'Uzes. The work is done thoroughly, and the natural history notes are better than the explanations of some of the foreign sporting terms; but the book is compiled for the enlightenment of those amongst whom it is counted a sin not to know the meaning of such words as "field-trials" and "mail-coach," and not for the use of experts. Contains 430 pp., and is illustrated with 50 vignettes and *culs-de-lampe*. Pairault, Paris, 1885. 8vo, 15 francs.

1402.—LIVRE DE TOUTES LES CHASSES. *E. Parent.* A compilation, and not a good one; a cyclopædia of field sports. Parent, Brussels; Tanera, Paris, 1865. 8vo, 2 vols.

1403.—CHASSE PRATIQUE. *E. Bellecroix.* An account of shooting societies, shooting grounds, game raising and watching, vermin destroying, etc. Didot, Paris, 1875 and 1879. 18mo.

1404.—CHASSEUR AU CHIEN D'ARRÊT. *Elzear Blaze.* One of a number of sporting books by a French writer, born at Cavaillon about 1786. His other works are "Chasseur au Chien Courant," "Causeries de Gourmets et Chasseurs." Tresse & Stock, Paris. Tenth edition, 1887, 12mo. The first edition, Montardier, Paris, 1836, second, Barba, 1837, third, Barba, 1839, all in 8vo; other Paris editions in 1846, 1854, 1858, 1862, 1868, 1872 and 1887. Belgian editions in 1836, 1844, 1852.

1405.—CHASSE AU CHIEN D'ARRÊT. *Dr. J. C. Chenu.* A treatise on shooting over dogs by an author well known as a writer of the "Encyclopædic Natural History" and of the "Ornithologie du Chasseur." Marcq, Paris, 1851. Picard, 1865; pp. viii, 184, 89 plates, 19 vignettes, in 12mo. Illustrated.

1406.—CHASSEURS EXCENTRIQUES. *C. d'Amezeuil.* A sporting souvenir. Dentu, Paris, 1875. In 18mo. 3 francs. Not of sporting interest.

1407.—CHASSEUR COSMOPOLITE. Dentu, Paris. 2 francs.

1408.—LIVRE DU CHASSEUR. *Charles Diguet.* A popular manual for the sportsman. Fayard, Paris, n.d. (1881). Gr. 8vo, 464 pp. [This may be regarded as a fair specimen of a class of sporting book for which there appears to have been a large demand in France. It is a book written in the style of a penny-a-liner round about shooting and natural history rather than of it, has many literary allusions, and is well studded with Latin quotations and sporting slang. The illustrations are in some cases of very fair quality, in others appear to have been taken from a cheap natural history book. An advantage of the book as a class was that it could be divided into various volumes, "Gibier à Plume," "Gibier à Poil," etc., and separately published with a coloured lithograph on paper cover.]

1409.—MANUEL ILLUSTRÉ DU CHASSEUR. *Robert Du Chêne.* A work by the editor of the "Almanach Manuel du Chasseur." A sportsman's calendar, illustrated by Emy. De la Rue, Paris, n.d.

1410.—MANUEL DES CHASSEURS. *Viscomte de Noe ("Cham").* Sixty-one caricatures. Martinet, Paris, n.d. 8vo.

1411.—GUIDE DU CHASSEUR. *F. Cassassoles.* A manual for sportsmen, with instructions for the use of setters, pointers, etc. A theoretical, practical and judicial treatise. Paris, n.d. In 24mo, illustrations. Another edition, Garnier frères, Paris, 1864.

1412.—GUIDE-CARNET DU CHASSEUR. *N. Libouille.* A small treatise on arms by a Belgian gunmaker, who was for some time editor of *Le Franc Tireur.* Dentu, Paris, 1879. 12mo.

1413.—GUIDE DU CHASSEUR. *C. Diguet.* A treatise on field sports. Paris, 1887. 12mo.

1414.—MANUEL DU CHASSEUR. *Leonce de Curel.* A book for young sportsmen, followed with the laws relating to game preserving in France. Metz, 1857, in 8vo, with plate. Dentu, Paris, 1858, 1861, and 1863.

1415.—CONSEILS AUX CHASSEURS. *H. Robinson.* A manual for sportsmen, treating of shooting, firearms, ammunition, and shooting requisites. Goin, Paris, 1860, 8vo, pp. 333, plates. Parent, Bruxelles, 1860, 1865. Another edition, Tanera, Paris, 1865. 3 fr. 50 c.

1416.—MANUEL DU JEUNE CHASSEUR. *Yonne Chatin de Mizelles.* Instructions for young sportsmen; How to become a dead shot; Game Register. Ceas et fils, Valence, 1869, 18mo. Other editions, Rothschild, Paris, n.d., 12mo; and later, with 37 vignettes, 70 pp., under new titles, by Melchior Chatin. 1 franc.

1417.—CHASSES DANS L'HIMALAYA. *C. Jules Basile Gerard.* An apocryphal work, similar to "Le Mangeur d'Hommes" by same author. Paris, 1862, 1863, 1865.

1418.—TUEUR DE LIONS. *C. J. B. Gerard.* Lion hunting and other sports in Algeria; highly coloured sketches of sporting adventures. Paris, 1854, with an illustration by Grenier. Other editions 1856, 1858, 1864, 1868, 1875, 1878, etc.

1419.—CHASSE AU LION. *C. J. B. Gerard.* Paris, 1852, 12mo; 1885, 12mo, engraving by G. Doré; Paris, Levy, 1862, 1869, has portrait of M. Gerard, 1874. There are some editions in 8vo with the Doré illustration which are much sought.

1420.—AFRIQUE DU NORD. *C. J. B. Gerard.* A history of the French territory, with some sporting notes. Dentu, Paris, 1860. Other editions without date.

1421.—CHASSES D'AFRIQUE. *C. J. B. Gerard.* A made-up book, 12 illustrations by Grenier and Moraine, in black or colour. Paris, n.d.

1422.—MES DERNIÈRES CHASSES. *Jules Gerard.* This work is preceded by a notice of the famous lion killer by A. Dumas. Calmann-Levy, Paris, 1877. 12mo.

1423.—MES CHASSES AU LION. *J. Chassaing.* With a preface by Garnier. Dentu, Paris, 1865, in 18mo. Second edition, 1879. Spanish edition, Madrid, 1868.

1424.—TIGRES EN COCHIN CHINE. *Duyateff.* Some particulars of tigers and tiger hunting in Cochin China, contributed to or incorporated with the "Rendezvous de Chasse." Barbon, Limoges, n.d. 8vo.

1425.—CHASSES AUX INDES. *Castillon.* Paris. 4to, 8 illustrations by V. Adam, two-coloured.

1426.—CHASSES EN AFRIQUE. *Castillon.* Courcier, Paris. 4to, oblong, 12 illustrations.

1426.—TUEUR DE PANTHÈRES. *H. Chevreuil,* the panther killer. An article reproduced from the *Débats* of August 4th, 1860. Aubry, Paris, 1860.

1427.—MES CHASSES. *Th. Anquetil.* Includes an account of tiger hunting, etc. Of little interest to sportsmen, and without technical value. Dentu, Paris, 1866. 18mo, 1 franc.

1428.—Aventures et Chasses dans l'extrême Orient. *Th. Anquetil.* Sport and adventure in the Far East. Includes "Men and Beasts," "Elephant Hunting and Tiger Hunting," which were separately published. Charpentier, Paris, 1874-76. In 18mo.

1429.—Chasse aux Bêtes Féroces. *E. Campagne.* Megard, Rouen, 1882. 12mo.

1430.—Chasse aux Lions. *A. Assolant.* With illustrations by Jules Girardet and Bembled. Third edition, 1892. Bardoin, Paris.

1431.—Chasse à la Becasse. *E. Jourdeuil.* A new edition, limited to five hundred copies, and a few on hand-made and special papers.

1432.—Expédition de Chasse au Nepaul. *Philippe* (Duc d'Orléans). C. Levy, Paris, 1892. 4to, 241 pp.

1433.—Art d'élever, de multiplier, et de chasser les Canards. *F. Routillet.* Paris, 1892. 18mo, 36 pp. Sketches.

1434.—Impressions de Chasse. *G. Azais.* Sporting sketches and notes on natural history. Hachette, Paris, 1870 and 1872. 12mo.

1435.—Chasse. *B. Asher* and *Ad. Belot.* Gives an account of a sporting tour in Spain, and of elephant hunting. Barbon, Limoges, n.d. 12mo.

1436.—Chasseur de Chamois and "Chasseur de l'Ours." *C. Buet.* Barbon, Limoges, n.d. 12mo.

1437.—Chasse au Mouflon. *E. Bergerat.* An account of sport in Corsica. Delagrave, Paris, 1891. 8vo, 383 pp., 43 plates, 55 illustrations in text, title-page in red and black.

1438.—Chasses aux Loups. *Baron Halna du Fretay.* Prudhomme, St. Brieuc, 1891. 8vo, 141 pp., frontispiece.

1439.—CHASSE DE LA CAILLE EN EGYPTE. *M. Magaud d'Aubusson.* Paris, 1891. 8vo, 4 plates.

1440.—CANARDS D'ÉGYPTE. *M. M. d'Aubusson.* This and the preceding are from a series of re-issues of ornithological papers from the " Revue des Sciences." Cerf et fils, Paris, 1891. 8vo, 7 plates.

1441.—CHASSE À L'OPOSSUM. *Oscar Wilde.* Oudin et Cie, Paris, 1891. 18mo, 64 pp., and illustrations.

1442.—CHASSE AUX PETITS OISEAUX. *E. Campagne.* Megard, Rouen, 1882. 12mo.

1443.—CHASSES D'AUTOMNE. *A. Grassal.* Pairault, Paris, 1886. In 16mo, 23 vignettes, 200 copies only.

1444.—LES CHASSES DU GLOBE. *P. Garnier.* A work of no great interest, by a voluminous writer; it is only one of many books of the same kind written possibly with a view to popularise foreign sport and adventure. J. Martin, Paris, 1887.

1445.—CHASSE ET PÊCHE. *Delphin Dastugue.* Practical treatise. Renoux et Maulde, Paris, 1886. In 18mo, pp. viii, 332. 3 francs.

1446.—CHASSE ET PÊCHE. *D. Dastugue.* A book of hints for sportsmen. Durand, Paris, 1868. 18mo.

1447.—CHASSE À LA BÉCASSE. By a " Chasseur Rustique " (*Varenne de Feuille*). A finely got up book; 111 copies printed. Bourg (printed by Perrin, Lyon), 1869, 8vo.

1448.—CHASSE À LA BÉCASSE. *G. Duwarnet.* " Pour chasser la Bécasse." Goin, Paris, s.d. In 18mo.

1449.—CHASSE AUX BÉCASSINES. *Léopold Elouis.* An account of shooting in marshes and on the sea shore in Normandy. Paris, n.d. 12mo, vignettes and coloured woodcuts. 3 francs.

1450.—CHASSES DE MER ET DE GRÈVES. *C. Diguet.* Marpon, Paris, 1886. In 12mo, 3 francs.

1451.—CHASSE AU MARAIS. *C. Diguet.* Treatise on wildfowling. Dentu, Paris, 1889. 18mo, 107 pp. 1 fr. 50 c.

1452.—TRAITÉ DE LA CHASSE DES ALOUETTES. *P. Garnier.* Some particulars concerning the use of a revolving mirror to attract larks.

1453.—DE LA CHASSE À L'ALOUETTE AU MIROIR ET AU FUSIL. *Nérée-Quepat.* Paris, Goin, n.d. 12mo. Two editions published.

1454.—GIBIER-PLUME; GIBIER-POIL. *Marquis de Cherville.* A book about sport. Another work of the kind is "Ornithologie du Chasseur."

1455.—SOUVENIRS DE CHASSES. *Viscount Louis de Dax.* Sporting recollections by a contributor to the *Chasse Illustrée*, concluding with particulars of game shooting in France. A second edition, "Nouveaux Souvenirs," published by Dentu, Paris, in 1860, is the more rare. Cartel, Paris, 1858. 12mo.

1456.—COMMENT L'ESPRIT VIENT AUX BÊTES. *C. d'Amezeuil.* What one sees when hunting. Not of great sporting interest or technical value.

1457.—SOIXANTE ANNÉES DE CHASSE. *J. A. Clamart.* Practical guide to sport and forestry. Afterwards appeared as an Illustrated Cyclopædia for Sportsmen, when 20 illustrations were added by A. Goin, who bought up the edition printed by Lelaurin at Mezières, and published by Letellier at Charleville, 1866. Petit says the Letellier edition is much sought after, and valuable. The illustrated editions are of less interest. First edition, "Cinquante Années," etc., Vouziers, 1854, 166 pp., no illustrations. Third edition the same, but added to by Goin, with new cover and title printed by Joüaüst. Subsequently reissued 1869.

1458.—LITTERATURE DE LA CHASSE. *E. Ritter.* A monograph on French sport in the Middle Ages, illustrated with 18 reproductions of old engravings. The text is in German, the citations in French. Neumann, Neudamm, 1886. In 8vo, 53 pp., 300 copies only printed, 6 fr.

1459.—HISTOIRE DE CHASSE. *Benoit-Champy.* A pamphlet, of which 100 copies only were printed. Pairault, Paris, 1886, 1 fr.

1460.—TECHNOLOGIE ARCHÉOLOGIQUE. *Dr. A. Peigne De la Court.* This work comprises "Chasse à la Haie," "Arts et Métiers de Goquet," "Chasse au Moyen-Age," etc. A work on the sporting methods of the Middle Ages and kindred subjects. The author wrote an etymological work, showing that the names Bruxelles and Louvain are derived from sporting terms. Peromie, 1873. 8vo.

1461.—ESSAI HISTORIQUE ET LÉGAL SUR LA CHASSE. *Marchand.* Le Jay, London and Paris, 1769. 12mo. Founded, it is said, on an earlier essay, "Calendrier, ou Essai Historique et Légal sur la Chasse," 1770.

1462.—TRAITÉ DU DROIT DE CHASSE. *F. De Launay*, author of "Nouveau Traité du Droit de Chasse." Paris, G. Quinet, 1681, 1685 (?).

1463.—LA CHASSE D'AUXERRES. *Abbé Le Bœuf.* Gives an account of the history of an old-established custom of hare hunting in Auxerre. Reproduced from the *Mercure de France*, 1725. Tochener, Paris. 12mo. (Vol. I. of "Collection of Dissertations.")

1464.—GUIDE PRATIQUE DU GARDE-CHASSE. *Ernest Bellecroix.* A manual for the gamekeeper, with notes on woodcraft based upon the treatise by A. De la Rue. Didot, Paris, 1886. 12mo, 3 fr.

1465.—GUIDE-MANUEL DU GARDE CHAMPÊTRE. *Marc Deffaux.* A text-book for the gamekeeper; gives particulars of vermin traps and gamekeepers' duties, also methods of sporting and fishing. Passard, Paris, 1853. 12mo, 2 fr.

1466.—MANUEL DES GARDES. *Jean Henriquez.* A work for the game preserver by the author of "Principes de Jurisprudence sur le Droit de Chasse" and "Code Pénal ... ou Précis Raisonné des Ordonnances," etc. Delalain, Paris, 1784. 12mo.

1467.—LA CHASSE, SON HISTOIRE ET SA LÉGISLATION. *Ernest Jullien.* A trustworthy, comprehensive book. Didier, Paris, 1868. 8vo, table, 6 fr.

1468.—DROIT DE CHASSE. *Charles Boulen.* A book on sporting rights and game laws, showing the property in game from the institution of the French monarchy to the present time. Paris, 1887. 8vo, 7 fr.

1469.—CODE FORESTIER. — *Dalloz.* The laws of forestry, sporting and fishing, with annotations. Paris, 1884. 4to, 30 fr.

1470.—LA CHASSE. — *Giraudeau.* Paris, 1882. In 12mo and in 4to.

1471.—TRAITÉ DE LA CHASSE. *J. B. Gail.* With an engraving of Diana by Chaudet. Paris, n.d., xxiii. et 227 pp.

1472.—SPORT À PARIS. *Eugène Chapus.* Chiefly relates to the turf, hunting, but also contains particulars of pistol shooting, rifle shooting, etc. Hachette, Paris, 1854. 12mo.

1473.—L'OUVERTURE DE LA CHASSE. A one-act play, by *Gustave Albitte* and *Desvergers.* Paris, n.d.

1474.—CHASSE AU TIR. Songs. 131 pp., 5 ill.

FRENCH BOOKS.

GUNS, GUN MANUFACTURE, GUNNERY.

1501.—EXTRAIT DU COURS SUR LES ARMES. *Cap. L. Panot.*
An instruction-book for the musketry instructor and for the use of non-commissioned officers. J. Dumaine, Paris, 1850. In 8vo.

1502.—TECHNOLOGIE DES ARMES À FEU. *Moritz Meyer.*
The best-known edition is the French translation made by M. Reiffel, and enlarged with many annotations. The work is a chronological history of firearms, and is in two parts: (1) from the invention of firearms, A.D. 40—1763; and (2) 1764—1832. Gen. Brackenbury, in his paper on the history of firearms, says of this publication: "Contains a series of assertions and assumptions unsupported by any evidence, or even by references, and in some cases carrying on their faces the stamp of improbability. It is, therefore, as regards that portion which relates to the archæology of cannon, utterly worthless to the student or antiquary." J. Correard, Paris, 1837. 8vo, 2 vols., 280 and 336 pp., exclusive of copious indices of 88 and 78 pp.

1503.—ARMES ET POUDRE DE CHASSE. *Louis Roux.* Lacroix, Paris, 1869. 12mo.

1504.—ARMES À FEU PORTATIVES. *Rodolphe Schmidt.* An account of hand firearms, from the date of their development from cannon until the present day. Translated by J. N. Cuttat, and illustrated with 400 chromolithograph drawings in 56 plates, forming a separate volume. This is a popular account of the development of military arms, and contains numerous descriptions of little known varieties of breechloaders. Ch. Tanera, Paris, 1877. Demy 4to, pp. 96, and atlas of 56 plates.

Guns, Gun Manufacture, Gunnery.   139

1504A.—FUSIL SUISSE À RÉPÉTITION. *R. Schmidt*. This is a manual for users of the 1889 model Swiss repeating rifle. H. Georg, Bâle, 1891. 16mo, 36 pp., and coloured folding plate.

1505.—MÉMOIRES D'UN FUSIL. *C. Diguet*. An autobiography of a sporting gun. Dentu, Paris, 1883. In 12mo.

1506.—FUSIL ET SES PERFECTIONNEMENTS, avec Notes de Chasse. *W. W. Greener*. A translation, by Georges Bonjour, of W. W. Greener's best known book. Firmin Didot, Paris, 1884 (London printed). 4to, pp. vi, 522, 500 illustrations.

1507.—MANIEMENT ET USAGE DES ARMES À FEU. *A. de Metz-Noblat*. A manual for all who use firearms; treats of accidents in the field and elsewhere, and the means to avoid them. Berger-Levrault, Paris, 1889. 18mo, 1 fr.; bound, 1 fr. 50 c.

1508.—ARMES DE CHASSE. *Arthur Guinard*. A short history of sporting firearms, descriptions of modern varieties, and practical hints on their use. A concise and clearly written little work. Dentu, Paris, 1882. 12mo.

1509.—CHASSE ET TIR. Album Galand. A gunmaker's catalogue. Paris, Author. 8vo, 111 pp., 70th edition, 1890.

1510.—FUSIL DE CHASSE, SES MUNITIONS ET SON TIR. *General Faure-Biguet*. Firmin Didot, Paris, 1891. 18mo, pp. vii, 186.

1511.—LES ARMES. *G. R. M. Maindron*. May et Motherez, Paris, 1891. 8vo, 344 pp., with illustration.

1512.—ARMES DE GUERRE. *Louis Figuier*. A popular treatise on weapons, for the most part extracted from the "Merveilles de Science," and produced "pour renseigner le public" on the occasion of the declaration of war against Germany. Paris, Furne, Jouvet et Cie, 1870. 4to, 582 pp., woodcuts.

1513.—Instruction Provisoire sur le Démontage, etc., du Fusil mod. 1869. An instruction-book for the Comblain rifle. P. Vanderlinden, Bruxelles, 1871. In 12mo.

1514.—Instruction sur la Nomenclature, etc., du Mosqueton modèle 1871. An instruction-book for the 1871 pattern musket. E. Guyot, Bruxelles, 1872. In 8vo, 1 p., 23 pp.

1515.—Armes Portatives. *R. Lachevre.* An instruction-book, being pt. 2, s. i. of the "Cours d'Artillerie." Lithographed for the use of students at the special schools. Various appendices have also been published in like manner. Fontainebleau, 1873. In 4to. Another edition 1879.

1516.—Les Armes Portatives. *R. Colard.* A description of the Werndl and Frühwerth rifles, and the Gasser revolver used in the Austro-Hungarian army 1874. 8vo, 3 plates, 2 fr. (*Rev. d'Artill.* reprints.)

1517.—Les Armes Portatives en Allemagne. A descriptive and critical account of the Bavarian Werder rifle, 1869 model, reprinted with additions from the *Rev. d'Artillerie* of 1874. Berger-Levrault, Paris. 8vo, plate, 1 fr. 50 c.

1518.—Les Armes Portatives en Allemagne. A description of the Mauser, 1871, model of the Prussian infantry. 2nd edition, 1877. 8vo, plate, 1 fr. The Mauser rifle, repeating model, 1882. 8vo, plate, 50 c. Fusil d'Infanterie, modèle 1871—1884. 8vo, plate, 1887, 75 c. Fusil, 1888 modèle. 8vo, plate, 1890, 75 c. These brochures consist of reprints of various articles in the *Rev. d'Artillerie*, which have been published by Berger-Levrault, Paris.

1519.—Les Armes Portatives en Russie. *L. Labiche.* A descriptive account of the Berdan and Krnka rifles (*Rev. d'Artillerie* reprint), 1875. 8vo, 2 plates, 2 fr.

1520.—LES ARMES PORTATIVES EN FRANCE. A description of the French 1874 model, Gras, infantry rifle, reprinted from the *Rev. d'Artillerie*, 1876. 8vo, plate, 2 fr.

1521.—FUSIL RATIONNEL. *E. Guillaumot*. A disquisition upon and specification of the Nagant infantry breech-loader. C. Muquardt, Bruxelles, 1884. 8vo, pp. 154, table and plates, illustrations in text.

1522.—ARMES À REPETITION. *J. Raenkel*. A descriptive account of the repeating rifles, other than French (*Rev. d'Artillerie* reprint), 1891. 8vo, 3 plates, 1 fr. 50 c.

1523.—LEBEL contre Mannlicher et Vetterli. *Colonel Ortus*. A criticism of the Lebel, Mannlicher, and Vetterli systems, and prophecies as to their use in the next war. Baudoin, Paris, 1892. 8vo, 88 pp.

1524.—DE LA RASANCE DES FUSILS DE PETIT CALIBRE. *E. Pagine*. Baudoin, Paris, 1892. 8vo, 88 pp.

1525.—TRANSFORMATION DES ARMES. *De Sparre*. A lecture on the principles which have permitted the conversion of firearms to newer systems. Lyon, 1892. 8vo, 25 pp., illustrations.

1526.—ARMURERIE. Nouv. man. complet de l'Armurerie, du Fourbisseur et de l'Arquebusier. *M. A. O. Paulin-Desormeaux*. This is one of the Manuels-Roret on the manufacturing arts, and is a practical treatise on gun-making, repairing, etc., with descriptions and illustrations of many varieties of firearms and firearms parts; now quite out of date. Roret, Paris, 1852, 18mo, 2 vols.: vol. i., pp. 396, vol. ii., pp. 792, 17 folding plates, with 1600 figures.

1527.—TRAITÉ DU FUSIL DE CHASSE ET DES ARMES DE PRÉCISION. *H. Mangeot*. This is a complete treatise, and quite up to the highest standard of the period at which published. Bruxelles, 1852; Bruxelles and Paris, 1854; Paris, 1857. Paris, Tanera, no date. All in 8vo, 6 to 8 fr.

1528.—COURS ELEMENTAIRES SUR LES ARMES PORTATIVES. *F. Gillion.* Contains a complete account of the method of manufacturing military arms in Liége. Liége, P. Gouchon, 1856, 8vo. 384 pp., 5 folding plates.

1529.—FABRICATION DES ARMES PORTATIVES. *M. Dumord.* A course of four lessons on gun-making by a *chef* of Artillery. October, 1874. In 4to.

1530.—MANUEL DE L'ARTIFICIER. A work for the Armourer Sergeant. E. Guyot, Bruxelles, 1877. In 8vo.

1531.—FABRICATION DES ARMES. *J. Piebourg.* A course of four lessons on practical arms manufacture by a professor attached to a French military academy, 1881. In 4to.

1532.—ETUDE SUR L'ORGANISATION DU SERVICE TECHNIQUE DANS LES MANUFACTURES D'ARMES. *G. Ply.* An extract from the *Revue de l'Artillerie.* Nancy and Paris, 1888. 8vo, pp. 260.

1533.—ENQUÊTE SUR LE MATÉRIEL. An official report of the committee appointed to investigate the stores used in the Franco-German war. Part 4 contains all that relates to small arms. J. Dumaine, Paris, 1871. In 8vo.

1534.—MÉTALLURGIE DU FER. *M. Dumord.* A treatise on metallurgy by a professor of gunmaking. Imp. Nat. Paris, 1876, in 4to; and E. Bourges, Fontainebleau, 1881.

1535.—L'EPREUVE DES ARMES À FEU, AU PAYS DE LIÉGE. *Alphonse Polain.* A history of the Liége firearms trade so far as shown by documents relating to the proof or possession of arms. The author was for many years director of the Liége proof-house. He collected a large number of legal documents and historical papers dealing with proof-house law, and his book was translated into English and largely circulated. H. V. Carmanne, Liége.

1536.—RECHERCHES HISTORIQUES, sur l'Epreuve des Armes à Feu au Pays de Liége. *Jules Polain.* This is a revised and enlarged edition of the work issued by the Director of the Liége proof-house, and it is the standard work upon proof tests and the history of gun-barrel proving and the practice followed in Belgium, etc. H. Vaillant Carmanne, Liége, 1891, large 8vo, 368 pp., 6 plates of plans, proof marks, etc., and woodcuts of proof marks in text, paper cover.

1537.—DES BANCS D'EPREUVES. *Jules Polain.* A brochure dealing with rules of foreign proof-houses, and the scale of charges imposed at Liége. H. V. Carmanne, Liége, 1892. 8vo, 28 pp. and folding table.

1538.—DES BANC D'EPREUVES, DE L'ORGANISATION. *Jules Polain.* A brochure describing the Liége proof-house, new rules relating to the proof of barrels thereat, and some remarks on the Hungarian proof law. H. V. Carmanne, Liége, 1892. 8vo, 32 pp.

1539.—BANC D'EPREUVES. *Jules Polain.* The law and rules of proof proposed in Germany. A brochure giving a translation of the Prussian Act to found proof-houses in the Empire of Germany. H. V. Carmanne, Liége, 1892. 8vo, 24 pp.

1540.—BANCS D'EPREUVES. *J. Polain.* A brochure giving further documents relating to the establishment of proof-houses in Germany. H. V. Carmanne, Liége, 1893. 8vo, 56 pp.

1541.—BANC D'EPREUVES. *Jules Polain.* An interesting brochure on "The influence the gun-barrel proving-houses exert upon the gun manufacturing industry," together with a review of the work done in the year 1892 at the English, French, Austrian, and Belgian proof-houses. H. V. Carmanne, Liége, 1893. 8vo, 56 pp.

1542.—DISPOSITIONS LÉGALES, Belges, Françaises, Anglaises, Autrichiennes et Allemandes, concernant la repression des frauds en matière d'épreuves d'armes à feu. *Jules*

Polain. A brochure giving precise details of the laws of various countries against forging proof-marks and possessing unproved arms. H. V. Carmanne, Liége, 1894. 8vo, 68 pp., pamphlet.

1543.—BALISTIQUE. Expérience sur la justesse comparée du tir à balles sphériques, plates, et longues. *Didion.* The author or writer of a treatise on ballistics published in nine parts at Metz, at various dates prior to 1860.

1544.—BALISTIQUE. Sur un appareil destiné à figurer le mouvement des projectiles oblongs dans l'air. *J. Perrodon*, 1875. 8vo, 4 illustrations, 1 franc. (*Rev. d'Art.* reprint.)

1545.—BALISTIQUE. De la résistance de l'air. *C. E. Page*, 1878. 8vo, 1 franc. (*Rev. d'Art.* reprint.)

1546.—BALISTIQUE. Sur l'établissement des tables de Tir de l'artillerie. *Beauvoir.* Trajectory formulæ, 1878. 8vo. 2 francs 50 cents. (*Rev. d'Art.* reprint.)

1547.—BALISTIQUE. Sur le mouvement des projectiles oblongs dans l'air. *E. Muzeau*, 1879. 8vo, 25 illustrations. 2 francs. (*Rev. d'Art.* reprint.)

1548.—BALISTIQUE CHRONOGRAPHE PENDULE DE M. CASPERSEN. *L. Cochard*, 1882. 8vo, plates. 50 cents. (*Rev. d'Art.* reprint.)

1549.—BALISTIQUE. Théorie élémentaire des phénomènes qui présentent le gyroscope, la toupie et le projectile oblong. *E. Jouffret*, 1874. 8vo, 1 franc. (*Rev. d'Art.* reprint.)

1550.—BALISTIQUE. Étude balistique sur les bouches à feu, etc. *J. B. V. Lefevre*, 1891. 8vo, 9 illustrations. (Reprint from the *Mémorial de l'Artillerie de la Marine.*)

1551.—BALISTIQUE. Influence de la diminution progressive des vitesses initiales données par les cartouches métalliques sur la portée du fusil d'infanterie. *J. B. V. Lefevre.* 1882. 8vo, 75 cents. (*Rev. d'Art.* reprint.)

1552.—BALISTIQUE. Détermination des vitesses des projectiles au moyen des phénomènes sonores. *Capt. Gossot.* 1891. 8vo, 1 franc 25 cents. (Reprint from the *Mém. de l'Art. de la Marine.*)

1553.—BALISTIQUE. Essai sur les principes de la balistique extérieure. *E. Vallier.* 1886. 8vo, 1 franc. (*Rev. d'Art* reprint.)

1554.—BALISTIQUE. Sur les méthodes actuelles de balistique. *E. Vallier.* 1890. 8vo, 1 franc 25 cents. (*Rev. d'Art.*)

1555.—BALISTIQUE EXTÉRIEURE. This is an annotated translation into French of the celebrated work of F. Siacci by *P. Laurent*, and is followed by a "Note sur les projectiles discoïdes," by F. Chapel. Berger-Levrault, Paris, 1892. 8vo, 60 illustrations, 490 pp., paper, 12 francs.

1556.—INSTRUCTION SUR LE TIR DU FUSIL RAYÉ. A text-book of musketry for the use of the French Infantry and Carabineers armed with rifles. Imp. Roy., Paris, 1861. 12mo.

1557.—TIR AU PISTOLET. *Adolphe d'Houdetot.* A treatise on revolver shooting, chiefly theoretical, but with practical hints. Four editions published. Charpentier, 1864 (last edition); the second edition 1843.

1558.—TIR AU FUSIL DE CHASSE. *A. d'Houdetot.* A complete work on the art of shooting with the shot gun, the target rifle, and the pistol. Charpentier, Paris, 1857, 1865. 12mo, illustrations, 3 francs.

1559.—RÈGLES DE TIR DU MOUSQUETON, m. 1871. An instruction-book. E. Guyot, Bruxelles, 1872. In 12mo, pp. i, 14.

1560.—INSTRUCTION SUR L'EMPLOI DU TUBE À TIR. A provisional order relating to the use of shooting tubes for practice. Imp. Nat., Paris, 1873. In 18mo, 48 pp.

1561.—INSTRUCTION DE TIR. A manual for the use of officers and military schools. Published with the approval of the Minister of War. J. Dumaine, Paris, 1873. In 8vo.

1562.—INSTRUCTION POUR TIR. A manual for the use of the musketry instructor of the Swiss infantry. K. J. Weiss, Berne, 1881. In 12mo.

1563.—FUSIL SUR L'ÉPAULE. *F. Pharaon (M. de Cherville)*. A book of no particular interest by the author of a treatise on Venerie, and writer of the notes "La Vie en Plein Air," in the Paris *Figaro*. These notes for 1885, 1886, were published separately in 12mo.

1564.—LE TIREUR INFALLIBLE. This is the French edition of "The Dead Shot," by "*Marksman*." The translation by H. Robinson. Goin, Paris, 1861. 8vo, illustrated.

1565.—TIR DE CHASSE RAISONNÉ. *T. Sourbe*. A theory of shooting based on the Franco-English method; dog-breaking, sporting hints, etc. Paris, 1885. 12mo, 3 francs.

1566.—TIR DU GIBIER. *Jules F. Petit*. On the art of wing shooting: why one misses, how one hits. Instructions for the young sportsman. Paris, 1885. 16mo.

1567.—CHASSE À TIR MISE À LA PORTÉE DE TOUS. *L. Boussenard*. A manual for sportsmen; hints on shooting, etc. Paris, 1887. One vol. 12mo.

1568.—LE CHAPITRE DES ACCIDENTS. *Maurice Alhoy*. A book illustrating the "accidents" of the chase. Paris, n.d.

1569.—CHAPITRE DES ACCIDENTS. *Maurice Alhoy*. With illustrations by Victor Adam. A book of pictures illustrating sporting episodes. Soulié, Paris, n.d. In 8vo oblong.

1570.—TIR. *L. D. A. J. Pons.* A brochure on the shooting of infantry in general. 1882. 8vo, 51 illustrations, table, 3 francs 50 cents. There is also a brochure, "Etude sur le Tir de l'Infanterie," 1883, 8vo, 9 illustrations, 2 francs 50 cents. Both are reprints from the *Revue Maritime.*

1571.—L'OUTILLAGE D'UNE ARMÉE. *G. Bethuys* and *C. Manceau.* A volume written to popularise military technics. There is a good introduction treating of the development of weapons from the stone age. The first ninety pages deal with small arms, the concluding portions of the volume of artillery, fortifications, etc. The illustrations are numerous, but of mediocre quality. Lecene, Oudin & Co., Paris, 1892. Gr. 8vo, 320 pp. Woodcuts and process blocks in text.

1572.—FUSIL DE CHASSE, "Hammerless," comment s'en servir. A translation by *A.* and *G. Guinard* of "The Breechloader, and How to Use it," by W. W. Greener. Paris, Firmin-Didot, 1894. 8vo, 390 pp., Plates and woodcuts in text, 3 francs.

MODERN GERMAN BOOKS.

GENERAL WORKS.—MILITARY RIFLES.—MUSKETRY.—GUN-MAKING.—SPORTING.

1601.—KRIEGSWAFFEN. *Emil Capitaine* and *Ph. von Hertling*. A periodical devoted to modern military armaments. The first volume illustrates a few leading principles of breechloading, and was published at Berlin in 1888. 8vo, pp. xii, 176 and 96, profusely illustrated. The fifth volume was published in 1893 by M. Babenzien, Rathenow, a 4to of 262 pp. In progress.

1602.—GESCHICHTE DER WAFFEN. *F. U. von Specht*. A complete and comprehensive work on weapons generally. The treatment is original, and the material has been gathered with care and well selected; the work is one of the most painstaking and thorough of any on the subject. Vol. I., Stone, Bronze, and Iron Age, 526 pp., 18 folding plates. II., Australasian and American, 674 pp., xxiv plates. III., African, etc., 902 pp., xvi plates, 1877. C. Luckhardt, Cassel and Leipzig, 1870, etc. 8vo, 2 vols.; 19 parts issued.

1603.—HANDFEUER WAFFEN, ihre Entstehung, etc. *Rud. Schmidt*. The original edition of "Armes à Feu portatives" (*q.v.*, No. 1504). The Atlas of 56 plates is the same. B. Schwabe, Basel, 1878. 4to, 2 vols.

1604.—NEUERUNGEN im Bewaffnungswesen der Infanterie. *R. Schmidt*. Forms a continuation of the earlier work, bringing it down to 1882.

General Works.—Military Rifles, etc. 149

1605.—NEUERUNGEN, etc. *R. Schmidt.* A supplement continuing the work to 1885.

1606.—ALLGEMEINE WAFFENKUNDE DER INFANTERIE. *R. Schmidt.* A treatise on modern military small arms. Volume of text and atlas of 23 engraved plates with 400 illustrations. B. Schwabe, Basel, 1888. 25 marks.

1607.—GESCHICHTLICHE ENTWICKELUNG DER HANDFEUER WAFFEN. *M. Thierbach.* An elaborate treatise on the development of the infantry rifle, the early portion chiefly from German sources. The first portion deals chiefly with the lock mechanism, the third wholly with breechloaders. C. Hockner, Dresden, 1888. Long 4to, 538 pp., 34 double-page coloured litho. plates, comprising 111 separate illustrations.

1608.—RUCKLADUNGSGEWEHRE. *Mattenheimer.* Fragments of a history of breechloaders and their development. Seidel, Vienna, 1876. 102 coloured plates. 9 florins. A supplement, "Neue Folge," sheets 103-11, 1890. 1 florin 68 kreuzers.

1609.—HINTERLADERGEWEHRE. *F. Hentsch.* A series of monographs on the small arms in use in the various European armies. No. 2, for instance, treats of the history of the breechloader in the Dutch army. Fr. Luckhardt, Leipzig, 1873. 8vo, 55 pp. and 5 lithographed plates. Sweden, Norway and Denmark are treated in another volume of 143 pp. and 6 plates, published in 1879; French arms in another published in the same year, 173 pp., 7 plates. The work is now to some extent superseded by the periodical *Kriegswaffen*, of which one volume appears annually. See No. 1601.

1610.—BESCHREIBUNG. A description of the French 1886 model gun. Seidel, Wien, 1888. 24 kreuzers.

1611.—REPETIR-GEWEHRE. A text-book of the 1888 model, with lithographed plate, 1888.

1612.—REPETIR-GEWEHRE. A history of the origin and development of repeating arms, with descriptions of the varieties in use. A well-arranged compilation, clearly printed in Roman type. E. Zernin, Darmstadt and Leipzig, 1882. 8vo, 256 pp., 56 woodcuts, numerous tables, paper covers.

1613.—GEWEHR, der Gegenwart und Zukunft, 1883.

1614.—GEWEHR. Gegenwärtige Stand de Bewaffnungsfrage der Infanterie. One lithograph, 1886.

1615.—GEWEHR. The new rifle and smokeless powder, with explanatory drawings. L. W. Seidel, Wien, 1890. Part I.

1616.—HANDFEUERWAFFEN. *Laukmayr.* Part IV. of " Waffenlehre " treats of hand firearms. Seven tables, four sheets of drawings. 1888.

1617.—HANDBUCH DES ÖSTERUNGEN HANDFEUERWAFFEN. *Laukmayr.* A military text-book. Seidel, Wien, 1888. Seven plates.

1618.—WICHTIGSTEN REPETIR-VERSCHLUSS-, Schloss- und Abzugs Mechanismus sammt, Kurzer geschichtlicher Entwicklung des neuen Österreichischen Armee-Gewehrs (188 m.). *Högg.* A short account of the 1888 Austrian Mannlicher rifle ; 2 plates, 80 figures. Seidel, Wien, 1888.

1619.—DREH- UND REPETIRPISTOLEN. *C. H. Schmidt.* A short practical treatise on the pistol and revolver and its manufacture. B. F. Voigt, Weimar, 1858. 8vo, 228 pp., 6 engraved folding plates of pistols and machinery.

1620.—INFANTERIE GEWEHR. *E. Thiel.* A technical treatise on the ballistics of the infantry rifle. Bonn, 1883. 8vo.

1621.—TECHNISCHE ENTWICKELUNG. *H. Weygand.* A treatise on the development of the infantry rifle as a weapon of precision. Berlin and Leipzig, 1876-8, 8vo, 3 parts.

General Works.—Military Rifles, etc. 151

1622.—BALLISTIK DER HANDFEUERWAFFEN. *A. Indra.* The ballistic qualities of small arms shown in a series of comparative tables. Seidel, Wien, 1879. 1 plate, 24 pp.

1623.—BALLISTIK. Theoretische aussere Ballistik nebst einer Anleitung zur praktischen Ermittlung der Flugbahn-Elemente. *Mieg.* 1884, 5 plates, 10 marks.

1624.—BALLISTIK. Rotation der Geschosse. *Pfister.* 1864, 1 plate.

1625.—BALLISTIK. Beurtheilung unserer ballistischen Rechenformeln. *Pfister.* 1882.

1626.—BALLISTIK. Theorie des schiessens der Handfeuerwaffen. *Hentsch.* A popular treatise on theoretical gunnery. Seedel, Wien, 1878, 2 parts, 4 illustrations.

1627.—BALLISTIK DER HANDFEUERWAFFEN. *Hentsch.* With 23 tables. 1876. 4to.

1628.—BALLISTIK. Theoretische Studien zur Ballistik zur gezogenen Gewehre. *Cranz.* Comparative ballistics. 8vo, 11 illustrations. 1887.

1629.—BALLISTIK. Neue Theorie der Flugbahn von Langeschossen auf Grund einer neuen Theorie der Drehung der Korper. Dahne, Vienna, 1888. 8vo.

1630.—BALLISTIK DER GEZOGENEN FEUERWAFFEN, mit einer mathematischer Einleitung. *Dam van Isselt.* One table. 1884.

1631.—DAS KLEINSTE KALIBER; oder das zukünftige Infantrie gewehr. *F. W. Hebler.* A mathematical treatise on calibres, velocity, etc. A Müller, Zurich and Leipzig, 1886. 8vo, 142 pp., 4 tables and 2 plates.

1632.—INSTRUKTION FÜR WAFFEN-OFFICIERE, etc. An official text-book for officers, and more particularly armourers, respecting the Werndl breech action. Hof & Staatsdruch, Vienna, 1878.

1633.—BETRACHTUNG über die Schiess übungen der Infanterie. A treatise on marksmanship and the handling of the rifle, by a Prussian staff officer. 1882. 8vo pamphlet.

1634.—ELEMENTARE SCHIESSTHEORIE. *Lauffer & Winch.* Seedel, Wien, 1884, 101 figures.

1635.—ZUKUNFTS GEWEHR, seine Wirkung. *K. Krnka.* With 1 plate. 1884.

1636.—WAFFENTECHNIK. Erfindung der Neuzeit auf dem Gebiete der Waffentechnik zur Erhöhung der Feuerschnelligkeit bei Handfeuerwaffen: *Kromar.* Four plates. 1885.

1637.—GRUNDRISS DER WAFFENLEHRE. *K. T. von Sauer.* A comprehensive technical book covering every variety of small firearms. Th. Riedel, Munich, 1876. Large 8vo, pp. vi, 568, and supplement of 76 pp., 12 plates of illustrations and 30 others bound, and a separate atlas.

1638.—

1639.—

1640.—

1641.—MODERNE GEWEHR FABRIKATION. *F. Brandeis.* An elaborate text-book or manual of instruction for the gunsmith. The principles of firearms construction carefully stated and numerous varieties of sporting gun mechanisms described. This work goes more fully into gunmaking details than any book since published, and is singularly free from theory and controversial matter. B. F. Voigt, Weimar, 1881. 8vo, 402 pp. An atlas 4to, 22 folio plates, with 430 figures.

1642.—DIE JAGDGEWEHRE DER GEGENWART. *Georg Koch.* "A handbook for sportsmen." A short treatise on firearms, covering much the same ground as W. W. Greener's "Modern Shot Guns," but having chapters on revolvers and rifled guns. B. F. Voigt, Weimar, 1891. Demy 8vo, 152 pp., 94 illustrations.

1643.—JAGD-, SCHIEBEN- UND SCHUTZ-WAFFEN. *Ig. Neumann.* A book on sporting weapons and target rifles. Voigt, Weimar, 1872. 8vo, 1 mark 50 pfge.

1644.—WESEN DER HINTERLADUNGS-GEWEHRE. *Ig. Neumann.* A complete treatise on breechloading mechanisms. Voigt, Weimar, 1880. 8vo, 27 litho. plates, 3 marks 75 pfge.

1645.—JAGD-FLINTE. *W. W. Greener.* A translation by *H. Leue* of "Modern Shot Guns" with additions; a chapter on rifles, and numerous fresh illustrations and full-page plates. Brockhaus, Leipzig, 1894. 8vo.

1646.—MODELLBUCH FÜR BÜCHSENMACHER. *C. Martin.* A book of illustrations of many varieties of guns, with simple descriptions intended to serve as a gunmaker's catalogue. Voigt, Weimar. 8vo, large folio, 32 plates, 2 marks.

1651.—DER JAGDLIEBHABER in der Schule der gerechten Waidmann's und Vogelstellers, unterhaltende Beleistigungen auf dem Lande mit der Jagd, dem Vogelfange . . . mit 2 litho. *Von Ehrenkreutz.* Weimar, Voigt, 1856. In 8vo.

1652.—DER DEUTSCHE SCHÜTZE in allen ihm vorkommenden Lagen und Verhaltnissen auf dem Scheibenstand, im Krieg, und auf der Jagd. Mit vielen Holschnitt. *C. Pistoris.* Warnberg, Zeh., 1862. Gr. in 8vo.

1653.—WALDSCHNEPFE UND IHRE JAGD. *R. A. v. Benburg.* Gärtner, Berlin, 1857, 1866.

1654.—PRAKTISCHE JAGER. *Rob. Bermisch.* A manual of instruction for sportsmen. Adler et Dictze, Dresden (2nd edition), 1859.

1655.—WAIDMANN'S-FAHRTEN. *A. v. Basedow.* Sporting rhymes. Leipzig, Schmidt, 1865. 8vo.

1656.—GESETZE ZUM SCHÜTZE DER FÖRSTER UND FORSTBEAMTEN. *F. J. J. Bank.* A treatise on the Prussian forest laws, fines, etc., etc. G. Renner, Berlin, 1867. 8vo.

1657.—DIE JAGD und ihre Wandlungen in Wort und Bild. *R. Corneli.* This book was the outcome of the Cleves Sporting Exhibition, and is a clever compilation. Harms, Amsterdam, 1883. Large folio, 384 pp., woodcuts.

MODERN ITALIAN BOOKS.

1701.—ARCHIBUSO DI NUOVA FOGGIA. *Domenico Berio.*
Relates to the use of fulminate. See p. 2, ch. v.,
Vol. XL., of the "Memoirs of the Academy of Science
of Turin." Not separately published.

1702.—TIRO DELL ARMI FUOCO. *Du Quesnay A. Delorme.*
Relates principally to the shooting of the Italian
infantry, but is denounced by military critics as a
useless publication. The work is that of A.
Desbordeliers. A version from the French was made
by Malagoli Vecchi of Modena, and another version
appeared in Genoa later. Florence, 1848, in 8vo;
Genoa, 1851, in 8vo.

1703.—STORIA DEL TIRO FEDERALE SVIZZERO. *Luigi Torrelli.*
Torino, 1851.

1704.—MANUALE DEL CACCIATORE. *Alberta Bacchi della
Lega.* Bologna, 1876.

1705.—MANUALE DEL CACCIATORE ITALIANO. *E. Azzi.* A
modern cyclopædia of shooting and sporting arms; the
gun portion written by Dr. Azzi, the kennel contributed
by F. Delor and N. Camusso. A carefully compiled
work, fairly written, and got up in an attractive style;
the illustrations are numerous, but not all original.
Dumolard Brothers, Milan, 1887. Demy 8vo, 907 pp.,
woodcuts and plates, half vellum, 25 lire.

1706.—ARMI A RIPETIZIONE. *Ippolito Viglezzi.* A
technical treatise on modern magazine guns. The
Kropatschek and Mannlicher systems are compared

in detail, and the whole question of military small arms thoroughly entered into. Voghera Carlo, Rome, 1890. 8vo, 262 pp., numerous figures in 40 engraved folding plates.

1707.—FUSILI DA CACCIA MODERNI. *W. W. Greener.* An English edition of "Modern Shot Guns." The translation, by the Marchese G. D'Adda Salvatera, is a very good one, and the edition is well printed on good paper. Preface by "Grilletto" (Dr. E. Azzi), who appears to have revised the translation. P. B. Bellini & Co., Milan, 1890. Large 8vo, 202 pp., illustrations as in English editions, 5 lire.

MODERN SPANISH BOOKS.

ARRANGED CHRONOLOGICALLY.

1801.—FABRICA DE FUSILS DE OVIEDO. *D. Manuel Paez Jaramillo.* An account of the firearms factory at Oviedo, included in the *Mem. Artilleria*, 1850; also published separately.

1802.—PROJECTO UNA ESCUELA DE TIRO. *D. Jose A. Berruezo.* The prospectus of a shooting school for Madrid. Madrid, 1851. 1 vol. 8vo.

1803.—CACERIAS EN MARRUCCOS. *J. Alvarez-Perez.* Authentic adventures of a Spaniard. Madrid, Printed for the Society of Instruction and Recreation. 8vo.

1804.—RESENA DE LAS ARMAS PORTATILES. *D. Santiago Loriga.* A writer on military subjects and contributor to the *Mem. Artilleria.* This paper forms a continuation to that published in 1852 on the "Fusil Reformado." Madrid, 1 vol. 8vo.

1805.—HISTORIA DE UN FUSIL, 1853. *D. Manuel d. Burto.* Appeared in the *Revista Militar.* Madrid, 1853.

1806.—FUSILES DE AGUJA FULMINANTE. *D. Luis de Anstegui y Doz.* An early notice of the Dreyse percussion gun; compare with Mosar's account, published in *Mem. Artilleria*, 1854. London, 1853, 10 pp. pamphlet.

1807.—ESTADO ACTUAL DE LAS ARMAS DE FUEGO. *D. J. M. Aparici y Bredma.* A translation from the French. See *Arts. et Rev. Mil.*, 1854, t. xv.

1808.—TIRO CON LA CARABINA. *D. Vicente Atienza y Martinez.* Lessons in military rifle shooting. Habana, 1859. 1 vol. 4to, 12 illustrations.

1809.—ESCUELA MILITAR DE TIRO. *D. Jose Coello y Quesada.* A study on the subject of military schools for the practice of musketry. Rivadeneyra. Madrid, 1859. 1 vol. 8vo.

1810.—ENSAYO TEORICO-PRACTICO SOBRE LAS ARMAS PORTATILES. *D. Miguel Correa* and *D. F. Martinez de Viergol.* Part I.: Infantry arms. Madrid, 1859. 1 vol. 8vo.

1811.—MANUAL DE TIRO. *D. M. Correa* and *D. F. Martinez y Viergol.* A text-book for sergeants and musketry instructors. Estrada, Madrid, 1864. 1 vol. 8vo, plates.

1812.—ARMAS PORTATILES CARGADAS POR LA RECAMARA. *D. J. Buega.* A treatise on military breechloaders, written in New York in 1866, and inserted in the *Mem. Artill.*, ser. 2, t. vi. Was translated into French and separately published. Correard, Paris, 1867. 1 vol. 8vo.

1813.—ARMAMENTO DE LA INFANTERIA. *D. E. Gonzalez Velasco.* A treatise on the arms actually in use with European armies, and a historico-descriptive summary of breechloading small arms. Madrid, 1867. 1 vol. 8vo, 6 plates.

1814.—CHASSEPOT. Particulars of the Chassepot rifle, translated into Spanish from the French. *Mem. Art.*, second series, t. vii., 1868.

1815.—EXAMEN CRITICO DEL ARMAMENTO FRANCES. A critique of the armament of the French during the German war. Madrid, 1870. 1 vol. 4to.

1816.—ARMAMENTO MODELO DE 1871. Report of the commission on the new gun, Remington, and the order in respect thereto. Madrid, 1871. 1 vol. 8vo, 108 pp.

1817.—REGLAMENTO PARA DE LA REAL MONTERIA, BALLESTERIA Y ARMERIA. *Baron Benifayo.* Madrid, 1871.

1818.—CAZA Y SU LEGISLACION. *J. Joaquin de Bada.* A treatise on sport, the use of arms and the game laws, more particularly the enforcement of the latter by local authorities. J. Miret, Barcelona, 1879. 8vo.

1819.—CURSO ELEMENTAL DE TIRO. *D. Jore Ferron y Saavedra.* An elementary course of lessons, theoretical and practical, on the art of rifle shooting. Cuevas y Menneras, Madrid. 1 vol. 8vo, 336 pp., 12 plates.

1820.—ESCOPETAS MODERNAS. *W. W. Greener.* A Spanish edition of " Modern Shot Guns " (*q.v.*). The translation, by Messrs. Arts y Ocon, is not good. Malaga, Gallegos y Urbano, 1893 (?). Small 4to, 222 pp., woodcuts as in 2nd English edition, 5 pesetas.

MODERN BOOKS (VARIOUS).

1901.—BIJDRAGEN tot de kennis van het getrokken geschut naar Schmoelzl, von feilitzen maievoky en anderen. *A. G. Kempers.* A book on gunnery, by an artillery captain. Utrecht, 1860. Demy 8vo, 176 pp., 5 litho. folding plates.

1911.—ILLUSTRERAD IDROTTSBOK HANDLEDNING I OLIKA GRENAR AF IDROTT OCH LEKAR. *V. Balck.* An encyclopædia of sports and pastimes, with instructions for every amusement, from playing the Jew's harp to driving a four-in-hand. The shooting portion by *O. B. Rydholm*, and the chapter on firearms by *C. Lempchen.* These portions are largely translations of the Badminton Library, and W. W. Greener's "Gun and its Development," from which illustrations have been reproduced. Issued in parts by C. E. Fritze, Stockholm. Commenced in 1886, 30 parts published to end of 1888. 8vo, 1 or 2 kroner each part, 1000 illustrations, woodcuts.

1921.—RUSSIAN. Instructions for shooting with the Smith and Wesson revolver. *Epichin.* Published for the Smith and Wesson Revolver Works, U₁S.A.

1922.—RUSSIAN. Roojia. *W. W. Greener.* A translation by L. Tarnovski of "The Gun and its Development." L. Sabanaev, Moscow, 1887. 4to, 2 vols.

PART III.
Appendices.

A SHORT BIBLIOGRAPHY OF EXPLOSIVES.

NOTE.—In addition to the works given below, particulars of the early use and manufacture of *gunpowder* are given in most of the early treatises on firearms, particularly Nos. 11, 13, 43, 123, 139, 143, 145, 147, 149, 173, 205, 232, 354, 360, 361, and 362 in Part I. For the *Invention of Gunpowder* see Daniel's "Histoire de Milice"; H. A. Hoyer's "Geschichte des Kriegskunst"; and Beckman's "History of Inventions." For *early use* in England, Harleian MSS., "Richard III., anno 1483," Eccleston's "English Antiquities," Smith's "Military Discourses in Ellis's Original Letters" (Camden Society's edition, p. 53); also for *Manufacture* Bohlen's "Alte Indien," vol. ii., p. 68. *See also* "List of Technical Papers, etc.," Nos. 2201 *et seq*.

BOOKS RELATING TO GUNPOWDER.

2101.—GUNPOWDER MANUFACTURE. A statement of facts relative to the savings which have arisen from manufacturing gunpowder at the Royal powder-mills; and of the improvements which have been made in its strength and durability since the year 1783. *Sir W. Congreve.* Dedicated to Lord Mulgrave, privately published, printed by J. Whiting, Finsbury Place, 1811. 8vo, 44 pp.

2102.—MANUFACTURE OF GUNPOWDER as carried on at the Government Factory, Waltham Abbey. *Major Fraser Baddeley.* A privately issued pamphlet. E. Littler. Sun Street, Waltham Abbey, 1857. Demy 8vo, 44 pp.

2103.—MEMOIR ON GUN-POWDER; in which are discussed the principles both of its manufacture and proof. *J. Braddock.* This book was printed at public expense,

300 copies only issued, and it is somewhat rare; the only copy I have been able to examine formerly belonged to M. Faraday, and is now in the Patent Library. Madras, 1829. 8vo, pp. viii, 138.

2104.—MEMOIR ON GUN-POWDER. *John Braddock*. This is the London edition of No. 2103; it was also translated into French as "Notes on Manufacture of Gunpowder in the East Indies, by *Ravichio de Peretsdorf*," Paris, 1840. London, 1832. 8vo.

2105.—SKETCH of the mode of manufacturing Gunpowder at the Ishapore Mills in Bengal, with a record of the experiments carried on to ascertain the value of charge, windage, vent, and weight, etc., in mortars and muskets; also reports of the various proofs of powder. *Col. W. Anderson*; with notes and additions by Lieut.-Col. Parlby. This is a comprehensive and apparently exhaustive work. J. Weale, London, 1862, 303 pp., plates, tables, etc.

2106.—HANDBOOK of the manufacture and proof of Gunpowder as carried on at the Royal Gunpowder Factory, Waltham Abbey. *F. Smith*. This is a serviceable handbook. Eyre & Spottiswoode, 1870. Demy 8vo, 132 pp., plates.

2107.—NOTES ON GUNPOWDER, by a manufacturer. A pamphlet issued gratuitously by Messrs. Curtiss and Harvey. Contains some practical hints on loading shot cartridges, and states the advantages which black gunpowder possesses when compared with the nitro compounds. 74, Lombard Street, London, 1890, etc. 8vo, cloth limp.

2108.—GUNPOWDER. Méthode suivie à la Poudrerie du Bouchet, pour les essais et analyses des salpêtres raffines. *F. Castan*, 1880. 8vo, 1 franc (*Rev. d'Art* reprint).

2109.—TEORIA CHIMICA DELLA COMPOSIZIONE DELLE POLVERE A FUOCO. *Carlo Sobrero*. A work of considerable interest, and based upon a long study of explosives.

The author was a Commandant of Artillery. Mil. Tip., Torino, 1852. 8vo.

2110.—INDEX TO THE LITERATURE OF EXPLOSIVES. *C. F. Munroe.* A Bibliography and Index to articles in Technical Magazines. Baltimore, 1893. 8vo, 195 pp.

MODERN HIGH EXPLOSIVES, ETC.

2111.—NEUMEYER'S INEXPLOSIVE GUNPOWDER. An inventor's description, etc. Published for E. H. Newby, 1867. 4to, 44 pp.

2112.—EXPLOSIVE AGENTS. *F. A. Abel.* A lecture on recent investigations and applications of explosives. Read before the British Association at Edinburgh, 1871. Edmonston & Douglas, Edinburgh, 1871. Demy 8vo, 40 pp.

2113.—EXPLOSIVE COMPOUNDS. *Perry F. Nursey.* The text of a paper read before, and discussion at, the Society of Engineers, November 1871. Privately printed, London, 1871. 8vo, 145 pp. (Patent Library, London.)

2114.—NOTES ON GUNPOWDER AND GUN-COTTON. *W. H. Wardell.* Extracts from Service Notes for the use of the Cadets at the Royal Military Academy, Woolwich. J. Cattermole, Woolwich, 1882. Demy 8vo, 52 pp.

2115.—EXPLOSIVES. *W. P. Bloxham.* Text of a paper read before the Science Society of King's College, London. W. Pile, Wallington. 8vo pamphlet, 40 pp., 6d.

2116.—REPORT. Experiments in Gunpowder made at Washington Arsenal, 1843-4. *A. Mordecai.* (Official.) Washington, D.C., 1845. Demy 8vo, 328 pp., 8 plates.

2117.—SHORT NOTES on the Manufacture of Gunpowder and Gun-cotton, prepared for the use of the Gentlemen Cadets of the R. M. Academy, Woolwich. *O. H. Goodenough.* Woolwich, 1872. 4to, 24 pp., 4 pp. plates.

2118.—RESEARCHES ON EXPLOSIVES. Fired Gunpowder. *Captain Noble* and *F. A. Abel*. Reprinted from the Philosophical Transactions of the Royal Society, Perth, 1875. Trübner & Co., London, 1875. 4to, 133 pp., illustrations in text and 11 plates.

2119.—MODERN HIGH EXPLOSIVES. *Manuel Eisler*. A handbook to nitro-glycerine and dynamite, their manufacture and use, and application to various purposes; pyroxiline or gun-cotton, the fulminates, picrates and chlorates, also the chemistry and analysis of the elementary bodies which enter into the manufacture of the principal nitro-compounds. Chiefly from the mining engineer's point of view. J. Urley & Sons, New York, 1884. Demy 8vo, 395 pp., woodcuts, etc.

2120.—HANDBOOK ON MODERN EXPLOSIVES. *M. Eisler*. "A practical treatise on the manufacture and application of dynamite, gun-cotton, nitro-glycerine and other explosive compounds, including the manufacture of collodion-cotton." Crosby Lockwood, 1890. Crown 8vo, 318 pp., 100 illustrations in the text.

2121.—EXPLOSIVES AND THEIR POWER. A condensed translation of *M. Berthelot*, by C. Napier Hake and W. Macnab, with a preface by J. P. Cundill. This gives the results of M. Berthelot's researches in a succinct form. J. Murray, London, 1892. Demy 8vo, 564 pp., illustrations.

2122.—SMOKELESS EXPLOSIVES. *Roos*. A pamphlet. McLure, Victoria Street, London, 1894.

2123.—DICTIONARY OF EXPLOSIVES. *J. P. Cundill*. Gives the composition of nearly all known explosives and the properties of many of them. W. J. Mackay & Co., Chatham, 1889. Demy 8vo, 104 pp., interleaved.

2124.—NOTES ON EXPLOSIVES. *Dr. W. R. Hodgkinson*. A pamphlet, 6d.

2125.—MODERN GUNS AND SMOKELESS POWDER. *Arthur Rigg* and *James Garvie*. E. & F. N. Spon, London. A short treatise on cordite and the use of smokeless explosives in ordnance. 1892. Demy 8vo, 84 pp., diagrams.

2126.—THE MANUFACTURE OF MODERN EXPLOSIVES. *Oscar Guttmann*. A practical treatise on factory and laboratory work. Whittaker & Co., London, 1894.

2127.—EXPLOSIVES. *W. J. Orsman*. A lecture delivered at University College, Nottingham, Nov. 25th, 1893, and giving in popular language a succinct history and description of the chemical composition of modern high explosives. London, 1894. 8vo pamphlet.

2128.—ROYAL GUNPOWDER FACTORY, Waltham Abbey. First Report of the Committee appointed to inquire into the accident on the 13th December, 1893, and also into the construction, etc., of the danger buildings at Waltham Abbey and the Royal Arsenal, Woolwich, together with minutes of evidence and appendices. Eyre & Spottiswoode, London, 1894. Fcap. folio, 2s.

2129.—EXPLOSIVES. Annual Report of H. M. Inspectors. The eighteenth (for 1893). Eyre & Spottiswoode, London, 1894. Fcap. folio, 1s. 4d.

2130.—HANDBOOK TO THE EXPLOSIVES ACT and Orders in Council. *V. D. Majendie*. A text-book for Explosive Inspectors, Explosive Manufacturers, and all interested in the licensing of persons and places as provided by the Explosives Act of 1875, and later Orders in Council relating thereto. Harrison & Sons, London, 1878, etc., various editions. 16mo, 2s.

2131.—POUDRE SANS FUMÉE ET LES POUDRES ANCIENNES. *A. Ponteaux*. Damidot, Dijon, 1892. 8vo, pp. xxv, 156.

2132.—EXPLOSIFS MODERNES. *Paul F. Chalon.* A practical and theoretical treatise on modern explosives, and dictionary of gunpowder and explosive substances. An exhaustive work. Bernard & Cie, Paris, 1889; n.e., 507 pp., illustrations.

2133.—SUR LA FORCE DE MATIÈRES EXPLOSIVES. *M. Berthelot.* The standard work on the thermal dynamics of explosives. Gauthier Villars, Paris. Third edition, 1883, 2 vols. 8vo, 405 and 445 pp. (See No. 2121.)

2134.—RAUCH FREIE PULVER. An anonymous pamphlet of 32 pp., published by R. Eisenschmidt, Berlin, 1889. 8vo.

2135.—GEPRESSTE SCHIESSWOLLE. *Franz Plach.* An exhaustive monograph of the use of pressed gun-cotton, more particularly with reference to torpedoes and submarine mining. Pola, 1891. 4to, 133 pp., 24 illustrations.

2136.—VOCABOLARIO DI POLVERI ED ESPLOSIVI. *Ferdinando Salvati.* A complete work on modern explosives, giving the composition of almost every known variety. Reprinted from the *Revista Maritima*.

AMMUNITION, GUN WOUNDS, ETC.

2140.—BORES AND LOADS FOR SPORTING GUNS. *W. A. Adams.* This is a short treatise on calibres and loads for various guns for British game shooting. H. Cox, 1894. Foolscap 8vo, limp cloth, 6*d*.

2141.—TABLES OF LOADS. "*Purple Heather.*" A pamphlet on the qualities of various loads for game shooting, more particularly with reference to the size of shot. Alexander & Shepheard, London, 1893. 8vo, paper.

2142.—TABLE OF LOADS for shoulder guns of all sizes, chokes and cylinders, and for punt guns. *Lewis Clement.* Field Office, 1880. Oblong 16mo, 6d.; n.e., 1881 (?), *Shooting Times* Office.

2143.—PROJECTILES, WEAPONS OF WAR, and explosive compounds. *J. Scoffern, M.B.* Treats of new weapons, rifled ordnance, Armstrong's breechloading cannon, etc. Longmans, London, 1859. 8vo, 376 pp., illustrated.

2144.—RIFLE AMMUNITION. *Captain Hawes.* Mitchell, 1859. 8vo, 14s.

2145.—TREATISE ON AMMUNITION. Official. A service handbook to ammunition of all kinds. Harrison & Sons, etc., 1892. Fifth edition. 8vo, 582 pp., 6s.

2146.—CARTOUCHES MÉTALLIQUES. An account of the metallic cartridges in use for war purposes. St. Petersburg, 1872. In 8vo.

2147.—NOTIONS SUR LE MATÉRIEL; ET LES MUNITIONS. (Official.) *Imp. Nat.*, Paris, 1889; 2nd edition, 1891, 1 fr. 50 c.

2148.—PATRONEN. *Mattenheimer.* Illustrated with two lithographs and a coloured copper-plate engraving. Vienna, 1868.

2151.—BOOKE OF OBSERVATIONS. *W. Clowes.* "A profitable and necessarie tretise for all those that are burned with the flame of Gunpowder, and also for curing of wounds made with musket and caliver shot." E. Bollifant (for T. Dawson), London, 1596. 4to.

2152.—SPAGERICKE ANTIDOTARIE FOR GUNNE SHOT. *P. A. T. Bombast von Hohenheim* (Paracelsus). A collection of 114 cases of treatment. London, 1596. 4to.

2153.—ACCIDENTS. *G. Piobert.* Sur les moyens de diminuer les dangers des explosions de la poudre. This consists of extracts from a paper read before the Académie des Sciences of "New Experiences of the Inflammation and Combustion of Powder." Bachelier, Paris, 1840. 4to, pamphlet, 12 pp.

2154.—MÉMOIRES SUR LES POUDRES DE GUERRE. *G. Piobert.*
This is a *résumé* of comparative trials of powders made by different processes in 1831-2 and 1836-7. Bachelier, Paris. 8vo, 96 pp., folding tables.

2155.—LES MILITAIRES BLESSÉS. *C. de Reincourt.* A history of the wounded and their treatment, and particularly of pensions and pensioners in France and abroad. Paris, 1875. 8vo, 2 vols.

TECHNICAL PAPERS, MAGAZINE ARTICLES, AND NEWSPAPER REFERENCES.

2201.—GUNPOWDER. *Gentleman's Magazine.* Invention of, x. 95 (1740); trial of, x. 315; mills blown up, xii. 49; of different strength, xviii. 165; accidents, xviii. 404; in rockets, xviii. 597; inwardly fatal, xix. 19; explosion at Ostend, xxiv. 480; at Moulsey, xxiv. 481; Duhamel on, xxiv. 491; experiments on, xxiv. 492; discovery to increase force of, xxv. 161; shipped to West Indies, xxv. 280; experiments on, xxv. 552; inflammation in firearms not instantaneous, *ibid.*; machine for proving, *ibid.*; proper charges for cannon, xxv. 553; what charge has greatest effect, *ibid.*; exportation prohibited, xxv. 570; prohibition continued, xxviii. 191, 449; xxx. 488; fired at Morpeth, xxviii. 448; explosion, xxix. 391; against exportation, xxxi. 233; explosion at Worcester, xxxii. 386; machines for testing, xxxiii. 73; prohibition removed, *ibid.*, 144; fired by ice, xxxiii. 94; experiments, xxxiii. 630; importers' trial, xxxvi. 197; accidents, xxxvii. 92, 142, 381, 560; Hounslow mills blown up, xlii. 41; explosion, xliii. 246; not to be exported, xliii. 578; explosion at Abbeville magazine, xliii. 580, 619; accident prevented, xliv. 40; exportation prohibited, xlv. 405; taken out of Dutch man-o'-war, *ibid.*; Carthagena magazine

blown up, xlv. 601; prohibited, xlvi. 93; force of
mixed, xlix. 310; debate on in Admiral Barrington's
fleet, l. 303; Strachey's account of, *ibid.*, 309; an
improvement in manufacture, lv. 916; introduction
into Russia, lvii. 392; Irish mills blown up, lvii. 446;
put in tobacco pipe is fatal, lvii. 644; Battle mill
blown up, lvii. 1189; lxxviii. 360; accidentally dis-
covered, lviii. 1041; Faversham mill blown up, lix.
950; inquiries about, lxi. 885; invention of, lxii. 517;
ivory-flask, lxii. 981, 1191; mill at Constantinople,
lxv. 155; accident, lxvii. 976; force of, lxviii. 501;
known in feudal times, lxx. 115 (1800); improved
way of preparing, lxxiii. 272; explosion at Leyden,
lxxviii. 77; at Cheam, *ibid.*; in London, lxxviii. 80;
disaster, lxxx. (2), 186; explosion, lxxx. (2), 279; uses
of, lxxxii. (1), 40; explosion of, lxxxiii. (2), 422, 695
(1818).

2202.—EXPLOSIVES. *Transactions and Journal of the
Society of Arts.* Substitutes for gunpowder, Abel, xx.
632; Pellet powder, xvi. 374; Schultze, xvii. 216,
289; Neumeyer's, xiv. 751, 768; Blast of gunpowder,
xix. 215; Explosion, xxxvii. 161; Gun-cotton, Austrian
reports on, xi. 715; xiv. 47, 585, 724; Present
knowledge of, xii. 357, 686; Gun-cotton, xix. 300;
Curious property of, xiv. 330; Punshon's trial, xx.
186, 427; Mackie's, xxiii. 227; Modern history of
gunpowder, xxvii. 437; New kind of gunpowder, xxi.
19; Improvements in gun-cotton, xxi. 470, 535;
Dering on explosives, xxxvii. 52; Cartridges, Coffin's
filling machine, xlv. 106; Jenner's shot cartridge,
xliv. 88; Percussion caps, xii. 486; Ammunition, xviii.
931.

2203.—EXPLOSIVES. *Journal United Service Institution.*
Gun-cotton, *Lieut. A. Walker*, 1864, viii. 396; Gun-
cotton cartridges, *J. Latham*, 1866, x. 328; Gale's
plan of rendering gunpowder non-explosive and re-
explosive, *W. Saunders*, 1866, x. 123; Norton's
percussion grenade for house defence, *Capt. J.*

Norton, 1866, x. 289; Gun-cotton and explosive agents, *F. A. Abel*, 1862, vi. 129; Gun-cotton, some new points in the application of, *F. A. Abel*, 1864, viii. 345; Gunpowder as a disruptive agent, *Capt. H. Schaw*, 1858, ii. 269; Explosives as substitutes for gunpowder, *F. A. Abel*, 1872, xvi. 457; Explosive force of gunpowder, *J. P. Morgan*, 1871, xv. 312; Schultze's granulated wood powder, *J. D. Dougall*, 1868, xii. 127; Special features in large and small grain gunpowders, *J. P. Morgan*, 1876, xx. 195; Cotton powder for military purposes, *S. J. Mackie*, 1877, xxi. 887; Recent inventions in gunpowder and other explosives, *W. H. Dering*, 1888, xxxiii. 603; Experiments with smokeless gunpowder, Gruson, c. 89, *W. G. Wickson*, 1890, xxxiv. 1069; Modern gunpowder as a propellent, *Major Barker*, 1890, xxxiv. 257; French small-arm smokeless powder (translation), 1893, xxxvii. 487.

2204.—CARTRIDGES AND PROJECTILES. *Journal of the United Service Institution.* New metallic cartridge for military purposes, *Dr. J. Millar*, 1866, x. 141; Gun-cotton cartridges, *J. Latham*, 1866, x. 328; Norton's rifle projectiles, *Capt. Norton*, 1858, ii. 338; Rifled projectile for smooth-bore artillery, *Capt. J. H. Selwyn*, 1866, x. 393; Cartridges for small arms, *Capt. O'Hea*, 1868, xii. 48, 105; Explosive bullets and their application to military purposes, *G. V. Fosbery*, 1868, xii. 48, 16; Modern rifle bullets and their effects, *C. H. Godwin*, 1892, xxxvi. 463.

2205.—EXPLOSIVES. Recent developments and applications of explosives. *V. D. Majendie.* Transactions Royal Artillery Institution, xviii. 223 (1890).

2206.—GUNMAKERS. *Gentleman's Magazine.* Gunmakers' trial, xvii. 101. The introduction of the firearms industry into Birmingham. *Gentleman's Magazine.* New Series, February 1869.

2207.—FIREARMS. *Gentleman's Magazine.* Why not carried by civil officers, vii. 806 (1737); practice recommended, xv. 596 (1745); improvement in, xlvi. 575; gradual progression of, lviii. 667; use in reign of Elizabeth, *ibid.*; firelock, lviii. 668. Of new metal, xix. 475 (1749); experiments, xxiii. 389; newly invented carriages for, xxiii. 390, 391; go off through touch-hole, xxiv. 445; from wreck of *Edgar*, xxv. 280; inscription upon gun at Dover, xxxvii. 499; Desagulier's improvements, xliii. 460; gun bursts, xliii. 517; first used in Spain by Moors, xlvii. 186; tax on proposed, lxv. 119; gun accident, lxvii. 610; penalty proposed for keeping a loaded one in a house, lxviii. 767; on the use of rifle barrel, lxxix. 937; remarkable one at Agra, lxxxviii.(2), 171.

2208.—FIREARMS. *Transactions of the Society of Arts.* These records date from 1783; after 1853 the references made are to the *Journal* of the Society. Baker's improvements, xxviii. 199; Warner's Safety, l. 71; Damascus iron, xliii. 105; l. (part ii.), 106; Hall's gun-lock, xxxvi. 80; Baker's screw for regulating mainspring, xl. 118; Dickenson's gun-lock, xliii. 125. Subsequent to 1852: Wilkinson's, i. 121, 141; ii. 601; rifle barrels, i. 122; Hawksworth's, ix. 600; Rifle shooting, ix. 474, 505, 519, 599, 600; Rifled ordnance, vii. 613; Rocket guns, vii. 342; Arms, xviii. 770; Revolving arms, Kerr's, ix. 7; Rifles, xxi. 489, 494, 532; Breechloading arms, xv. 400; Rifles, xviii. 931; Mackay's, xii. 359; Centrifugal, xv. 426; New gun, xix. 44, 423; Chassepot, xv. 184; American, xii. 34.

2209.—GUNNERY AND MISCELLANEOUS. *Society of Arts Transactions and Journal.* Depressing guns, xxix. 91; Lady Bentham on gunnery, *Journal*, ii. 807; iii. 157, 643; iv. 41; Whitworth's system, xviii. 143; Gun-making by machinery, *Journal*, xix. 423; Museum of firearms at Birmingham, xxii. 953; Bullet mould, xxxix. 101; Cartouch box, xxxvii. 79; Firing cannon, xxxi. 211.

2210.—FIREARMS. *Journal of the United Service Institution.*
Breechloaders for the army, with addendum on gun-cotton, *Lieut. A. Walker*, 1864, viii. 396; Early breechloaders, *J. Latham*, 1865, ix. 88; Breechloading, Montstorm's system, *F. A. Braendlin*, 1864, viii. 280; Carbine and pistol, *Lieut. A. Steinmetz*, 1861, v. 454; Davidson's telescopic rifle-sight, *Lieut. Davidson*, 1864, viii. 426; Errors of the rifle, *Capt. Arbuckle*, 1864, viii. 158; Gun-locks, their history, *R. Pritchett*, 1859, iii. 307; Arms of precision, *Capt. Schaw*, 1870, xiv. 59, 377; Arms of precision and cavalry, *Major-Gen. Smith*, xii. 49, 147; Progress of breechloading small arms, *J. Latham*, 1875, xix. 83, 631; Military breechloading small arms, *V. D. Majendie*, 1867, xi. 44, 190; Rifles and rifling, *J. B. O'Hea*, 1873, xvii. 72, 356; Rifles of France, Prussia and England, *Mervin Drake*, 1871, xv. 64, 438; Russell's electric guns and ammunition, *Major Seyton*, 1886, xix. 134, 541; Remington-Lee rifle, *Major Armstrong*, 1886, xxx. 529; Magazine rifles, *G. V. Fosbery*, 1882, xxvi. 456; *Ibid.*, 1883, xxvii. 777; Repeating rifles, *J. Walter*, 1878, xxii. 1090; Repeating rifle question, *J. Walter*, 1880, xxiv. 778; Magazine and repeating rifles, *Capt. W. James*, 1887, xxi. 135; Modern military rifles and firelocks, *Col. Slade*, 1888, xxii. 899; Martini magazine repeating rifles, *Major Harston*, 1889, xxxiii. 39; Repeating rifles in war, *T. A. Marsh*, 1891, xxxv. 1167; Military small arms, *G. V. Fosbery*, 1891, xxxv. 707; Magazine refrigeration (translation), 1892, xxxvi. 1323; Magazine rifles, their latest development and effects, *Capt. W. H. James*, 1892, xxxvi. 931; The Mannlicher 6·5 mm. rifle (translation), *J. Fraenkel*, 1893, xxxvii. 291.

2211.—RIFLE. *Journal of the United Service Institution.* Its influence on modern warfare, *Lieut.-Col. Dixon*, 1857, i. 95; Necessity for its introduction as a universal infantry weapon, *Lieut.-Col. Welford*, 1857, i. 238; Rifle and rampart, *Capt. Tyler*, 1860, iv.

331; Rifle and spade, *Capt. Tyler*, 1859, iii. 170; Modern effect of on siege operations, *Capt. Tyler*, 1858, ii. 225; On the improvement of the rifle as a weapon for general use, *Lieut.-Col. Lane-Fox*, 1858, ii. 453; Rifles and rifle trajectories, *Lieut. A. Walker*, 1862, vi. 436; The Mannlicher rifle, 6·5 mm. calibre, *J. Fraenkel* (a translation), xxxvii. 291.

2212.—BALLISTICS. *Journal of the United Service Institution.* Minie expansion system, *J. Boucher*, 1858, ii. 144; Parabolic theory of projection for ranges in vacuo, *Lieut.-Col. Fox*, 1861, v. 497; Flight of projectiles, with a description of an instrument taken to show the trajectory of a ball from a given elevation and range, together with the initial velocity and force of striking, *Major-Gen. Anstruther*, 1865, ix. 472; Swiss targets and rifle ranges, *J. Latham*, 1861, v. 110; Trajectories, *Lieut. Walker*, 1862, vi. 436; Trajectory of balls, *Major-Gen. Anstruther*, 1861, v. 309; Revolution in gunnery and science, *Lieut.-Col. Hope*, 1885, xxviii. 127, 965; Photography of flying bullets, *C. V. Boys*, 1893, xxxvii. 855.

2213.—MISCELLANEOUS. *Journal of the United Service Institution.* Sight: On certain conditions of sight which affect accurate shooting, *Litton Forbes*, 1882, xxvi. 811; Safety rifle ranges, *Major Hurst*, 1889, xxxi. 413; Range finding, *Lieut. White*, 1890, xxxiv. 279.

2214.—PROCEEDINGS OF THE ROYAL ARTILLERY INSTITUTION. *Miscellaneous Papers and References.* Experiments in fire of infantry, 1839, vol. i., p. 23; The science of gunnery and force of gunpowder, *Capt. Boxer*, 1854, vol. i., p. 275; Velocity tables, *Capt. Noble*, 1862, vol. ii., p. 11; Belgian experiments on the proof of gunpowder, *Lieut.-Col. Younghusband*, 1858, vol. iii., p. 110; Austrian report on gun-cotton, vol. iii., p. 114; Report on Lenk's gun-cotton, vol. iii., p. 367; Gun-cotton, *Major Miller*, vol. iv., p. 65; Phenomena of gun-cotton, *F. A. Abel*, vol. iv., p. 127; Causes of deviation unconnected with rifling, *Lieut. W. F. Richardson*, vol. iv., p. 455; Ancient cannon in Europe, *H. Brackenbury*, vol. iv., p. 287; vol. v., p. 1; Military breechloading rifles and their ammunition, *Capt. R. Haig*, vol. v., p. 240; Boxer ammunition for Snider rifle, *C. O. Browne*, vol. v., p. 261; Ballistic experiments by the Ordnance Survey Committee, vol. vi., p. 9; Proof of gunpowder at Waltham, vol. vii., p. 50; English guns and foreign critics, *V. D. Majendie*, vol. vii., p. 90; Merits of large bores and small bores with reference to artillery and small arms, *J. Sladen*, vol. vii., p. 273; Tables of remaining velocities, *F. Bashforth*, vol. vii., p. 367, vol. viii., p. 1; Notes on ditto, vol. xii., pp. 64, 516; Explosive force of gunpowder, *J. P. Morgan*, vol. vii., p. 413; Bavarian revolver cannon, *E. Baring*, vol. viii., p. 28; Flat trajectories, small arms, *J. Sladen*, vol. viii., p. 74; Many-barrelled rifle batteries, or mitrailleurs, *J. F. Owen*, vol. viii., p. 419; Pebble powder, *J. P. Morgan*, vol. ix., p. 87; Motion of projectiles, *E. Kensington*, vol. ix., p. 159; List of gunpowder explosions, *V. D. Majendie*, vol. ix., p. 246; Accidental explosions, *F. A. Abel*, vol. ix., p. 259; Service small arms, manufacture and repair, *F. S. Stoney*, vol. ix., p. 303; Application of Prof. Bashforth's general tables to problems in practical gunnery, *J. Sladen*, vol. ix., p. 320; On the rotation required for the stability of an elongated projectile, *A. G. Greenhill*, vol. x., p. 577, vol. xi., pp. 103, 119, 124, 131, vol. xii., p. 17; Shooting properties of small arms in use in Europe, *A. Indra* (translation), vol. xi., p. 1; Improved shape for moulding gunpowder, *M. Tweedie*, vol. xi., p. 467; Extracts from *Russian Small Arms Magazine*, vol. xi., p. 603; Experiments with small shot, *W. McClintock*, vol. xii., p. 332; Problems in gunnery, *W. McClintock*, vol. xii., p. 351; Notes on "gun," "gyn," and "pillet," vol. xii., p. 499; Wild-fowl and punt guns, *W. McClintock*, vol. xii., p. 555; Rifles for large game,

W. McClintock, vol. xii. p. 569; Military rifles, vol. xii., p. 578; Gunpowder works in Bengal, *F. W. Stubbs*, vol. xiii., p. 1; Calculation of trajectories, vol. xiii., p. 53, vol. xiv., p. 373, vol. xv., pp. 81 523, 597, vol. xvii., pp. 81, 181, 389; Visit to Spanish gun factories, vol. xiii., p. 204; Revolvers, *W McClintock*, vol. xii., p. 211; A good shot, *H. H. Maxwell*, vol. xiv., p. 84; Explosives, *J. P. Cundill*, vol. xiv., p. 141; Picric powders, *W. H. H. Waters*, vol. xv., p. 293; Dictionary of explosives, *J. P. Cundhill*, vol. xv., p. 541, vol. xiii., pp. 25, etc.; Small arms *v.* Machine guns, *J. T. Rowan*, vol. xiii., p. 31; On vertical drift of elongated projectiles, *Bashforth*, vol. xvii., p. 33; Recent developments of explosives, *V. D. Majendie*, vol. xviii., p. 223; Berthier rifle, *W. B. Hemans*, vol. xviii., p. 511; On the motion of elongated projectiles, *G. T. Walker*, vol. xviii., p. 187; Velocities, *H. A. Bethell*, vol. xviii., p. 423; Soldiering and sport in Mashonaland, vol. xx., p. 69; Gunpowder and cordite, *F. W. J. Barker*, vol. xx., p. 269.

SELECTED BOOKS ON OLD ARMS, FOREIGN ARMS, ETC.

2301.—ANCIENT ARMS AND ARMOUR. *E. J. Brett.* A pictorial and descriptive record of the origin and development of Arms and Armour. This is a comprehensive work, embodying the results of much research, and well illustrated with specially drawn plates from the author's own fine collection. It is the fullest and most recently written work on the subject of which it treats. Sampson Low & Co., London, 1894. Imperial 4to, 650 pp., 133 plates, with about 1200 illustrations. £5 5s.

2302.—ANCIENT ARMOUR AND WEAPONS IN EUROPE to end of XVII. century. *John Hewitt.* An account of Arms and Armour in the Royal Armoury, with supplement. Oxford and London, 1855-60. 8vo. 3 vols.

2303.—A CRITICAL INQUIRY INTO ANTIENT ARMOUR, as it existed in Europe, particularly in Great Britain, from the Norman Conquest to the Reign of King Charles II. Illustrated with a series of illuminated engravings, with a glossary of military terms of the Middle Ages. *Sir Samuel Rush Meyrick.* Jennings, London. 2nd edition. 3 vols. 1842.

2304.—ENGRAVED ILLUSTRATIONS OF ANCIENT ARMS AND ARMOUR from the collection of Llewelyn Meyrick, Esq., at Goodrich Court, Herefordshire; after the drawings and with the descriptions of Dr. Meyrick. *Joseph Skelton.* Gives in the preface an explanation of the difficulties which attended the production of the "Critical Inquiry," and the fact that "three successive proprietors became bankrupt before the whole work was in the hands of the actual publisher" as the reason for producing this work; "which is the more accurate in detail and of greater value to the antiquary." Printed by G. Schultze, London, for theauthor, 1830. Folio, 2 vols., 130 plates.

2305.—WEAPONS OF THE ANCIENTS. *John R. Williams.* "An essay on Defensive and Offensive Weapons and Engines of the Ancients and of the Middle Ages, their relation to the Constitution and Handling of Armies, and their effect upon the Art of War." Printed at the Artillery School, Fort Monroe, Virginia, 1886. 4to, 28 pp.

2306.—EVOLUTION OF ARMS AND ARMOUR. *J. C. Kimball.* J. H. West, New York, 1890. 10 cents.

2307.—ARMS AND ARMOUR. *C. Boutell.* (Translated from M. P. Lacombe.) This is a description of weapons and armour in antiquity and the middle ages, with a descriptive notice of modern weapons. A popular work, well illustrated. Cassell, London, 1859. 8vo, 296 pp., 70 woodcuts.

2308.—ARMS AND ARMOUR. *Auguste Demmin.* A popular illustrated history of weapons and armour from the earliest period to 1870; it was translated by Mr. T. C. Black, of the South Kensington Museum, and is perhaps the most useful and comprehensive of all publications as an introductory text-book to Arms and Armour. G. Bell & Sons, London, 1877. 8vo, 596 pp., 200 illustrations.

2309.—RESUMEN SACADO, ETC. *D. Ig. Abadia.* An account of the arms, etc., in the Royal Armoury, Madrid. Madrid, 1793. 1 vol., 8vo.

2310.—SCHIOPPI NELL' ANNO 1347. *Luigi Cibrario.* An article on early artillery, taken from vol. vi. of the "Memoirs of the Academy of Science," and a second edition, with the title of "Delle Artiglierie dal MCCC al MDCC," was published in 1851. Royal Press, Turin, 1844. In 8vo.

2311.—QUELLEN ZUR GESCHICHTE DES FEUER WAFFEN. This is a series of reproductions of original drawings of weapons, etc., in the German museums, to serve as a source for a history of firearms. Leipzig, 1872. 4to.

2312.—ILLUSTRATIONS OF ANCIENT FIREARMS. In the Archæological Album; or Museum of National Antiquities, by *T. Wright*. Illustrations by F. W. Fairholt, pp. 121-128. London, 1845.—Museo Español Antigüedades, J. G. Dorregaray. Vol. V., pp. 9, 123, Madrid, 1875.—Guns and Pistols of XVIth Century, Munitoli, Vorbilder, etc. Vol. i. Portfolio 82, Art Lib. S. K. Mus.—Musée de l'Artillerie de Paris. Portfolio 366, Art Lib. S. K. Mus.—Old German Gunstocks. 1600-1628, from Augsburg, now in the Imperial Armoury, Vienna. See Portfolio 225, Art Lib. S. K. Mus.—History of Hand Firearms. S. R. Meyrick, "Archæologia." Vol. xxii., 1829.

2313.—REPORTS ON MODERN ARMS, Collections, Exhibitions, etc. *Arabian* firearms, photographs of arms in the Real Armeria, Turin. Portfolio 377, Art Lib. S. K. Mus. London Exhibition, report of the French Jury, vol. iv., Paris, 1862.—*Indian* Firearms at the Madras Exhibition, see Portfolio 34 at the Art Lib. S. K. Mus. Paris Exhibition, 1867, see Capt. V. Majendie's report. London, 1868. Vol. iv.—*Italian*, Milan Industrial Museum, reproductions, Portfolio 559, Art Lib. S. K. Mus. Report on Military and Sporting Arms and Weapons at the Philadelphia Exhibition, 1876, by Maj. W. H. Noble. London, 1877. Report on Small Arms at Vienna Exhibition, by W. H. Russell. London, 1874. Reports, vol. ii.

CATALOGUES OF COLLECTIONS OF ANCIENT ARMS.

2351.—ARMERIA ANTICA E MODERNA del Re Carlo Alberto. Fontana, Turin, 1846. In 8vo.

2352.—CATALOGO DE LA REAL ARMERIA DE MADRID. Aguado, Madrid, 1849. 1 vol. 4to, plates. A second edition, 1863, in 8vo.

2353.—CATALOGO DE LOS OBJETOS QUI CONTIENE EL REAL MUSEAR MILITAR. Tejado, Madrid, 1856. 1 vol., 393 pp.

2354.—MUSÉE D'ARTILLERIE, PARIS. *O. Penguilly L'Haridon.* Catalogue of the best French collection of firearms. This catalogue is now superseded, and is valuable only for its notes. Mourgues frères, Paris, 1862. 1004 pp., paper. 5 francs.

2355.—MUSÉE D'ARTILLERIE EN 1889. *L. Robert.* Volume IV. contains particulars of the small arms; and, in addition to giving details of 2448 arms and accessories in the collection, has useful historical notices, some notes and references. Imp. Nat., Paris, 1893, vol. iv. 8vo, 403 pp., paper. 1½ francs.

2356.—ARMES ET ARMURES. *E. van Vinkeroy.* Catalogue of the Museum at La Porte de Hal, Bruxelles. The collection is but the *débris* left by or recovered from the successive conquerors of the Netherlands. The original collection dates back to the fifteenth century, when A. de Bourgogne commenced the collection afterwards known as the "Royal Arsenal," and which was for the last time most seriously despoiled by the Austrians on their evacuation in 1794. The present collection has been got together since 1835, and is constantly being added to. Lelong, Brussels, 1885. 8vo, 498 pp., woodcuts, paper. 3 francs.

2357.—ARTILLERISKAVO MUSEA. *N. E. Brandenburg.* Catalogue of the Arms collection in the Artillery Museum of the St. Petersburg Arsenal. The collection is a rich one, particularly in breech-loading cannon of early dates, revolving arms, etc. Part I. has interesting historical notes, and deals with arms dating prior to 1809. Bokrama, St. Petersburg, 1877. Large 8vo, woodcuts, 314 pp., paper.

2358.—DRESDEN, GEWEHR GALLERIE. *F. Nollain* and *Carl Clauss.* An intelligently compiled, illustrated catalogue of a very fine collection, which is particularly rich in ornamented arms and seventeenth-century wheel-locks. H. Schönfeld, Dresden, 1873. 8vo, 164 pp., 18 fine woodcuts, paper boards.

2359.—ARMERIA. *Vittorio Seyssel d'Aix.* A description of the antique and modern arms in the collection of S. M. Carlo Alberto, the Turin Armoury. 1554 articles enumerated. The historical notes are scanty and too anecdotal. Fontana, Turin, 1840. Large 8vo, 452 pp., 3 folding lithographic sheets of drawings, some inferior woodcuts, stiff picture boards. Second edition, 1846.

2360.—OROUJENAIA PALATA. Catalogue of the Royal Armoury in the Kremlin, Moscow. French editions also published. Mamontoff, Moscow, 1882. 8vo pamphlet, 42 pp.

2361.—ROYAL ARMOURY, WINDSOR CASTLE. The Turkish firearms in this collection will be found illustrated in Portfolio 2, at the Art Library, South Kensington.

2362.—SOUTH KENSINGTON COLLECTION.—Catalogue of the munitions of war in the S. K. Museum, London. 8vo. 1875.

2363.—SOUTH KENSINGTON COLLECTION.—A collection of photographs from specimens in the Museum, selected by J. C. Robinson. Portfolio 113, at the Art Lib., South Kensington.

2364.—SOUTH KENSINGTON.—Catalogue of the wheel-lock guns, etc., in the loan collection, 1862. London, 1862. 8vo, pp. 364.

2365.—AMBRASER COLLECTION, VIENNA. The firearms in this collection are illustrated in a series contained in Portfolio 210, at the Art Library, South Kensington.

2366.—NURNBERG COLLECTION. Illustrations of the firearms in this collection will be found in Portfolio 250, at the Art Library, South Kensington.

2367.—HAMMER MUSEUM, STOCKHOLM. The firearms of this collection will be found illustrated in Portfolio 499, at the Art Library, South Kensington.

2368.—OFFICIAL CATALOGUE of the Tower Armouries. *John Hewitt.* London, 1859. 12mo.

2369.—TSARSKOE ZELOE. Baumann, St. Petersburg, 1860. A supplement thereto, 188—.

BIBLIOGRAPHIES.

SPORTING—MILITARY—ENCYCLOPÆDIAS AND TECHNICAL DICTIONARIES.

2401.—SPORTING: LATIN. BIBLIOTHECA SCRIPTORUM VENATICORUM. *G. C. Kreysig.* Altenburg, 1750. 8vo, 190 pp., 18 folio tables.

2402.—SPORTING: GERMAN. LITERARISCHEN Erscheinungen Land und Haus wirtschaft. *E. Bauldamus.* Three separate publications, one covering eleven years, 1856-66. Reichenecker, Leipzig, 1866, 8vo; the second, 1866-1870, Hinrichs, Leipzig, 1871, 8vo; the third, German books, 1871-75, Hinrichs, 1876, 8vo.

2403.—SPORTING: FRENCH. BIBLIOGRAPHIE GÉNÉRALE DES OUVRAGES SUR LA CHASSE, LA VENERIE ET LA FAUCONNERIE. *R. Souhait.* This is a general descriptive catalogue of Sporting Books, from the fifteenth century to 1885, and has critical notes and sale prices. Part I. arranged alphabetically according to authors' names. Part II., anonymous and periodicals. Rouquette, Paris, 1886. 4to, 754 pp.

2404.—SPORTING: FRENCH. QUELSQUES ADDITIONS, etc., to the above work. *Paul Petit.* Contains also numerous bibliographical and biographical corrections, but treats of French books only. Fifty copies only printed. Louviers, 1888. 8vo.

2405.—BIBLIOGRAPHICAL: FRENCH. BIBLIOTHÈQUE DES AUTEURS QUI ONT TRAITÉ DE LA CHASSE. N. & R. Lallemant. A bibliography and biography of authors who have written on sport. Rouen, 1763. 8vo, 226 pp.

Sporting—Military—Encyclopædias, etc. 185

2406.—SPORTING: SPANISH. BIBLIOGRAPHIA VENATORIA ESPAÑOLA. *J. Gutierrez de la Vega.* 25 copies only reprinted from the bibliographical introduction to the "Biblioteca Venatoria." Tello, Madrid, 1877. 8vo, 112 pp.

2407.—BIBLIOTHECA HISTORICO-MILITARIS. *Johann Pohler.* A work which is to comprehend the books on every war and in every tongue to the year 1880. The 16th volume will contain a bibliography of artillery, etc. Cassel (Germany), 1886, etc. 8vo. In progress.

2408.—MILITARY: GERMAN. ALLGEMEINE LITERATUR DER KRIEGSWEISENSCHAFTEN. *H. F. Rumpf.* Arranged chronologically, with subdivisions as to subjects and sizes of books. C. Reimer, Berlin, 1824. 8vo, 2 vols.

2409.—BIBLIOGRAFIA MILITAR DE ESPAÑA. *D.Jose Almirante.* A very complete work, arranged alphabetically according to authors, but furnished with indices to subjects. Madrid, 1876. 4to, 988 pp.

2410.—BIBLIOGRAFIA MILITARE: ITALIANA. *Al. D'Ayala.* A complete book; the third edition, "Artigliera," is the one of chief interest, about 32 pp. of the book of 450 pp. Royal Press, Turin, 1854. Demy 8vo, 450 pp.

2411.—MILITARY: ENGLISH. List of Works on Artillery, etc. *J. H. Lefroy.* This list is given in 12 pp., Vol. II., of the "Proceedings of the Royal Artillery Institution."

2412.—MILITARY: ENGLISH. Some old and rare books in the Library of the Royal Artillery Association. Not all devoted to military subjects. See "Proceedings of the R. A. Inst.," Vol. xv., p. 37.

2413.—MILITARY: ENGLISH. A list of 81 books on Artillery, etc., taken from the Catalogue of the Paris Exhibition, 1889. "Proceedings of the R. A. Inst.," vol. xvii., p. 509.

2414.—ANCIENT ARMS: ENGLISH. CATALOGUE OF BOOKS AND PHOTOGRAPHS in the National Art Library, illustrating Armour and Weapons. Compiled for the use of students and visitors to the South Kensington Museum Library. London, 1883. 8vo, 68 pp., 6*d*.

2415.—MILITARY DICTIONARY; comprising terms, scientific and otherwise, connected with the science of War. Compiled by Maj.-Gen. G. E. Voyle, assisted by Captain G. De Saint-Clair-Stevenson. This work appeared originally as a "Dictionary of Artillery and other Military and Scientific Terms," and was published by Thacker, Spink & Co., Calcutta. The third edition, the first under this title, by W. Clowes, London, 1876. 8vo, 582 pp., and 38 pp. supplement.

2416.—MILITARY DICTIONARY; comprising technical definitions, information on raising and keeping troops; actual service, including makeshifts and improved *materiel*, and law, government, regulation, and administration relating to land forces. *Col. H. L. Scott.* This is an illustrated encyclopædia. D. Van Nostrand, New York, 1861. 8vo, 674 pp., woodcuts.

2417.—MILITARY DICTIONARY AND GAZETTEER. *Thomas Wilhelm.* Comprises "Ancient and modern military technical terms, historical accounts of all the American Indians, as well as ancient warlike tribes; also notices of battles from the earliest period to the present time, with a cursive explanation of terms used in heraldry and the offices thereof." The work also gives geographical information, and has an appendix containing the articles of war. L. R. Hamersly & Co., Philadelphia, 1879. Revised edition, 1881. 8vo, 660 pp., 32 litho. plates.

2418.—MILITARY ENCYCLOPÆDIA. Dictionary of Military Knowledge. *E. S. Farrow.* A comprehensive work, well written, and illustrated with maps, plates, and about 3000 woodcuts. Author, 240, Broadway, New York, 1885. 4to. Vol. I., A—G, 821 pp.; Vol. II.,

H—R, 832 pp.; Vol. III., S—Z, 668 pp., and plates.
This work is under constant revision, and supplements
are issued at irregular intervals.

2419.—ANGLO-FRENCH. An Universal Military Dictionary
in English and French, in which are explained the
terms of the principal sciences that are necessary for
the information of an officer. *Charles James.* T. Egerton,
London, 1802. The 4th edition, 1816, is the best.
8vo, pp. xii, 1006, portrait.

2420.—GERMAN-ENGLISH-FRENCH. Technological Military
Dictionary. *Capt. G. F. Duckett.* The German-English-
French part, 452 pp.

2421.—FRENCH-GERMAN-ENGLISH-RUSSIAN. Military Technological Dictionary. *And. Engel.* St. Petersburg,
1863. First part, A—C, 424 pp. The book is scarce,
and has been long out of print.

2422.—RUSSO-GERMAN. Military Technological Dictionary.
J. S. Kuznetsovi. Devrient, St. Petersburg, 1872.
8vo, 452 pp., with supplementary appendix, 44 pp.

2423.—FRANCO-GERMAN. Kriegs-Ingenieur-Artillerie-See-
und-Ritter Lexicon. *Jacob von Eggers.* This is a
glossary of technical and military terms in French, with
German equivalents, and *vice versâ.* G. C. Walther,
Dresden and Leipzig, 1757. 8vo, Vol. I., 1420 columns,
710 pp.; Vol. II., 1420 columns and 28 folding plates.

2424.—FRENCH. Nouveau Dictionnaire Militaire. Compiled by a committee of officers. This is a military
encyclopædia, well written, and the information given
in most succinct form. Text illustrated with 310
figures. L. Baudoin, Paris, 1892. 8vo, 854 pp.

2425.—GERMAN. Handworterbuch der Gesamten Militair-
wissenschaften. *B. Paten.* An encyclopædic military
technological dictionary, published in nine quarto

volumes, with illustrations. Velhagen & Klasing, Bielefeld and Leipzig, 1877-80.

2426.—SPANISH. Diccionario Militair. *D. Jose Almirante.* An etymological, historical, technological, military dictionary, with vocabularies of French and German technical terms. Dept. of War, Madrid, 1869. 4to, 1218 pp.

Index.

INDEX.

Abel, F. A., 2112, 2118.
Adam, Victor, 519.
Adams, W. A., 1293, 2141.
Afflito, Maria, 173.
Agrippa, Cornelius, 106.
Ahadia, Ig., 348, 2309.
Aikins, Dr. J., 279.
Aix, V. S. d', 2359.
Ajello d'Ayalo, 113.
Alberghetti de Venezia, S., 212, 239.
Albitte, G., 1473.
Aldington, J., 269.
Alejo de Puella, 2.
Alenzo Martinez del Espinar, 165.
Alhoy, M., 1568, 1569.
Alison, G. C., 613.
Alken, H., 428.
Allich, L., 624, 625.
Almirante, J., 809.
Alvarez Perez, J., 1803.
Amezeuil, C. St., 1406, 1456.
Ammon, 1625.
Anderson, Col., 2105.
Anderson, R., 198, 226, 229, 232.
Anquetil, T., 1427, 1428.
Anreo, J. de B., 176.
Anschutz, H., 663.
Anstegui y Doz, L., 1806.
Aparici y Biedma, J. M., 1807.
Apperley, C. J., 451, 1216.
Arcania, J. G., 805.
Arcy, d', 341.
Ardesoif, J. P., 272.
Arellanus, J. M. de, 322.
Arena, P. A., 704.
Armiger, C., 436.

Arts, F., 1820.
Asher, B., 1435.
Assolant, A., 1430.
Atienza y Martinez, D. V., 1808.
Auban, Marquis de St., 336, 592.
Aubusson, M. D', 1439, 1440.
"Avon," 1295.
Azais, G., 1434.
Azzi, Dr. E., 1705.

Babington, J., 147.
Bacchi della Lega, A., 1704.
Bacellar, A. H. de, 801.
Bada, J. J. D., 1818.
Baddely, Fraser, 2102.
Bado, Anreo, 176.
Bailey, H., 1358.
Bailey, T., 252.
Bailly, Bixio, 523.
Baines, T., 1301.
Baker, Ez., 451.
Baker, Sir S. W., 1317, 1323, 1324, 1348, 1349, 1350, 1351, 1352, 1353.
Balch, V., 1911.
Bank, F. J. J., 1656.
Barber, E. C., 1176.
Barclay, 1232.
Barret, E., 1154.
Barriff, W., 164.
Barry, W., 1268.
Bartlett, W. A., 1018.
Barwick, H., 28.
Basedow, A. de, 1655.
Bashforth, F., 1162—1168.
Bate, J., 145.
Beaufoy, Captain, 411.

Beauvoir, 1546.
Bellecroix, E., 1403, 1464.
Benburg, R. A. v., 1653.
Benifayo, Baron, 1817.
Benoit-Champy, 1459.
Bergerat, E., 1437.
Bermusch, Robert, 1654.
Beroaldo-Bianchini, 612.
Berrieczo, D. J. A., 1802.
Berthelot, M., 2133.
Bethuys, G., 1571.
Bianchini, B., 612.
Biedma, J. M. A., 1807.
Bigot de Morogues, 316.
Biquet, Gen. F., 1510.
Binet, Etienne, 132.
Binney, Thomas, 260.
Birago, F., 138.
Birnie, R., 1040.
Bixio Bailly, 523.
Blaine, D. P., 454.
Blakely, T. A., 1159.
Blakey, R., 1009.
Blanc-St.-Bonnet, Ch. de, 506.
Blaze, E., 1404.
Bliss, H. C., 1256.
Bloxham, W. P., 2115.
Blunt, S. E., 1180.
Bocca, D. Mazzo, 9.
Bœuf, Abbé le, 1463.
Bogardus, H., 1252.
Bond, Lt.-Col. H., 1021.
Boner, C., 1320.
Bonfadini, V., 153, 175.
Bonnet, Ch. de Blanc St., 506.
Bordino, S. M., 701, 703.
Borer, F. C., 1260.
Borio, D., 1701.
Bossi, G., 134, 203.
Botelho de Oliviera, B., 305.
Bouchage, Ch. de, 575.
Boucher, J., 1109.
Boulen, C., 1468.
Bourne, William, 20.
Boussenard, L., 4567.
Boutell, C., 2307.
Bowers, G., 1222.
Brandeis, F., 1641.

Brandenburg, N. E., 2357.
Brandock, J., 2103, 2104.
Brandt, J. D., 1157.
Braun, 208.
Brechtel, 43.
Brett, E. J., 2301.
Brewin, R., 1114.
Bridgeman, J. V., 1175.
Bridges, T. W., 1156.
Brinck, T. N., 207.
Brinckman, A., 1326.
Bromley-Davenport, W., 1296.
Brown, Sir B., 1185.
Brown, H., 274.
Bry, Theo. de, 123.
Buchiers, 209.
Buega, D. J., 1812.
Buet, C., 1436.
Bulliard, 342.
Bumstead, J., 1258.
Bunning, 224.
Burger, Kaspar, 30.
Burgess, F. F. R., 1019.
Busca, Gabriele, 7.
Bush, D. M. D., 1805.
Butler, Sir W. F., 1399.
Butler, J. S., 1130.
Buxton, E. F., 1338.
Buxton, E. N., 1317a.

Campagne, E., 1429, 1442.
Campbell, E. S. N., 433.
Campbell, Walter, 465.
Campion, J. S., 1399d.
Capitaine, E., 1601.
Capobianco, A., 40.
Carleton, W., 468, 474, 479.
Carnegie, W., 1233.
Casimir Simienowicz, 256.
Cassassoles, F., 1411.
Castan, F., 2108.
Castillon, 1425, 1426.
Cataneo, Girolamo, 14, 15.
Cerda, T., 168, 332.
Chalon, P. F., 2132.
"Cham" (*see* Noë), 1410
Championniere, M., 520.
Champy, B., 1459.

Index.

Chapman, J. R., 477.
Chapus, E., 1472.
Chassaine, J., 1423.
Chatin de Mezelles, Y., 1416.
Chaugrain, de, 335.
Chene, R. du, 1405.
Chenu, Dr. J. C., 1405.
Cherville, Marquis de, 1454.
Chevigué, Comte de, 514.
Chevillard, 180.
Chevreuil, H., 1426.
Chincherni, A., 154.
Chrestman, W. K., 619.
"Christopher Idle," 1263.
Cibrario, L., 2310.
Clamart, J. A., 1457.
Clauss, Care, 2358.
Clement, Lewis, 1273-75, 2142.
Cleveland, H. W. S., 1178.
Cobb, S., 1052.
Cochard, L., 1548.
Codies, J., 804.
Coehorn, 189, 238.
Coello y Quesada, J., 1809.
Colard, R., 1516.
Collado, L., 160.
Colliado, Luigi, 19.
Colomberini, G. B., 228.
Colombina, G. B., 157.
Colquhoun, J., 455, 1287.
Colson, 211.
Congreve, Sir W., 2101.
Cook, J., 224.
Cooper, A. W., 1278.
Coote, Hon. R., 264.
Corballis, J. H., 1214.
Corneli, R., 1657.
Cornelius Agrippa, 106.
Correa, M., 1810, 1811.
Cotty, M. H., 503, 505.
Coudray, T. de, 330.
Couteur, J. Le, 1103.
Cox, Nic, 234.
Cradock, C., 1341.
Cranach, U. von, 192.
Cranz, 1628.
"Craven" (*see* Carleton), 468, 474, 479.

Crealocke, H. H., 1218.
Crevelli, A., 702.
Creyke, Mrs. W., 1201.
Cross, D. W., 1373.
Cundill, J. P., 2121, 2123.
Curel, L. de, 1414.
Cyprian Lucar, 23.

Dahne, 1629.
Dailly, Pierre, 187.
D'Aix, V. S., 2359.
Dalloz, 1469.
D'Amezeuil, C., 1456.
Danford, G., 1321.
Daniel, Geo., 1207.
Daniels, W. B., 404.
D'Arcy, 341.
Dastugue, D., 1445, 1446.
D'Aubusson, M., 1439, 1440.
Davelcourt, D., 109, 112, 114, 120.
Davenport, W. B., 1296.
Dawson, Captain, 1398.
Dax, Vcte L. de, 1455.
D'Ayalo, Santa Ajello, 113.
Deane, J., 1003.
De Bada, J. J., 1818.
De Cherville, 1454, 1563.
De Curel, L., 1414.
De Dax, Vcte L., 1455.
Deffaux, M., 1465.
De Feuille, V., 1447.
De la Court, P., 1460.
Delaunay, F., 1462.
Della Lega, A. B., 1704.
Delorme, Du Q. A., 1702.
De Metz-Noblat, A., 1507.
Demmin, A., 2308.
De Mezelles, Y. C., 1416.
De Riencourt, C., 2155.
Desormeaux, M. A. O. P., 1526.
De Sparre, Vcte, 1525.
De Viergol, F. M., 1810.
D'Ewes, J., 1305.
Deyeux, Theoph., 516.
D'Houdetot, A., 1557, 1558.
"Diane Chasseresse" (*see* Creyke).
Didion, 1543.

Diego de Morales, 185.
Diego Ufano (Anglicé Uffans, *q.v.*), 116, 131.
Dietrich, Jes., 202.
Diezel, C., 618.
Diguet, Ch., 1408, 1413, 1415, 1451, 1505.
Ditchfield, 1208.
Domenico Borio, 1701.
Donneaud du Plan, 509.
Douet, 150.
Dougall, J. D., 1014, 1121, 1253, 1290.
Dove, P. E., 1105.
Doz, L. d. A., 1806.
"Dragon," 1222.
Drayson, W. W., 1347.
Du Chêne, Robert, 1409.
Du Fretay, Baron H., 1438.
Dumord, M., 1529, 1534.
Dupuys, 334.
Du Quesnay, 1702.
Durand, M., 129.
Durfey, T., 200.
Duro, D. V., 808.
Duwarnet, G., 1448.
Duyateff, 1424.
D'Yauville, 221.
Dyke, Th. S. van, 1379, 1392.

E. J. F. (*see* F.), 1234.
Edel, 231.
Edie, G., 273.
Ehrenkreutz, 1651.
Ehrenswerd, 320.
Eichenlaub, E., 615.
Eisenkramer, 204.
Eisler, M., 2119, 2120.
Eldred, W., 170.
"Ellangowan," 1292.
Elliott, R. H., 1344.
Elorza, D. F. A. de, 806.
Eloues, D., 1449.
Elrichs, M. F., 621, 622.
Elton, R., 172.
Elzear Blaze, 1404.
Epichin, 1921.
Erasmo di Valvasone, 104.

Escaler, F. T. de l', 177.
Espinar, A. M., 163.
Esteban Guillelmi, D., 809.
Eugenii, 214.
Eugenio Gentilini, 31.
Ewes, J. D', 1305.

F., E. J., 1234.
Fairfax, Thos., 223.
Faulder, 282.
Faure-Biguet, 1510.
Fawkes, F., 270.
Fellows, R. B., 1265.
Fenton, C. H., 1184.
Ferro, Alfonso, 10.
Ferron y Saavedra, J., 1819.
Ferrufino, J., 29.
Feuille, Vcte de, 1447.
Figuier, L., 1512.
Fioscono, C., 309.
Fitch, C. H., 1041.
Fittis, R. S., 1289.
Folkard, H. C., 1271.
Forrester, Frank (*see* Herbert), 488.
Fowler, J. K., 1213.
Frances, F., 1278.
Frankland, Sir Thomas, 402.
Fretay, Baron H. du, 1438.
Friederich, 326.
Fucar, Pablo del, 6.
Fuchs, 346.
Furttenbach, J., 139, 163.

Gail, J. B., 1471.
Galand, 1509.
Gale, F., 1209.
Galezzo Gualdo Priorato, 161.
Garnier, P., 1423, 1444, 1452.
Garvie, J., 2125.
Gatti, A., 122.
Gautier, 225.
Gay, J. D., 1333.
Gaya, L. de, 199, 206.
Geisler, 302, 307.
Gentilini, E., 31, 158.
Gerard, C. Jules Basel, 1417, 1418, 1419, 1420, 1421, 1422.

Gerstæcker, F., 1363.
Gheya, J. de, 111.
Giles, Jacob, 253, 254.
Gillion, F., 1528.
Gillmore, Parker, 1306-14.
Girard, 319.
Girardin, C. de, 511.
Giraudeau, 1470.
Girolamo Cataneo, 14, 15.
"Gloan," 1013.
Godwin, F., 1048.
Goldman, N., 169.
Gonzalez Velasco, E., 1813.
Gonzalez y Arcaina, J., 805.
Goodenough, O. H., 2117.
Goodman, J. D., 1051.
Gosset, Capt., 1552.
Gould, A. C., 1029, 1101, 1386.
Graevnitz, 326.
Grasshoff, F. B. G., 602.
Grassol, A., 1443.
Gravius or Greaves, J., 213.
Gray, J., 257.
Greener, W., 443, 462, 1002, 1055.
Greener, W. O., 1037.
Greener, W. W., 1012, 1015, 1016, 1023, 1027, 1506, 1572, 1645, 1707, 1820, 1922.
Greenwood, W., 284.
Grenville-Murray, E. C., 1224.
Gresse, G. de, 32.
Greville, B. Violet, 1202, 1203.
Gribeauval, 336.
Grignon, 338.
Grimble, A., 1283.
Grinnel, G. B., 1389.
Groben, 329.
Grose, Francis, 293, 294, 295.
Grundels, 301.
Gryndall, W., 35.
Guilano Bossi, 134.
Guillaumot, E., 1521.
Guillelmi, D. E., 809.
Guinard, Arthur, 1508.
Guserio, Jordam, 309.
Guttmann, O., 2126.

Hake, C. N., 2121.

Halford, Sir H., 1190.
Hall, H. B., 476, 490, 491, 1217.
Hall, Lucullus, 1225.
Hallock, C., 1374-76.
Halma du Fretay, 1438.
Hamilton, D., 1343.
Hanger, Col. G., 416, 418.
Hardy, C., 1362.
Haridon, O. P. L', 2354.
Harris, Sir W. C., 449, 453, 456, 469, 1381.
Harrison, W. B., 1042.
Harting, J. G., 1272, 1297.
Hartley, W. G., 1108.
Hasenbank, 304.
Hassell, J., 427.
Haubruck, T. S. (pseudonym), 483.
Hawes, Capt., 2144.
Hawker, Col. P., 415.
Hazelet, Lorrain, 149.
Heath, H., 1188.
Heaton, —, 1183.
Hebler, F. W., 1631.
Heinsius, 313.
Henriquez, J., 1466.
Henshall, J. A., 1395.
Hentsch, F., 1609, 1627.
Herbert, H. W., 488.
Hertling, Ph. v., 1601.
Heurt, J., 2302, 2368.
Heurteloup, M., 517.
Hodgkinson, W. R., 2124.
Hoffman, C. F., 452.
Hoffman, L., 616.
Högg, 1618.
Hohberg, W. H. v., 306.
Holliday, F., 266.
Hooper, J. J., 1266.
Horsfield, K., 1280.
Houdetot, A. de, 1557, 1558.
Hovel, H. de B., 1189.
Howett, J., 460.
Howitt, Sam., 410-14.
Howlett, Robt., 1233.
Hubbard, J., 1399.
Hunter, H. E., 1371.
Hunter, S. J., 1365.
Hyde, J. T., 1158.

Indra, A., 1622.
Inglis, Hon. J., 1339, 1340, 1399, e, f, g.
Irving, J. T., 446.
Isodoro, Soler, 349.
Isselberg, 126.
Isselt, Dam van, 1630.

J., K. C. A., 1342.
Jacob, J., 1186.
Jacob de Gheyn, 111, 127.
Jacquinet, 182, 1038.
Jaramillo, D. M. J., 1801.
Jeans, T., 1220.
Jervis, J. W., 1004.
Jewett, L., 1110.
Joao Rodrigues, 308.
Johnson, Daniel, 1322.
Johnson, T. B., 420, 421, 423, 424, 437, 470, 1006, 1264.
Josephus Furtenbach, 139.
Jouffret, E., 1549.
Jourdeuil, E., 1431.
Julien, Ch. de St., 108.
Jullien, E., 1467.
Justus Lipsius, 36.

K. C. A. J., 1342.
Karr, H. W. S., 1302.
Karsten, 326.
Kaspar Burger, 30.
Kebbel, T. E., 1281, 1282.
Keep, F., 1260.
Kempers, A. G., 1901.
Kennedy, Admiral, 1399b.
Kestner, Sig., 191.
Kimball, J. C., 2306.
Kincaid, J., 432.
King, S., 431.
Kinloch, A. A. A., 1332.
Kipling, J. L., 1345.
Knight Horsfield, 1280.
Koch, G., 1642.
Krnka, K., 1635.
Kromar, 1636.

Labiche, L., 1519.
Lachevre, R., 1515.

Lacombe, F., 350.
Lacy, R., 464.
Lancaster, Chas., 1251.
Lander, O., 1050.
Lankmayr, 1616, 1667.
Lascelles, Robert, 419.
Lauffer, 1634.
Launay, F. de, 1462.
Laurent, P., 1555.
Lawrence, J., 425.
Leale, Miss, 1203.
Le Blond, 323.
Le Bœuf, Abbé, 1463.
Leech, J., 1219.
Lefevre, J. B. V., 1550, 1551.
Leffingwell, W. B., 1357, 1388.
Lega, A. B. d', 1704.
Lempschen, C., 1911.
Lennox, Lord W., 1204, 1205, 1206.
Leonardo da Vinci, 243.
Leue, H., 1645.
Leutmann, A., 314.
Leveson, H. A., 1327-31, 1337.
Lewis, E. J., 1361.
L'Haridon, O. P., 2354.
Libioulle, N., 1412.
Liebault, J., 44.
Liebnechts, 311.
Lipsius, Justus, 36.
Llave, P. de la, 810.
Lloyd, L., 434.
Lomdomo, S. de, 26.
Long, J. W., 1397a.
Lord, W. B., 1301.
Lorescha, J. de, 802.
Loriga, D. S., 1804.
Lorrain Hazelet, 149.
Lucas, T. J., 1359.
Lydekker, R., 1226.

MacGregor, J., 1174.
Macnab, W., 2121.
Maindron, G. R. M., 1511.
Majendie, V. D., 1126, 2130.
Malpeyre, M. de, 523.
Malthus, F., 143, 174.
Manceau, C., 1591.

Mangeot, H., 1527.
Manley, J. J., 1227.
Manuel de Arellanus, J., 322.
Marchand, 1461.
Markham, F., 1325.
Markham, Gervase, 44, 137.
Markland, A., 255.
"Marksman," 1254.
Marolles, M. de, 285, 345.
Martin, C., 1646.
Martinez, D. V. A., 1808.
Martinez del Espinar, A., 165.
Mason, F., 1270.
Mast, J., 1369.
Mateos, D. J., 146.
Mattenhamer, 2148.
Mattenheimer, 1608.
Maxwell, W. H., 438, 440, 1286, 1288.
Mayer, J., 471.
Mayer, A. M., 1304.
Mazzo Bocca, 9.
McLennox, K., 280, 281.
Medrano, S. F. de, 240.
Meneses, D. F. S., 806.
Merseuni, 166.
Metz-Noblat, A. de, 1507.
Meunier, V., 1315.
Meyer, M., 1502.
Meyrick, 2303.
Mezelles, Y. C. de, 1416.
Millais, F., 1298.
Mills, J., 475.
Mitford, B., 1223.
Montague, G., 288.
Morales, Diego, 185.
Moray or Murray, Sir R., 220.
Mordecai, A., 2116.
More, Sir Jonas, 210.
Moretti, 195.
Morogues, B. de, 316.
Mountain, W., 263.
Muller, J., 262, 265, 267.
Munroe, C. F., 2110.
Murphy, J. M., 1397.
Murray (*see* Moray), 220.
Murray, E. C. Grenville, 1224.
Muzeau, E., 1547.

Napier, E. H. D. E., 467.
Naylor, J., 178.
Neree-Quepat, 1453.
"Nessmuk," 1394.
Neumann, Ig., 1643, 1644.
Neumeyer, 2111.
"Newtonensis," 1010.
Niccols, R., 119.
Nicolls, J. A., 1554.
"Nimrod" (*see* C. Appesley), 451.
Noblat, A. de M., 1507.
Noble, Capt., 2118.
Noe, Viscomte de, 1410.
Nollain, F., 2358.
Norton, Robert, 140.
Nursey, F. N., 2113.
Nye, N., 190.

Oakleigh, T. (*see* Wilson, J.)
Ocon, M., 1820.
O'Connor, R., 484.
Okes, G. C., 1231.
"Old Gamekeeper," 1257.
"Old Shikaree" (*see* Leveson), 1327, etc., 1337.
Oliviera, B. Botelho de, 305.
Orlandi, 105.
Orleans, P. Duc d', 1432.
Orsmann, W. J., 2127.
Ortus, Col., 1523.
Osbaldeston, W. A., 290.

Paez Jaramillo, D. M., 1801.
Page, C. E., 1545.
Page, Thomas, 268.
Pairault, A., 1401.
Panot, L., 1501.
Panzera, F. W., 1151.
Papin, N., 218.
Paquée, E., 1524.
Paracelsus (P. A. T. Bombast von Hohenheim), 2152.
Parent, E., 1402.
Partington, C. F., 1043.
Paulin-Desormeaux, M. A. O., 1536.
Payne-Gallwey, Sir R., 1020, 1024, 1276-7.

Peake, R. B., 450.
Peigne de la Court, 1460.
Peirander, 242.
Penn, R., 448.
Perez, J. A., 1803.
Pergæus, Apollonius, 278.
Perrodon, J., 1544.
Petit, J. F., 1566.
Petrini, A., 156.
Pfister, 1624, 1625.
"Pharaon, F." (*see* Cherville), 1563.
Philippe, Duc d'Orléans, 1432.
Piebourg, P., 1531.
Pietro Sardi, 128.
Pinkney, R., 1113.
Pinto y Velarde, A. C., 328.
Piobert, G., 2153, 2154.
Pistoris, H. C., 1652.
Plach, F., 2135.
Plan, Donneaud du, 509.
Plunket, Thomas, 222.
Plutonei, 315.
Ply, G., 1532.
Polain, A., 1535.
Polain, J., 1536-42.
Pollok, Lieut.-Col. F., 1335.
Pons, L. D. A. J., 1570.
Ponteaux, A., 2131.
Powell, W. B., 1399, *g*.
Preuss, v., 5.
Price, Gwynne, 1259.
Price, Sir R. L., 1372.
Pringle, Sir J., 275.
Priorato, Galazzo Gualdo, 161.
Prosser, C. E., 1036.
Puelles, Alejo de, 2.
"Purple Heather," 1025, 1026.
Pye, H. J., 276, 283, 287, 408.

Quaritch, B., 1038.
Quepat, N., 1453.
Quesada, J. C., 1809.
Quesnay, A. du, 1702.

Raenkel, J., 1522.
Rafter, Captain, 1104.
Ramelli, 22.

Randall, J., 1213.
Rawlings, E., 206.
Ray, John, 201.
Reed, F. M., 1368.
Reid, Capt. Mayne, 1129.
Remy, S., 235, 323.
René, François, pseudonym (*see* P. Binet), 132.
Revoil, B. H., 1364.
Reynardson, E. T. S. B., 1303.
Reynolds, C. B., 1236, 1237.
Riche, B., 21.
Riencourt, C., 2155.
Rigg, A., 2125.
Ritter, E., 1458.
Robert, L., 2355.
Roberts, J., 153.
Roberts, T., 403.
Robins, Benj., 258.
Robinson, H., 1415, 1564.
Rodrigues, Joao, 308.
Roosevelt, Th., 1378, 1389, 1391, 1393.
Routillet, F., 1433.
Roux, Henri, 507.
Roux, J. W., 606, 627.
Roux, Louis, 1503.
Rudolph, Prince, 1321.
Ruscelli, 125.
Russell, W. H., 1107.
Rydholm, O. B., 1911.

S. H. (*see* Howitt), 410
Saavedra, J. F., 1819
St. Amezeuil, C., 1406.
St. Auban, Marquis, 522.
St. Bonnet, Ch. Blanc, 506.
St. John, C., 1284, 1285.
St. John, Hon. F., 1319.
St. Remy, 235.
Sales, D. de, 502.
Saltzer, C. F., 608.
Salvati, F., 2136.
Sanderson, G. P., 1336.
Santiago Loriga, 1804.
Sardi, Pietro, 128.
Sauer, K. T. v., 1637.
Scheel, 340.

Schild, Gunther, 609, 611.
Schmidt, C. H., 1619.
Schmidt, E. O., 623, 626.
Schmidt, R., 1504.
Schmidt, Rudolph, 1603-6.
Schreiber, G., 179, 237.
Schrenck, J., 101.
Schwachii, 133.
Scoffern, J., 2143.
Scott, W. H., 422.
Scrope, W., 447.
Sears, M. U., 1132.
Seaton-Karr, H. W., 1302
Selous, F. C., 1356, 1357.
"Seneca," 1385.
Shelvock, G. S., 256.
Shields, G. O., 1382-4.
Shirley, H., 152.
Shotterel, R., 200.
Siacci, F., 1555.
Siemenowicz, Cas., 171, 256.
Simon, J. B., 317.
Simons, F. C., 1152, 1160.
Skelton, 2304.
Slade, C. G., 1131.
Smith, F., 2106.
Smith, G. P., 1235.
Smith, Hawkes, 458.
Smith (Smyth), Sir John, 27, 33, 142.
Smythe, Thomas, 42.
Sobrero, C., 2109.
Soler, I., 349.
Somerville, W., 297.
Sourbe, T., 1565.
Spadoni, N., 197.
Sparre, Vcte de, 1526.
Specht, F. U. V., 1602.
Speedy, T., 1291.
Sponek, C. F. v., 604.
Sponeman, A., 617.
Stables, W. G., 1316.
Stahl, J. F., 325, 339.
Starr, G. O., 1189.
Starrat, W., 261.
Stelle, G. P., 1042.
Sterndale, R. A., 1346.
Stevens, Charles, 44.

Stevens, Capt. J. H., 442.
Stockbridge, V. D., 1030.
Straton, B., 1377.
Surflet, R., 44.
Surtees, W., 441.

Talberg, 1221.
Tamarez de la Escaler, 177.
Taplin, W., 292, 405.
Tarnovski, 1922.
Tartaglia, Nicolas, 8, 23.
Tennent, G. E., 1007-8.
Thackeray, Capt., 1177.
Thiel, E., 1620.
Thierbach, M., 1607.
Thierry, M., 518.
Thompson, 478.
Thompson, J., 286.
Thompson, M., 1396.
Thon, C. F. G., 607, 614, 620.
Thornhill, R. B., 407.
Thornton, N., 1111.
Thrasher, H., 1367.
Timaeus, G. E. L. v., 347.
Tolfrey, F., 463, 473.
Torelli, L., 1703.
Torricelli, 167.
Townshend, J. K., 487.
Tozer, B., 1022.
Tronson de Coudray 330.
Tupper, M. F., 1106.

Ufano, Diego, 116.
Uffans, D., 116, 131.
Utrecht, W. C. v., 159.

Vallier, E., 1553, 1554.
Valturius, Robertus, 1.
Valvasone, Erasmo de, 104.
Vandelli, F. de, 331.
Van Isselt, D., 1630.
Van Utrecht, W. C., 159.
Van Vinkeroy, C., 2356.
Van Zedlitz, F., 184.
Varenne de Feuille, 1447.
Velasco, E. G., 1813.
Velarde, A. C. P., 328.
Venn, Thos., 194.

Victor, Adam, 519.
Viergol, T. M. de, 1810, 1811.
Viglezzi, J., 1706.
Vinci, Leonardo da, 243.
Vinkenroy, En., 2356.
Vita Bonfadini, 155, 175.
Vogel, H., 318.
Von Basedow, A., 1655.
Von Benburg, R. A., 1653.
Von Cranach, U., 192.
Von Ehrenkreutz, 1651.
Von Hertling, 1601.
Von Sauer, 1637.
Von Specht, F. W., 1602.
Von Sponek, C. G., 604.

Walford, E. C., 1123.
Walker, A., 1124.
Walker, D., 457.
Wallhausen, V., 121.
Walsh, J. H., 1005, 1017, 1056, 1102, 1171, 1262.
Walsingham, Lord, 1299.
Ward, 1044.
Ward, Ed., 1267.
Wardell, W. H., 2114.
Warren, T. K., 1366.
Watson, B. A., 1380.
Watt, W., 444.

Webb, G., 1001.
Weygand, H., 1621.
Whitworth, Sir J., 1134.
Wilcox, C. M., 1122.
Wilde, Oscar, 1441.
"Wildfowler" (*see* Clement), 1273, etc.
Wilhelm Claesz v. Utrecht, 159.
Wilkins, J., 1218.
Wilkinson, H., 461.
Willard, G. L., 1187.
Williams, 2305.
Williamson, Thos., 409.
Willoghbœus, F., 201.
Wilson, J., 445, 459, 466.
Winch, 1634.
Wingate, G. W., 1181.
Winkrat, 1685.
Wolley, C. P., 1028, 1390.
Wolverton, Lord, 1355.

Xibaja, J. de, 185.

Yauville, D', 221.
Yonne, C. de Mezelles, 1416.

Zedlitz, F. v., 184.
Zuebler, 117.

APPENDIX.

Some Recent Books and Omissions.
1895.

ENGLISH BOOKS.

FIREARMS.

01.—THE BREECH-LOADER AND HOW TO USE IT; WITH NOTES ON RIFLES. *W. W. Greener.* An enlarged edition (*v.* No. 1027) of a sportsman's handbook. The additional matter consists of chapters treating of "Rifles of the Past and Present," "The Sporting Rifle," "Rudiments of Rifle Shooting," "Long Shots," "The 303 as a Sporting Weapon," and a general index. There are also fresh illustrations and some alterations in the general arrangement of the book, and fresh notes on shot guns, powders, etc. Fifth edition, Cassell & Co., London, 1895. 8vo, 405 pp., illustrated, paper boards, 2s. 6d.

02.—PRACTICAL HINTS TO SPORTSMEN on the purchase of their weapons. *J. H. Crane.* This is little more than an amplified catalogue of weapons made by Mr. Crane, who is given as the author of "Modern Military Small Arms," but it contains some interesting particulars of the methods of gunmaking current in Birmingham a quarter of a century ago. Thompson & Sons, Hatton Garden, London, 1872. 8vo, 44 pp. and woodcuts.

03.—TEXT BOOK FOR MILITARY SMALL ARMS. *Official.* Contains a short history of the military musket, descriptions of those formerly used in the British Army, and those now forming the equipment of Modern Armies, with particulars for their identification and that of their ammunition, their ballistic value, etc. Eyre & Spottiswoode, etc., London, Edinburgh, and Dublin, 1894. 159 pp., plates, 2s. 6d.

04.—RIFLES. A chapter and some notes on "A Course of Instruction in Ordnance and Gunnery." *Capt. H. Metcalfe.* J. Wiley, New York, 1891.

05.—MANNLICHER RIFLE. A monograph of the Mannlicher Rifle, its varieties, and the ballistics of the various calibres in use. Schwarte & Hammer, London, 1895. Privately printed.

06.—ACCLES MACHINE GUN. *J. G. Accles.* A monograph on the improved form of Gatling Machine Gun, illustrated with photographs, diagrams, etc. Mole, Birmingham, 1895. 8vo, privately printed.

07.—THEORY AND PRACTICE OF TARGET SHOOTING. *A. G. Foulkes..* Practical hints on the use of military and match rifles, a description of the effects of different atmospheric conditions, and instructions in the use of various aids to rifle shooting by a well-known expert shot. Illustrated with numerous diagrams, etc. The contents include :—

Introduction to Target Shooting and its Uses.—Use of Rifling.—Gunpowder and Explosives.—Cordite,—Points of an Ideal Rifle.—Hints as to Choice of a Martini.—Care of the Rifle.—Necessity of Scientific Knowledge.—Official Positions and Discussions thereon.—The Four Rules for Aiming and Discussions thereon.—The Eye in its relation to Shooting.—Theoretical Principles.—Flip.—Forces to which the Bullet is Exposed.—Description of Shooting Instruments (Verniers, etc.), and Hints as to their Use.—Targets.—Rules to be Observed in Learning to Pull Off.—Causes of Failure in Rifle Shooting.—Blowing Off.—Team Shooting.—Training.—Match Rifles and Hints on their Selection.—Record Scores.—Rules.—Rifle Sights and Adjustments.—Index.

H. Cox, London, 1895. Demy 8vo, illustrated, 21 plates, 228 pp., 10s. 6d.

08.—MODERN RIFLE SHOOTING. "*A Marksman.*" A handbook for Volunteers. J. S. Phillips, London, 1895. 8vo, 174 pp., 2s. 6d.

SHOOTING.

010.—A YEAR OF SPORT AND NATURAL HISTORY. Edited by *Sir Oswald Crawfurd*. Aims at sketching sports at every season of the year: deer stalking, grouse driving, rabbit shooting are included in the series, which embraces every variety of sport found in the British Isles; and has chapters on birds of prey, the nidification of birds, and the habits of British wild birds and animals. Many illustrations by F. Feller, A. T. Elwes, and others. Chapman & Hall, London, 1895. Demy 4to, £1 1s.

011.—SKETCHES IN GROUSE-LAND. *E. G. Mackenzie*. Essays. Swan Sonnenschein, London, 1895. 8vo, pp. viii, 248.

012.—ART OF WILDFOWLING. *Abel Chapman*. This book is far more than it professes to be: instead of being confined to "first lessons," it is one of the ablest treatises on the most general of British sports, and the one that has of late attracted most attention owing to the fact that modern methods of shooting gratify those only who delight in successful marksmanship. Sportsmen who take pleasure in hunting their game more and more resort to wildfowling, and the literature of this branch of the sport of shooting is rapidly increasing. Mr. Chapman, after devoting twelve chapters to the practice of wildfowling and the habits of wildfowl at home and abroad, adds five chapters of reminiscences, of which the best are "Two Seasons on Home Waters," and "Two Seasons in Southern Spain." Mr. Chapman was part author of "Wild Spain," and his writings afford valuable information for sportsmen seeking sport near Great Britain. This volume has thirty-six illustrations by the author, and three by Charles Whymper. London: H. Cox, 1896. 8vo, illustrated, 268 pp., 10s. 6d.

013.—PRACTICAL WILDFOWLING. *H. Sharp.* Instructions for beginners, reprinted, with additions, from *The Exchange and Mart*, illustrated with process blocks from drawings of wildfowl, etc., by H. Sharp, and woodcuts of guns and gear. Part I., Outfit and Accessories; II., Wildfowling; III., Shore-birds and Shore-bird Shooting. L. Upcott Gill, London, 1895. 8vo, 291 pp., price 12s. 6d.

014.—WILDFOWL AND SEAFOWL OF GREAT BRITAIN. "*A Son of the Marshes.*" Edited by *J. A. Owen.* Twelve illustrations by Bryan Hook. Descriptions of wildfowl and their haunts, and sketches of marshland folk, with some gossip, legend, and folklore. Chapman & Hall, London, 1895. Demy 8vo, chh. xxv. 12 plates, 14s.

015.—BRITISH GAME BIRDS AND WILD FOWL. *B. R. Morris.* A standard work on ornithology for naturalists and sportsmen. This—fourth—edition is edited by *W. B. Tegetmeier*, and has 60 hand-coloured plates. J. C. Nimmo, London, 1895. 2 vols., royal 8vo, 400 pp., 30s. net.

016.—THE GAME BIRDS AND WILD FOWL OF THE BRITISH ISLANDS. *Charles Dixon.* A handbook for the naturalist and sportsman. "Full of interest for the bird lover, and full of information for the sportsman, besides being copious and exact from the purely scientific point of view." Illustrated by A. T. Elwes; a special edition with coloured plates. Chapman & Hall, London, 1895. Demy 8vo, 484 pp., 18s.

017.—THE GROUSE.—A book of the "Fur and Feather Series." The natural history by the *Rev. H. A. Macpherson*, the shooting by *A. J. Stuart-Wortley*, the cookery by *George Saintsbury*. A companion book to "The Partridge," by the same authors (see No. 1299). Thirteen illustrations by A. J. Stuart-Wortley and A. Thorburn, and diagrams in the text. Similar monographs in the same series are announced as follows:—"The Pheasant," by A. J. Stuart-Wortley, the Rev. H. A. Macpherson, and A. J. Innes-Shand. "The Hare and the Rabbit," by the Hon. Gerald Lascelles. "Wildfowl," by the Hon. John Scott-Montagu. "Red Deer," by Cameron of Lochiel. Longmans, Green & Co., London, 1894. Crown 8vo, 5s.

018.—PRACTICAL PHEASANT REARING: with an Appendix on Grouse Driving. *R. J. L. Price.* H. Cox, London. Post 8vo, 3s. 6d.

019.—GAME BIRDS AND SHOOTING SKETCHES. *J. G. Millais.* Illustrating the habits, modes of capture, stages of plumage, and of hybrids and varieties. Coloured plates and other illustrations, and a Frontispiece by Sir J. E. Millais. For an earlier edition see No. 1298. Sotheran, London, 1894. 4to, pp. xii, 72.

020.—GAME BIRDS AT HOME. *T. S. Van Dyke.* Sporting sketches. Sampson Low, London, 1895. Crown 8vo, 220 pp., 7s. 6d.

021.—LAND BIRDS AND GAME BIRDS OF NEW ENGLAND. *H. D. Meriot.* A book for naturalists. New York and London, 1895.

022.—NORTH AMERICAN SHORE BIRDS. *D. G. Elliott.* A reference book for the naturalist and sportsman. Suckling, 1895. 8vo, 268 pp., 10s.

023.—SPORT IN ENGLAND: PAST AND PRESENT. *Col. E. C. C. Hartopp.* Chiefly relates to shooting. The contents include:

CONTENTS.—Useful Hints to Young Beginners.—Young England as a Sportsman.—The Poaching of Paired Birds.—The Egg Season and its Enemies.—Landlord and Tenant Rights.—Crop Cutting.—"St. Grouse": Past and Present.—"St. Partridge": Past and Present.—"Longtails": Past and Present.—"Covert Shooting."—Good Shots, and others.—Funny Facts in Sports.—A Few Hints on Shooting Kits.—Ferrets and their Management.—Trapping, Netting, and Snaring.—Poaching and How it is Done.—Small Days and

Pot Hunting.—Turning Down Live Bought Pheasants.—How and Where Rabbit-farming can Pay.—The Gamekeeper and his Duties.—Guns and Gunmakers.—Sport, as I have Found it.—The Woodcock.—The Partridge.—The Cat.—The Stoat.—The Weasel.—The Rat.—Recipes for Diseases in Dogs.—Retrievers of the Present Day,

H. Cox, London, 1895, post 8vo, 3s. 6d.

024.—DAYS IN THULE WITH GUN AND ROD. *John Bickerdyke.* An illustrated record of times past in a shooting lodge in the Hebrides. Constable, London, 1894. 12mo, 196 pp., 3s. 6d.; another edition 16mo, 1895, 2s. 6d.

025.—THOUGHTS ON SPORT. *H. R. Sargent.* Simpkin, London, 1895. 8vo, 454 pp., 10s. 6d.

026.—DIARY OF COLONEL PETER HAWKER. Extracts from the records and rough notes made by the author of "Instructions to Young Sportsmen," with an introduction by *Sir Ralph Payne-Gallwey, Bart.* Two portraits and eight illustrations taken from the last edition of the "Instructions." The cream of the diaries was extracted by the colonel himself for the various editions of his own books; the information here given consists chiefly of personal details and quaint remarks; but there is an interesting account of shooting-trips to the north for grouse shooting. Longmans, Green & Co., London, 1894. 2 vols. 8vo, 32s.

027.—SONGS AND BALLADS OF SPORT. *W. W. Tomlinson.* Old sporting songs. Scott, London, 1895. 16mo, 318 pp., 1s.

028.—CONVERSATIONAL HINTS FOR YOUNG SHOOTERS: a Guide to Polite Talk. *R. C. Lehman.* A facetious work reprinted from *Punch.* Chatto, London, 1894. 8vo, pp. viii, 114.

029.—NEW SPORTING STORIES. *G. G.* Chiefly racing and hunting. Bellairs, London, 1895. 8vo, 226 pp., 3s. 6d

030.—TALES FROM THE NOTE-BOOK OF A SPORTSMAN. *I. S. Turgeniev.* Sketches of life in Russian villages; political rather than sporting. Translated by *E. Richter.* Lamley, London, 1895. 8vo, 260 pp., 3s. 6d.

031.—HUNTERS THREE. *T. W. Knox.* Stories.

032.—POACHERS AND POACHING. *John Watson.* A book which game-keepers and game-preservers may study with advantage. Chapman & Hall, London, 1894. Frontis., crown 8vo, pp. viii, 327, 7s. 6d.

033.—MAKING A SHOOTING. *Anonymous.* A pamphlet giving the author's experiences in game-rearing, and some practical hints. Sonnenschein, London, 1894. 8vo, 92 pp., 1s.

034.—GAMEKEEPER'S SHOOTING MEMORANDUM BOOK. "*I. E. B. C.*" A book for registering number of game shot, sent for sale, etc. London, H. Cox. Pocket diary form, price 1s. 6d.

FOREIGN SPORT.

035.—GUN, RIFLE AND HOUND IN EAST AND WEST. "*Snaffle.*" Sketches of sport, chiefly hunting. Illustrated by H. Dixon. Chapman & Hall, London, 1894. Demy 8vo, pp. x, 376; 14s.

036.—TEN YEARS' TRAVEL AND SPORT IN FOREIGN LANDS; or, Travels in the Eighties. *H. W. Seton-Karr.* A new enlarged edition with portrait (see No. 1302). Chapman & Hall, London, 1894. Cr. 8vo, ill., pp. lx, 445; 5s.

037.—HUNTING IN MANY LANDS. Edited by *Theo. Roosevelt* and *Geo. Bird Grinnell.* The book of the American Boone and Crockett Club, treating of the sporting adventures and experiences of various members in

East Africa, California, Canada, India, Russia, Mongolia and elsewhere in search of big game. It is a book of sport undertaken for sport's sake; and some parts have much offended naturalists and those who hope to see the preservation of large wild game. Douglas, Edinburgh, 1895. 8vo, 448 pp.; 15s.

038.—THIRTY YEARS OF SHIKAR. *Sir E. Braddon.* Recollections of sport, chiefly in the East. Blackwood, Edinburgh, 1895. 8vo, 372 pp.; 18s.

039.—A SPORTING PILGRIMAGE. *C. P. Whitney.* Of no interest to shooters: consists of studies in such British sports as golf, football, etc. Osgood, New York, 1895. 8vo, ill., pp. xii, 397.

040.—THE SPORTSMAN'S MANUAL. *R. H. Tyacke.* A guide for those in search of game in Spiti, Bara, Bagahab, etc. Thacker, Spink, Calcutta, 1893. pp. vi, 128.

041.—SHOOTING AND YACHTING TRIPS IN THE MEDITERRANEAN. *Col. Bayot.* Allen, London, 1887; n.e. 1895, pp. viii, 224.

042.—TRAVELS, SPORTS, AND POLITICS IN THE EAST OF EUROPE. *Marquis of Huntly.* Contains little of shooting. Chapman & Hall, London, 189–. Crown 8vo, ill., pp. viii, 311; 12s.

043.—SPORTING DAYS IN SOUTHERN INDIA: being Reminiscences of Twenty Trips in Pursuit of Big Game, chiefly in the Madras Presidency. *Lieut.-Col. A. J. C. Pollock.* The contents include: three chapters devoted to Tiger Shooting and to Bear Shooting, and two each to the Panther, Bison, Elephant, Deer and Antelopes. There is a chapter on the Ibex, and two chapters on Miscellaneous game. The book is well illustrated by Whymper and others. H. Cox, London, 1895. Royal 8vo, pp. xx, 252; 16s.

044.—INCIDENTS OF FOREIGN SPORT AND TRAVEL. *Col. Pollock.* Adventures and experiences of hunting big game (see No. 1335). Illustrated by A. T. Elwes. Chapman & Hall, London, 1895. Demy 8vo, pp. vi, 427; 16s.

045.—TIGER SHOOTING IN THE DOON AND ULWAR. *Fife Cookson.* Records of shooting trips and experiences, and sketches of life in India. Chapman & Hall, London, 1887. Ill., pp. xi, 257, 8vo.

046.—SPORT IN LADAKH. *F. E. S. A.* Contains five chapters, each treating of a day's shooting, after the Ibex, Bushel, Ovis Ammon, Goa, and the Shapoo. H. Cox, London, 1895. Demy 4to, ill., 38, pp. boards, 5s.

047.—RIFLE AND SPEAR WITH THE RAJPUTS. *Mrs. Alan Gardner.* A narrative of a winter's travel and sport in Northern India. Chatto, London, 1895. Imperial 8vo, ill., 352 pp., 21s.

048.—SPORT ON THE PAMIRS. *C. Sperling Cumberland.* An account of a shooting expedition on the Pamirs and the Turkestan steppes. Frontispiece and map. Blackwood, Edinburgh, 1895. 8vo, pp. x, 278.

049.—SPORT IN INDIA AND SOMALI LAND. *J. S. Edye.* Contains some hints to sportsmen. Gale & Polden, Aldershot, 1895. Crown 8vo, 170 pp., 6s.

050.—LION HUNTING IN SOMALI LAND; also an account of "Pig-sticking the African Wart Hog." *C. J. Melliss.* Illustrated from photographs by the author and C. Aldin. Chapman & Hall, London, 1895. 8vo, 182 pp, 7s. 6d.

051.—IN HAUNTS OF WILD GAME. *F. V. Kirby.* "Maquaquamba." An account of the wanderings of a naturalist. Contains much sporting information relating to the Kahlamba-Limpopo district. Blackwood, Edinburgh, 1895. Large demy 8vo, portrait, and illustrations by C. Whimper, 25s.

052.—SPORT IN ASHANTI. *J. A. Skertchley.* Seems to have appeared in 1876 as "Melinda the Caboceer; or Sport in Ashanti," by the author of "Ashanti as it is." It is a tale of the Gold Coast. London, 1895. 8vo, ill.

053.—BEAR HUNTING IN THE WHITE MOUNTAINS; or, Alaska and British Columbia Revisited. *H. W. Seton-Karr.* Chapman & Hall, London, 189 . Crown 8vo, map and ill., pp. vi, 156, 4s. 6d.

054.—GUNSHOT INJURIES. *T. Longmore.* The history, characteristic features, complications and general treatment of bullet wounds, and statistics concerning them. Longmans, London; n.e. 1895. 8vo, 864 pp., 78 woodcuts, 31s. 6d.

055.—HOW I SHOT MY BEARS. *Mrs. R. H. Tyacke*, edited by *E. E. Cathell.* A record of two years' camp life in Kullu, and of sport in the Himalayas. Low, London, 1893. 8vo, maps and ill., pp. xi, 318, 10s. 6d.

056.—THE DEAD SHOT. "*Marksman.*" Purports to be a complete guide for the sportsman; a treatise on the use of the Gun, with lessons in the Art of Game-shooting, Game-driving, Wildfowling, and Trap-shooting. Longmans, London, 1895. New (seventh) edition, 12 ill., crown 8vo, 10s. 6d.

FOREIGN BOOKS.

0101.—LA CHASSE DE GIBIER DANS L'EST. *C. Velin.* A treatise on game preserving and forestry in the eastern provinces of France. G. Frassen, Epinal, n.d. 8vo, 180 pp.

0102.—BALISTIQUE EXTÉRIEURE. *Col. Zaboudskie.* A course of lectures delivered at the St. Petersburg Academy of Science.

0103.—DICTIONNAIRE MILITAIRE. By *A Committee of Officers*. A military encyclopædia and polyglot dictionary of technical terms in use. In addition to definitions, descriptions, etc., the equivalent terms are given in German, English, Italian, Spanish, and Russian; the last in Roman characters with accented pronunciation. Now issuing in 20 parts; will be comprised in 2 large 8vo vols., double cols., of 1280 pp. each vol. Paris, Berger-Levrault et Cie, 3 fr. each part.

0104.—DIE GEHEIMNISSE der Englischen Gewehr-fabrikation und Buchsenmacher-Kunst ; so wie der Erzeugung der Verschiedenen Eisenforten zu den feinsten Jagdgewehren. *William Greener*. Translated by *Ch. H. Schmidt*. Practically "The Science of Gunnery" (No. 462), but with many additions, some not found in any of the English additions. B. F. Vorgt, Weimar, 1842. 8vo, 344 pp., 16 litho plates.

0105.—SELBTSPANNER GEWEHRE. *W. Witte*. A brochure on Automatic guns. Eisenschmidt, Berlin, 1895. 8vo.

0106.—SCHOSS. *Brandeis*. A brochure on shooting. Hartleben, Vienna, 1895. 8vo.

0107.—EXPLOSIVES. Präparate und der Geschoss-construction. Siedel & Sohn, Vienna, 1895. 8vo.

0108.—GEMEINFASSLICHE WAFFENLEHRE. *W. Witte*. A handbook for self-instruction. Gives a short history of early firearms and precise details of the powers and uses of various modern military rifles. Seigfried, Mettler & Sohn, Berlin, 1887, etc. 8vo, 247 pp., 7 litho plates.

0109.—FORTSCHRITTE und Vervänderungen im Gebiete des Waffenwesens in d. Neuster Zeit. *W. Witte*. This is an appendix to the preceding. Three parts. Lebel's Buchhandlung, Berlin, 1894. Large 8vo, 258 pp., woodcuts in text.

ARTICLES IN CURRENT LITERATURE.

0121.—SHOOTING. Ontario's big game. *Canadian Magazine*, vol. iv. Extermination of great game in South Africa. *H. A. Bryden. Fortnightly Review*, lvi. 538. Winter's Sport in the Rockies. *W. B. Grohman, English Illustrated Magazine*, xii. 19. Climbing for white goats in America. *G. B. Grinnell, Scribner*, xv. 643. Famous hunting parties of the plains. *Cosmopolitan*, xvii. Stray shots in Mexico, *O. H. Howarth, Outing*, xi. 52. The American Sportswoman. *E. C. Barney, Fortnightly Review*, lvi. 263.

0122.—RIFLES. The Russian "Mark" 3 rifle in Abyssinia. An article in the *Russki Invalid* for 1894, p. 237, etc. The magazine rifle; its development and use, *Lieut. W. A. Campbell, United Service Magazine*, 1894, xii. 403. Dr. A. Demosthen's Experiments with the Roumanian 6·5 m.m. Mannlicher. *Med. Mon.* iii. 1894. Effect of the small-bore bullet on horses. *Vet. Cap. F. Smith, Journal R. U. S. I.*, xxxviii. 172. Magazine rifle trials in the United States. *Cap. F. L. Nathan, Journal R. U. S. I.*, xxxviii. 175. First systematic attempt (by M. Blanc) at interchangeability in firearms. *W. F. Durfie, Cassier's Magazine*, v. 469.

0123.—OLD ARMS. Illustrations and descriptions of the weapons of the middle ages are given in *T. A. Dodge's* "Gustavus Adolphus: a History of the Art of War, etc." Boston, 1895. 8vo. Notes on Armour in the Tower of London. *Viscount Dillon, Antiquary*, xxix. 25, 193. Ancient Arms and Armour. *Antiquary*, xxix. 15. Arms and Armour. *Col. C. King.* An illustrated article in the *United Service Magazine*, cxxx. 45. The Beginnings of the British Army. *Macmillan*, lxx. 265.

0124.—MISCELLANEOUS. Projectiles and Explosives in War. *Edinburgh Review*, clxxx. 447. Amberite. *Chambers' Journal*, xi. 191.

NAMES OF AUTHORS IN THE SUPPLEMENT.

A., F. E. S., 046.
Accles, J. G., 06.

Bagot, Col., 041.
Barney, E. C., 0121.
"Bickerdyke, John," 024.
Braddon, Sir E., 038.
Brandeis, F., 0106
Bryden, H. A., 0121.

C., I. E. B., 034.
Cameron of Lochiel, 017.
Campbell, Lieut. W., 0122.
Chapman, Abel, 012.
Cookson, Fife, 045.
Crane, J. H., 02.
Crawfurd, Sir Oswald, 010.
Cumberland, C. Sperling, 048.

Dillon, Viscount, 0123.
Dixon, C., 016.
Dodge, T. A., 0123.
Dyke, T. S. V., 020.

Edye, J. S., 049.
Elliot, D. G., 022.

"F. E. S. A.," 046.
Foulkes, A. G., 07.

"G. G.," 029.
Gallwey, Sir R. P., 026.
Gardner, Mrs. Alan, 047.
Greener, W., 0104.

Greener, W. W., 01.
Grinnell, G. B., 037, 0121.
Grohman, W. B., 0121.

Hartopp, Col., E. C., 023.
Howarth, O. H., 0121.
Huntly, Marquis of, 042.

"I. E. B. C.," 034.
Innes-Shand, A. J., 017.

Karr, H. W. Seton-, 036, 053.
King, Col. C., 0123.
Kirby, F. V., 051.
Knox, T. W., 031.

Lascelles, Hon. G., 017.
Lehman, R. C., 028.
Longmore, T., 054.

Mackenzie, E. G., 011.
Macpherson, H. A., 017.
"Marksman," 08.
Meriot, H. D., 021.
Metcalfe, H., 04.
Millais, J. G., 019.
Morris, B. R., 015.

Nathan, F. L., 0122.

Owen, J. A., 014.

Payne-Gallwey, Sir R., 026.
Pollock, Col. A. J. C., 043, 044.

Price, R. J. L., 018.

Richter, E., 030.
Roosevelt, T., 037.

Sargent, H. R., 025.
Schmidt, Ch. H., 0104.
Scott-Montagu, Hon. J., 017.
Seton-Karr, H. W., 036, 053.
Sharp, H., 013.
Skertchley, J. A., 052.
Smith, F., 0122.
"Snaffle," 035.
"Son of the Marshes," 014.
Stuart-Wortley, A. J., 017.

Tegetmeier, W. B., 015.
Thorburn, A., 017.
Tomlinson, W. W., 027.
Turgeniev, I. S., 030.
Tyacke, Mrs. R. H., 055.
Tyacke, R. H., 040.

Van Dyke, T. S., 020.
Velin, C., 0101.

Watson, J., 032.
Whitney, C. P., 039.
Witte, W., 0105, 0108-9.

Zaboudskie, Col., 0102.

www.ingramcontent.com/pod-product-compliance
Lightning Source LLC
Chambersburg PA
CBHW022018220426
43663CB00007B/1124